Center Stage

Media and the Performance of American Politics

Gary C. Woodward

ROWMAN & LITTLEFIELD PUBLISHERS, INC.
Lanham • Boulder • New York • Toronto • Plymouth, UK

ROWMAN & LITTLEFIELD PUBLISHERS, INC.

Published in the United States of America
by Rowman & Littlefield Publishers, Inc.
A wholly owned subsidiary of The Rowman & Littlefield Publishing Group, Inc.
4501 Forbes Boulevard, Suite 200, Lanham, Maryland 20706
www.rowmanlittlefield.com

Estover Road, Plymouth PL6 7PY, United Kingdom

British Library Cataloguing in Publication Information Available

Library of Congress Cataloging-in-Publication Data
Woodward, Gary C.
Center stage : media and the performance of American politics / Gary C. Woodward.
p. cm. — (Communication, media, and politics)
Includes bibliographical references and index.
ISBN-13: 978-0-7425-3564-0 (cloth : alk. paper)
ISBN-10: 0-7425-3564-9 (cloth : alk. paper)
ISBN-13: 978-0-7425-3565-7 (pbk. : alk. paper)
ISBN-10: 0-7425-3565-7 (pbk. : alk. paper)
1. Communication in politics—United States. 2. Rhetoric—Political aspects—United States. 3 Mass media—Political aspects—United States. 4. Journalism—Political aspects—United States. 5. United States—Politics and government. 6. Discourse analysis—Political aspects. I. Title. II. Series.

JA85.2.U6W66 2007
320.97301'4—dc22

2006011873

Printed in the United States of America

∞™ The paper used in this publication meets the minimum requirements of American National Standard for Information Sciences—Permanence of Paper for Printed Library Materials, ANSI/NISO Z39.48-1992.

Center Stage

Communication, Media, and Politics
Series Editor
Robert E. Denton, Jr., Virginia Tech

This series features a range of work dealing with the role and function of communication in the realm of politics, broadly defined. Including general academic books and texts for use in graduate and advanced undergraduate courses, the series encompasses humanistic, critical, historical, and empirical studies in political communication in the United States. Primary subject areas include campaigns and elections, media, and political institutions. *Communication, Media, and Politics* books will be of interest to students, teachers, and scholars of political communication from the disciplines of communication, rhetorical studies, political science, journalism, and political sociology.

RECENT TITLES IN THE SERIES

Political Campaign Communication: Principles and Practices, Fifth Edition
Judith S. Trent and Robert V. Friedenberg
The Rhetoric of Redemption: Kenneth Burke's Redemption Drama and Martin Luther King, Jr.'s "I Have a Dream" Speech
David A. Bobbitt
Reelpolitik II: Political Ideologies in '50s and '60s Films
Beverly Merrill Kelley
New Frontiers in International Communication Theory
Edited by Mehdi Semati
News Narratives and News Framing: Constructing Political Reality
Karen S. Johnson-Cartee
Leading Ladies of the White House: Communication Strategies of Notable Twentieth-Century First Ladies
Edited by Molly Meijer Wertheimer
Entertaining Politics: New Political Television and Civic Culture
Jeffrey P. Jones
Presidential Candidate Images
Edited by Kenneth L. Hacker
Bring 'Em On: Media and Politics in the Iraq War
Edited by Lee Artz and Yahya R. Kamalipour
The Talk of the Party: Political Labels, Symbolic Capital, and American Life
Sharon E. Jarvis
The 2004 Presidential Campaign: A Communication Perspective
Edited by Robert E. Denton, Jr.
Women's Political Discourse: A Twenty-first-Century Perspective
Molly A. Mayhead and Brenda DeVore Marshall
Making Sense of Political Ideology: The Power of Language in Democracy
Bernard L. Brock, Mark E. Huglen, James F. Klumpp, and Sharon Howell
Transforming Conflict: Communication and Ethnopolitical Conflict
Donald G. Ellis
Towel Snapping the Press: Bush's Journey from Locker-Room Antics to Message Control
James E. Mueller

To Brian Lamb
and the idea of C-SPAN

Where the mind is without fear and the head is held high; Where knowledge is free;
Where the world has not been broken up into fragments by narrow domestic walls;
Where words come out from the depth of truth;
Where tireless striving stretches its arms towards perfection;
Where the clear stream of reason has not lost its way into the dreary desert sand of dead habit;
Where the mind is led forward by thee into ever-widening thought and action—
Into that heaven of freedom, my Father, let my country awake.

—Rabindranath Tagore, *Gitanjali* (1910)

Contents

Acknowledgments

The author gratefully acknowledges permission to quote from Gary C. Woodward, "The Rules of the Game: The Military and the Press in the Persian Gulf," in *Media and the Persian Gulf War*, edited by Robert E. Denton Jr., copyright © 1993 by Robert E. Denton Jr. Reproduced with permission of Greenwood Publishing Group, Inc., Westport, Conn. I also acknowledge permission to quote from Gary C. Woodward, *Perspectives on American Political Media*, published by Allyn and Bacon, Boston, Mass. Copyright © 1997 by Pearson Education. Reprinted by permission of the publisher. Rabindranath Tagore's song poem is from *Gitanjali*, a collection of prose translations made by the author from the original Bengali with an introduction by W. B. Yeats. (New York: Macmillan, 1912, 1913).

The cartoon on p. 19 is © The New Yorker Collection 2005 Mike Twohy from cartoonbank.com. All Rights Reserved.

The cartoon on p. 46 is © The New Yorker Collection 2003 J. C. Duffy from cartoonbank.com. All Rights Reserved.

The cartoon on p. 65 is © The New Yorker Collection 2004 Drew Dernavich from cartoonbank.com. All Rights Reserved.

The cartoon on p. 70 is © The New Yorker Collection 2005 Jack Ziegler from cartoonbank.com. All Rights Reserved.

The cartoon on p. 134 is © The New Yorker Collection 1987 Dana Fradon from cartoonbank.com. All Rights Reserved.

The cartoon on p. 173 is © The New Yorker Collection 1997 Arnie Levin from cartoonbank.com. All Rights Reserved.

Preface

This book treats national politics as the process of managing and staging—*performing*—the choices made by the press and political institutions. Because for most of us events in the nation's civic life are largely mediated, we understand them as a form of managed presentation, another kind of theater that is offered to us via television, newspapers, Internet sites, and related media.

To start with the assumption that politics is a subset of performance may seem to suggest a central reason our civic life is—at least for many Americans—so disappointing. In common usage, to "stage," "display," or "perform" is to substitute an imitation for the real, hoping that the appearance of authenticity is enough to keep us from missing the genuine. Certainly in some ways this *is* the case. But the cliché of politics as an endless carnival of distraction is facile and misses something basic about who we are.

Although it is demonstrably true that we have an ailing political culture, the impulse for drama that is the model for this book is not presented as the primary cause. If we fall short of having media and political institutions that keep us from engaging in significant national conversations (and most thoughtful analysts have reached this conclusion following many different pathways), it is not because political agents are forced into an alien world of second-rate dramaturgy. Rather, it is because they and their audiences collectively lack the imagination to be effective dramatists of the nation's choices and possibilities. Political events are not phony or less valuable because they have been staged. Instead, they fail when their presentation conceals rather than clarifies political choices. As Curtis White has noted, media and politics are among "the great antagonists of the imagination."[1] The problem is not that they exist in dramatic forms but that we have reduced both to being worthy of no more than a few disposable minutes of our leisure time. We have come to accept so little from resources that could give us so much.

The dramatic perspective builds on a long and useful tradition of communication analysis and criticism. Many have argued that it functions as more than a metaphor, representing the essence of how we organize our knowledge about everyday affairs. Eric Gorham notes that politics is inherently representational and symbolic, thereby inducing even the politically passive to awareness and judgment.[2] Like all forms of communication, it is understood largely through its assigned *motives* and the processes of rhetorical characterization. Similarly, Kenneth Burke observes that we instinctively treat "language and thought *primarily as modes of action*."[3] We offer our ideas to others for approval and immediate understanding. In doing so, we strive for what Erving Goffman called "expressive coherence." We want to meet the implicit "expressive requirements" of situations, carefully managing the impressions that we communicate to others.[4] Bruce Gronbeck rightly observes that "*all* political communication is fundamentally dramaturgical in function and force."[5] Like other contexts of sociality, it feeds on our nature as *Homo narrans*: creatures who make sense of their world through the structures and rhythms of storytelling.[6]

Even those with the most latent of theatrical impulses could rise to the occasion. The famously undemonstrative George Washington still knew how to construct a persona that would stimulate the adulation of the new nation.[7] In his own way, he was just as conscious of how his actions shaped public perceptions as the current occupants of the White House.

The anemic state of American political culture that will shadow us throughout this study flows from other causes. This book takes its place with many others that also worry about the well-known problems that contribute to a downward spiral of citizen interest in public life.[8] Modern political institutions already start with two strikes against them: a polis that lacks even elementary knowledge of their political institutions, and reporting in the most popular media that is generally too simple-minded to advance the nation's understanding of complex issues. For the minority of Americans who wish for more, the crude logics and self-referential orientations of politics geared to the lowest common denominator offer their own reasons for discouragement. The result is a disengaged nation fed on discourse as stale and predictable as a Broadway revival of *Cats*.

Consider the more complex pathways that millions of Americans follow through their own lives every day. They go to work and school, contribute time and energy to community institutions and places of worship, and negotiate the difficult terrain of scores of personal relationships. In these interactions, Americans routinely understand fine distinctions in communicative emphases, nuances of meaning reflected in language, subtle lapses in logic, and the probable consequences of choices made by others. By contrast, the "retail" messages seeping into our consciousness through the "newer" media of television and radio look quaintly primitive. Compared with the variegated textures of daily life, the rhetoric of campaigns, or the endless hours of "news talk" that fill our airwaves, all seem like mutant forms of discourse—species of rhetoric that appear to have left the stream of evolutionary progress to languish in their own dead ends.

We are left with political information that exists in two starkly unequal parts. On one hand, reporting in most of mainstream media rarely verges from the safe center of preferred narratives and predictable perspectives. On the other hand, the *strategic* uses of money, professional staffs, and audience research make the design of political discourse ever more sophisticated. Put another way, the *content* of political messages is not very rich or specific, but the *processes* for managing political attitudes have grown more complex.

All of this comes at a time when there is increasing skepticism about the ability of American journalism itself to serve as a check on the power and excesses of government. The 2005 annual report by the Project for Excellence in Journalism offers some somber conclusions about the general decline in the credibility of mainstream news sources. The study found that between 1985 and 2002,

- the number of Americans who thought news organizations were highly professional declined from 72 to 49 percent;
- the number who thought news organizations were moral fell from 54 to 39 percent;
- those who felt news organizations tried to cover up their mistakes rose from 13 to 67 percent;
- the number who thought the press got the facts straight fell from 55 to 35 percent;
- those who thought news organizations were biased politically rose from 45 to 59 percent.[9]

Even if incomplete, the study suggests a nation with a growing sense of discomfort about its traditional sources of information. If members of a society feel that they are not getting accurate information, their faith in the democratic process cannot but be eroded.

This book reflects a growing sense of urgency for another reason. Woven into its various sections is the fear that a number of core values are being abandoned by key media and political institutions. These are norms that have been honored by imitation around the world, including

- a commitment to open discussion and argument,
- deference for the sovereignty and opinions of other nations,
- respect for social diversity and the rights of minorities,
- a willingness to engage in bilateral communication and compromise, and
- protection of the weakest among us from the forces of an unregulated marketplace.

These Wilsonian values have existed for decades in the aspirational rhetoric of both Democratic and Republican administrations. And they were enacted in noble responses such as Lend-Lease and the Marshall Plan during World War II, Mexican loan guarantees during the Clinton years, and the second Bush administration's commitments to fund HIV care worldwide. But signs that they are under challenge are everywhere: in political conduct defined by fierce winner-take-all campaigns, in what David Remnick describes as the "political porn" of best-selling diatribes of character assassination,[10] and in philosophies of governing that marginalize minorities at home as well as America's traditional allies. The related tendency to equate politics with personal self-interest also deflects attention and resources away from the humane intentions that used to be associated with American liberal democracy. The shadows of these concerns are cast on virtually all of the communication settings—traditional and "new" journalism, the presidency, the Congress, and courts—that we will consider in these pages.

Thanks are due to a number of friends and colleagues who provided ideas, criticism, and materials for this manuscript. They include Elisa Barbetti, Michael C. Donaldson, Kathy Grace, Terry Byrne, Susan Ryan, Paul D'Angelo, Ann Li, John Pollock, Janet Robbins, Carol Rowe, and Hilary Woodward. Three anonymous reviewers offered a number of helpful comments and suggestions. As ever, Mary Adamson-King kept the office running when I was distracted with the details of this project. Thanks are also due for data on media use provided by the Pew Research Center for the People and the Press, Andrew Tyndall, the Center for Media and Public Affairs, and the Vanderbilt News Archive, among others. Of course, the conclusions I have reached from their information are mine alone.

The College of New Jersey provided time and a cheerful place to work on this project. Allyn and Bacon/Pearson granted permission to quote passages from a related study completed in 1997. Praeger/Greenwood granted permission to quote excerpts from my earlier survey of military–press relations. I also received encouragement and support from longtime friend and colleague Robert E. Denton Jr. and from Brenda Hadenfeldt at Rowman & Littlefield.

NOTES

1. Curtis White, *The Middle Mind: Why Americans Don't Think for Themselves* (New York: HarperSanFrancisco, 2003), 7.

2. See Eric Gorham, *The Theater of Politics* (Lanham, Md.: Lexington Books, 2000), 23.

3. Kenneth Burke, *A Grammar of Motives* (Berkeley: University of California Press, 1969), xxii.

4. Erving Goffman, *The Presentation of Self in Everyday Life* (New York: Anchor, 1959), 55–56.

5. Bruce Gronbeck, "Electric Rhetoric: The Changing Forms of American Political Discourse," *Vichiana: Rassegna di Studi Classici* 3 (1990): 152.

6. Walter Fisher, *Human Communication as Narration* (Columbia: University of South Carolina Press, 1987), 62.

7. Forrest McDonald, *The Presidency of George Washington* (New York: Norton, 1974), 25.

8. See, for example, Roderick P. Hart, *Seducing America* (New York: Oxford University Press, 1994); Jeffrey Scheuer, *The Sound Bite Society* (New York: Four Walls, 1999); Thomas Patterson, *Out of Order* (New York: Knopf, 1993); Larry Sabato, Mark Stencel, and S. Robert Lichter, *Peepshow: Media and Politics in an Age of Scandal* (Lanham, Md.: Rowman & Littlefield, 2000); James Fallows, *Breaking the News* (New York: Pantheon, 1996); and Robert Entman, *Democracy without Citizens: The Media and the Decay of American Politics* (New York: Oxford University Press, 1989).

9. "Overview: The State of the News Media 2005," Project for Excellence in Journalism, Journalism.org, http://www.stateofthemedia.org/2005/narrative_overview_publicattitudes.asp?cat=7&media=1 (accessed May 25, 2006).

10. David Remnick, "Political Porn," *New Yorker*, July 4, 2005, 29.

Prologue: News, Politics, and the Public Interest on September 10, 2001

The summer of 2001 had been hot in most parts of the nation, especially the northeastern states. As September gained a foothold against the heat, New Yorkers noted with relief that forecasters called for cooler and drier temperatures. The *New York Times*' color weather page predicted that a cold front from the north would produce temperatures in the mid-seventies on the 11th, creating a day that might live up to the song lyrics about Manhattan's clear autumn air. Residents as well as the "bridge and tunnel" crowd of migrant office workers were now back in the city after August vacations in New England and the Jersey shore. Some were still reading the popular beach novels of the summer, including potboilers by Clive Cussler and Catherine Coulter with the usual quotient of international spies and domestic sleuths. Others drifted in and out of movie theaters, passing time with forgettable end-of-summer films like *The Musketeer*, *Rush Hour*, and *Rat Race*.

September traditionally ends the summer hiatus away from the cares of the world. Vacations are over. School is back in session. And many Americans begin to reconnect to the national news circuit that, as much as anything, offers portraits of their hopes and excesses in predictable twenty-four-hour cycles. On Monday the 10th, it was hard for the cable news networks to find a reason to flash their "Breaking News" graphics. And the day's papers were equally thin.

Readers of the *Times* found a front-page story about the city's lethargic but typically hostile mayor's race. Rudolf Giuliani, who could not run again, was beginning to wrap up his municipal career; its final act about to unfold in a nightmare no one could envision.[1] Readers also glanced at a page-one article about a Canadian pilot's successful attempt to land a crippled passenger airline in the Azores. Others focused on the economic recession, medical malpractice insurance, and a tough new policy on visas that forced many Chinese students to cancel trips to the United States. An article on page 3 offered familiar details of death and retribution in the West Bank. And on its opinions page, the paper complained about the new president's reluctance to push for national energy conservation. A second editorial criticized attempts by the free-spending pharmaceutical companies to influence the drug prescription choices of doctors.[2]

In its circular "goldfish bowl" studio on West 57th Street, just two miles north and fourteen hours away from what would become Ground Zero, Dan Rather began the first feed of the *CBS Evening News*. The slow news day meant that the normally energized Rather would have to keep his cowboy hyperbole in check. The best CBS could do was to start with a two-"package" opening focusing on health care. Reporter Bob Orr got a spacious three-minute block of time for a story about the dangers and false claims of dietary supplements. His journalistic peg was footage from Senate hearings featuring a physician who claimed that under current law, anyone could get away with selling grass clippings as supplements. Reporter Sharyl Attkission followed up with a two-minute story on the power of the pharmaceutical industry to dictate the outcomes of medical studies.[3]

These were typical of the "news you can use" stories that the networks preferred to carry over into the new decade. The larger world outside intruded less on the sensibilities of television viewers than at any time since the days of the Cold War. Overseas bureaus had been closed. Reporters covering Congress and the federal regulatory agencies found little interest from New York producers, upstaged in part by the young female faces the networks preferred at the stock exchanges and White House. Lead stories now frequently carried datelines no farther away than the medicine cabinet, the workplace, or the family counselor's office. To be sure, a segment buried near the end of the thirty-minute newscast tentatively struck a few notes that would later be hammered as the twin towers fell a day later. David Martin's piece about airplanes outside their assigned airspace perhaps seemed less urgent, because the guilty parties were American military aircraft who got too close to civilian airports. But pictures of the wreckage from a midair collision were reminders of how quickly the routine of flight can turn into disaster.

Readers of *Time* magazine found a more reassuring world. The wife of the congressman and alleged philanderer Gary Condit wondered whether her married life would ever regain its previous "twinkle." And a longer cover story noted the similarities between the economic recessions that accompanied both of the Bush presidencies.

A sense of how much was about to change in the next twenty-four hours was evident in *Time*'s misplaced observation that the future of the president's political agenda rested in his ability to work with Dennis Hastert, Speaker of the House of Representatives.[4] On that Monday, it was a considerable stretch to conclude that Bush's political fortunes could have depended on a camera-shy legislator few Americans could even identify—possible only because Bush seemed to have so little interest in the rest of the world and only a vague desire to shape a domestic agenda. His clearest objectives were to push failing schools to reform and to shape national priorities on a doctrine of self-reliance modeled around the sparse social services of his native Texas.

By 8:46 A.M. on Tuesday, this old political agenda would be swept aside by four commercial airliners inexplicably commandeered and turned into flying bombs. George W. Bush was probably as prepared as any president can be to deal with the kind catastrophic human crisis that the immediate attacks on the World Trade Center and Pentagon represented. Terrorism as a political wildcard had already worn itself into the national psyche. For decades, presidents had received daily briefings about the efforts of others to—in Bill Clinton's words—"kill the innocent and . . . strike fear and burn hatred into the hearts of the rest of us."[5] Where Bush was different was that he was arguably the least willing of any recent White House resident to deal with the far-reaching international causes that would soon recast his presidency. After officially disowning a series of international agreements early in his administration and casting foreign and military policy in a unilateralist mold, he would have to backtrack and seek international help in Afghanistan and Iraq. But that awkward U-turn was still months in the future, after worldwide sympathy from 9/11 had been eroded by his decision to use the American military as his primary instrument of foreign policy.

With the attacks in New York, the most prominent physical landmark in the city took its place with another symbol of national disaster. Americans reached back to the catastrophe of the Japanese attack on Pearl Harbor to find a moment of such appalling national horror. The attack was massive, sudden, and unexpected. In New York, 2,749 office workers, airline passengers, and rescuers perished in the jet-fueled infernos. Thousands more barely escaped what seemed the unimaginable collapse of the twin 110-story towers.[6] With the simultaneous attack on the Pentagon, the nation experienced a sense of vulnerability unknown since the early years of World War II.

Within three hours, nearly all Americans had heard about the attacks. One study of a university community indicates that about half learned the news from another person; others, from radio and television.[7] Soon after, millions began the familiar ritual of sitting out a national crisis tuned to a cable news channel or network for hours and sometimes days.

National crises turn Americans into spectators of distant traumas where narratives of terrorism, assassination, or war momentarily connect them to each other. Recast through a nationalist screen, these are then converted into predictable secondary narratives of defiance and resolve.

The World Trade Center, moments after the first attack. Many of the first images came from midtown cameras two miles north.
Source: Courtesy of Prints and Photographs Division, Library of Congress.

The more Americans watched the unfolding horrors of the attacks, the more unsettled they reported themselves to be.[8] Many no doubt sensed what is now a cliché: that the attacks had changed not only the landscape of fourteen acres in Lower Manhattan but the political landscape as well. Live and via endless taped replays, television's insistence that Americans rewitness the evident horrors of the attack meant that the nation would mobilize in a massive political response and an ideological reversal.

With the events of that Tuesday morning, a sentimental American preference for a Cold War agenda of competing superpowers was finally put to rest. Compared with the United States' old Soviet adversaries, the stateless enemy that attacked New York and Washington was far more elusive and evocative of endless doomsday fantasies. In the process of turning the sluggish vessel of American power into these unpredictable winds, a struggling and unpopular president would convince others that he had finally found his bearings. In a stunning act of simplistic compression, Bush used his 2002 State of the Union address to identify a collection of dysfunctional states—Iraq, Iran, and North Korea—as an "axis of evil."[9] Others such as Afghanistan were added later because they were controlled by leaders or tribes beyond the influence of the Western democracies.

In different ways, each served Bush's new "strike first" doctrine by apparently harboring "known terrorists" such as Osama bin Laden or plausibly threatening to use "weapons of mass destruction" against neighboring states.

This confusing reduction of geopolitics to a hit list of miscreants served its purpose. The point was not that the nation needed immediate clarity about the root causes of 9/11. National crises feed the search for simplistic measures. The prime need was for a list of enemies and a clear declaration that the world's most powerful government was about to be deployed to bring about their destruction. Bush must have calculated that a populace will follow a leader who promises security and asserts military power to guarantee it.

And so the nation and the president were swept into a rhetorical campaign that mixed grim warnings of retribution with nervous celebrations of American exceptionalism. Military campaigns would soon follow in Afghanistan and, later, in a full-scale invasion and occupation of Iraq. In the process, national priorities and different news templates were established.

Not since the Vietnam era had military plans dominated national headlines and affected so many families. American troop levels just in Iraq quickly swelled to nearly 250,000, with many reservists called to active duty. Congress quickly passed budget resolutions to enlarge the Pentagon budget by $87 billion. And a steady diet of news about Americans killed in action returned to the nation's living rooms. As with Vietnam, most Asian, Latin American, and European allies declined to contribute to the American occupation. And similar to that period, a president disliked by many Europeans traveled to ostensibly friendly capitals like London heavily guarded against citizens ready to take to the streets in protest.[10]

Even in the face of growing isolation of the United States, most news organizations readily accepted the White House premise that the nation was now in an open-ended war at home and overseas.[11] As thousands of troops were committed to Iraq, Afghanistan, and forward support bases in Europe and the Middle East, networks jockeyed for retired generals to explain how forces would dominate the enemy. Daily news accounts of Americans lost in action were inevitably paired with the circular logic of honoring their memory by seeing the "global" struggle through to its illusory end. Journalistic organizations picked up the lexicon of the policy and military strategists, with their talk of "regime change," "preemptive self-defense," "shock and awe bombing," "weapons of mass destruction," "terrorist cells," and "homeland security."

In further echoes of the Vietnam era, White House aides complained that news organizations were spending more time on military casualties overseas than on reconstruction in places like Iraq. In fact, it was not true for television news, which clung to the president's emphasis on "nation building."[12] However, by September of 2003, two years after 9/11, the United States' news agenda appeared to be set for years to come, put into play by ten fanatics bent on attacking New York and the Pentagon and sustained by rhetorical and military campaigns against a growing list of "rogue" states. Prior to 9/11, the news database LexisNexis catalogued a little more than fifty foreign and American news articles a day about terrorism. By 2004, the number had increased sixteenfold to nearly nine hundred in a twenty-four-hour news cycle.[13]

As if the ghosts of anti-Communism required their own resurrection, there reemerged within our own modern *terrorspeak* many of the same tropes that were common at the start of the Cold War. Terrorism as an idea flourishes because we have linguistic and psychological habits that assure its survival. Those certain that the nation is at grave risk find comfort in terms and fantasies suggesting that larger forces are behind worldwide acts of political retaliation. We are probably more likely to be struck by lightning than by terrorists.[14] And by some measures, the world has never been as peaceful.[15] But substitute "terrorists" or Al Qaeda for the older poison represented by Communism, and most of the rhetoric still works. *They* are largely unseen but organized and unified. *Their* "operatives" have betrayed our hospitality and infiltrated our cities. And *they* have taken credit for inflicting wounds on the infidels of the West—something we "know," after all, from *their* boastful websites. The collective pronoun simplifies real-world realities that would otherwise require understanding diverse and sometimes contradictory political motivations. We let our imaginations build an enemy of mythic dimensions, one that is all the more powerful because of its anonymity.

The fiction of a single collective pronoun repeats the mistake of the early Cold War that assumed Chinese, Russian, or Vietnamese Communists were all part of a coordinated global effort. In these constructions, our war is with a persistent and cunning foe. In spite of all we know about the dysfunctions of dispersed organizations, we look for signs that "cells" in London, Iraq, Madrid, or New York are part of a single "cancerous" source.[16] For publics who will usually trade curiosity for simple reassurance, there is comfort in the rhetorical construction of so formidable an enemy.

Religion also has its own role in descriptions of the adversary. In a period of American life when political leaders in the White House and Congress believe they are waging a battle to preserve the presumptively Christian soul of the nation, a war fought on the hallowed ground of religious belief has its advantages. In its day, invective that linked Communism to the "godless" and "atheistic" worked its magic.[17] Today the religious markers are different. The enemy this time *has* a religion, but the wrong one. Islamic fundamentalism is widely viewed to be the motivating force for most acts of violence against the West. Never mind that some research suggests that suicide terrorists in Iraq,

Israel, and elsewhere have individual rather than religious motivations. Robert Pape's analysis of hundreds of such bombers suggests that they were provoked less by religion than the more logical motivation of expelling foreign occupiers out of the Middle East, especially the Palestinian territories and Iraq.[18] But it would be more discomforting to reach the conclusion that the motives of "terrorists" in Iraq and elsewhere are not dissimilar to the motives of American insurgents who waged their own war against British occupiers.[19] After all, that insight might suggest that our interventionist policy seeds the very kinds of terrorist acts we seek to end.[20]

To be sure, the doctrine of military preemption that is reviled internationally never gained widespread acceptance even within the United States.[21] But the national turn to the political right that started in the contested presidential election of 2000 benefited from the new war against America's political enemies. As a bottomless source of both fear and reassurance,[22] terrorism assured the 2004 reelection of George W. Bush and Republican majorities in the Congress. As these pages reflect, its promise of an endless struggle is firmly entrenched as an organizing principle of our national life.

NOTES

1. The World Trade Center had been attacked in 1993. A car bomb had been placed in a garage under the buildings, with smoke damage and six fatalities. But no one thought the center itself could be completely destroyed, even after a direct hit by an airliner. See Jim Dwyer and Kevin Flynn, *102 Minutes* (New York: Holt, 2005), 7–11.

2. *New York Times*, September 10, 2001.

3. Abstract of the *CBS Evening News*, September 10, 2001, Vanderbilt Television News Archive, http://tvnews.vanderbilt.edu/TVN-displayfullbroadcast.pl?SID=20060607978820800&UID=&CID=45842&auth=&code=TVN&getmonth=9&getdate=10&getyear=2001&Network=CBS&HeaderLink=642363&source=BroadcastSelect&action=getfullbroadcast (accessed June 7, 2006).

4. *Time*, September 17, 2001.

5. Bill Clinton, speech at George Washington University, August 5, 1996.

6. A detailed account of how many survived and others perished is told in Dwyer and Flynn, *102 Minutes*.

7. Stacey Kanihan and Kendra Gale, "Within 3 Hours, 97 Percent Learn about 9/11 Attacks," *Newspaper Research Journal*, Winter 2003, 78–83.

8. Kanihan and Gale, "Within 3 Hours," 87–88.

9. George W. Bush, "State of the Union Address," *New York Times*, January 30, 2002, A22.

10. In February 2003, an estimated one million British citizens turned out on one day to protest American plans to attack Iraq. Later in the year, an army of American and British police were mobilized for the visit of George Bush on a state visit to

Britain, America's major ally in Iraq. Scott Lindaw, "Bush Heads to London to Discuss Iraq," Associated Press, November 18, 2003, http://news.yahoo.com (accessed November 18, 2003).

11. Generally, the mainstream media accepted the president's assumption that the nation was "at war," with serious dissent about its consequences left to smaller opinion magazines and a host of Internet sites. Bruce Williams, "Saying What We Want When We're Supposed to Watch What We Say: The New Media Environment, Internet Chat Rooms, and Public Discourse after 9/11," paper presented at the National Communication Association Annual Meeting, Miami Beach, Florida, November 22, 2003.

12. *Tyndall Weekly*, October 18, 2003.

13. Comparison of articles in the LexisNexis newspaper database with *terrorism* in the headline on September 30, 2001, and September 3, 2004.

14. Nassim Taleb, "Scaring Us Senseless," *New York Times*, July 25, 2005, sec. 4, 13.

15. Gregg Easterbrook, "The End of War?" *New Republic*, May 30, 2005, 18.

16. For alternate views of the mythic Al Qaeda, see Jason Burke, "Al Qaeda," *Foreign Policy*, May–June 2004, 18–20, 22, 24, 26; and Kimberly McCloud and Adam Dolnik, "Debunking the Myth of Al Qaeda," *Christian Science Monitor*, May 23, 2002, 11.

17. For a representative sample, see Joseph McCarthy's 1950 speech at Wheeling, West Virginia, in "Remarks," *Congressional Record*, 81st Congress, 2nd session (Washington, D.C.: U.S. Government Printing Office, 1951), 1954–57.

18. Robert Pape, *Dying to Win: The Strategic Logic of Suicide Terrorism* (New York: Random House, 2005), 3–7.

19. The colonial revolt was essentially against British occupation, with its economic and political prerogatives. Moreover, although George Washington never liked it, much of the American insurgency was fought by separate militias against a more organized British command—a pattern that shares some similarities with the Iraqi insurgency. See Walter Millis, *Arms and Men: America's Military History and Military Policy from the Revolution to the Present* (New York: Capricorn Books, 1956), 22–29.

20. Analysts such as Robert Jervis predict just this unintended effect of the Iraqi intervention. Robert Jervis, "Terrorism, Preventive War and the Bush Doctrine," Politics Forum lecture, the College of New Jersey, November 10, 2005.

21. In October 2005, fully half of the nation thought that "using force in Iraq" was the "wrong decision." "Plurality Now Sees Bush Presidency as Unsuccessful," poll from the Pew Research Center for the People and the Press, October 13, 2005, http://people-press.org/reports/display.php3?ReportID=259 (accessed May 25, 2006).

22. Fully 86 percent of Republicans defined terrorism as an "issue that mattered most" in 2004, compared with 14 percent of Democrats. Katharine Q. Seelye, "Moral Issues Cited as a Defining Issue of the Election," *New York Times*, November 4, 2004, P4.

Chapter One

Frames of Reference in an Era of Casual Spectatorship

> The ingenuity of the human mind in constructing worlds and the capacity of language to indulge that talent are subtle and concealed, but they are also the fundamental influences upon politics.[1]
>
> —Murray Edelman

When Americans are asked to think about politics, they are likely to respond from a reservoir of preexisting frames. For an increasing number of citizens, the chatter surrounding the nation's civil life has become a numbing clamor of predictable opinions that sometimes obscure rather than clarify issues and choices. Even as their own party identification has declined, their leaders in Congress and state legislatures have turned into ideological warriors. Legislative politics is *more* partisan and bitter, intensifying feelings of a disconnect between citizens and their political institutions. In this frame, political life is often seen as a *performance for the public* by agents who in reality serve a different and privileged group of "special interests." For many Americans, huge corporations and their K Street advocates in Washington are the true patrons of the political process.[2]

The rhetoric of performance is equally dismissed by the news media as predictable ritual, providing justification for focusing on the game of politics, with its infinitely variable combinations of moves and countermoves. In the words of one campaign pollster, "the culture of political analysis has completely overtaken the culture of ideas."[3]

The result is often a public that is indifferent and sullen—moods that get reflected back to them in the media's own reporting. When political attitudes do capture the imagination, they often seem to be energized more by rebellion than by ideas. These days Americans are often clearer about what they like or oppose than what they endorse. This reactive state of mind explains a great deal, ranging from public acceptance of a fear-driven "war on terrorism," to the voters' willingness to turn over governorships in Minnesota and California to entertainers who made lucrative careers acting out fantasies of revenge.

From a less judgmental *structural* frame, politics has actually changed very little. It is still about the management and control of the resources of the state. And it is represented on a daily basis by what happens in the White House and Congress, as well as their counterparts at the state and municipal levels. We cherish the idea that any citizen can enter the fray. And there are still enough citizen-politicians in the mix to keep the romance alive. But most American leaders still come from the ranks of legal and professional elites.[4] And like Washington, Adams, and Madison before them, they are still governed by evolving constitutional prerogatives that divide power between executive, legislative and judicial branches.

Today's political leaders differ from their earlier counterparts largely through their dependence on public relations professionals and celebrity-journalists for representations of their work. The effects of this professionalization are, in various ways, the subject of most of this book. Three remaining frames—labeled here as staging, media, and alternative—are our primary focus. While staging is our dominant theme, each frame provides clarity about the others. To understand the possibilities of staging, we must also survey the scope and power of the mass media as the primary engines of political consciousness. And while we lament a national tendency for spectatorship rather than participation, we also want to look at alternative routes to political consciousness: ways to engage the world that can transcend the limits of prepackaged events. A recurring theme in these pages is the wish that we exploit the inherent powers of drama to rekindle the nation's impaired capacity for political imagination.

THE STAGING FRAME

The problems and opportunities of approaching politics from the perspective of staging can be seen from a small but representative moment: a contrived photo opportunity at what was supposed to be the end of the 2003 war in Iraq. On May 1, White House advisers arranged a dramatic arrival of President George W. Bush by fighter jet onto the perilously small deck of the aircraft carrier *Abraham Lincoln*. The idea was that he would personally thank the sailors onboard for their work in support of the invasion and at the same time arrive by the most photogenic means possible. A huge sign, "Mission Accomplished," was draped over the ship's superstructure to complete the carefully constructed tableau.

The normal route for such a visit would be by presidential helicopter from nearby San Diego. But that would not have had the panache of an arrival aboard a navy S-3B Viking jet, its tail hook just catching the deck wire of the short runway. Carrier landings are among the riskiest maneuvers navy pilots are likely to undertake. But true to the event's cinematic potential, cameras were ready to capture the president emerging from the cockpit, as one reporter recalls, "in full olive flight suit and combat boots, his helmet tucked jauntily under his left arm. As he exchanged salutes with the sailors, his ejection harness, hugging him tightly between the legs, gave him the bowlegged swagger of a top gun."[5]

A "stunt photo-op," some concluded.[6] Others decried the president's "ham-fisted theatrics."[7] But few press outlets missed the captivating pictures of the commander and chief on the carrier and his remarks thanking the *Lincoln*'s sailors for their dedication and hard work.

At least initially, the event seemed to work, as master publicist Michael Deaver described it, as a "powerful visual, not only of Bush as commander in chief, but of his strength as world leader."[8] Others noted that Bush had produced perfect footage for ads yet to be made for the coming 2004 presidential campaign.

But a moment of high theater designed to contribute to national support for an administration can sometimes undermine it. Even carefully chosen symbols can provide their own triggers for useful public discussion, and this event raised two issues that would touch on the character of the president and his war policy. The first was that, to some, the landing looked *too* calculated. Not since the days of Teddy Roosevelt had a president dressed up in full military gear, a fact made more ironic by much public discussion of Bush's limited military experience in the Texas National Guard. "I do not begrudge his salute to America's warriors on the carrier Lincoln," noted West Virginia's plain-spoken senator Robert Byrd. "But I do question the motives of a deskbound president who assumes the garb of a warrior for the purposes of a speech."[9] Others observed that the carrier was actually delayed in returning to its home port in order to accommodate the presidential visit. They also debunked a White House story that the *Lincoln* was too far out at sea to receive the president by more conventional means.[10]

The second problem was the large "Mission Accomplished" banner. In the days to follow, the crisp military certainty of its wording would be undone by more bloodshed. Carefully placed in the background to frame the president as he stepped off the navy jet, the banner was clearly intended to suggest an activist leader guiding the military as it made the world safe from nations building "weapons of mass destruction." Not only were no such weapons found in Iraq, but the war itself was not really over. Continuous news of casualties in Iraq began to undermine the message of the event, especially when the number of "postwar" deaths of GIs surpassed those during the war itself.

The staff on the carrier later tried to fall on their swords by declaring that the sign was their doing, not the White House's. And the president was only too happy to help. "I know it was attributed somehow to some ingenious advance man from my staff," he said. But "they weren't that ingenious."[11] Yet the White House was soon forced to admit that the entire event and banner were their work,[12] a fact that made sense given their meticulous efforts in staging other presidential visits.

This small moment illustrates several conclusions that are at the heart of this book. First and obviously, politics is naturally about the management of impressions through what can generally be called "theatrical" processes. To be "political" is to think often in terms of the effects of decisions and actions on constituents and media. Announcements, speeches, "town meetings," and hearings are designed for the camera and the microphone. Words are carefully chosen for their potential as sound bites. And the calendar of political activities builds on the recurring observances of national life. Second, these events create their own levels of discourse. They are subject to endless interpretation and reinterpretation. They invite favorable or negative assessments of motive. And they are, in equal measure, *spurs to public discussion* as well as pathways taken to subvert it.

In the case of the Bush White House, the objectives and costs of the Iraq war were promoted in a variety of ways, including the carrier landing. By taking the bold and perhaps reckless step of verging out of the presidential persona, the president called attention to the values he wished to enact through his choice. In short, this minor spectacle created its own contested meanings that—like all discourse—would be measured against specific facts, attributed motives, and their intended audiences.

To "manage" or "stage" an event is not to escape politics or its hard choices but to invite assessment of the event's meaning in terms of known facts and the credibility of its authors. The generative sources of this perspective lie most clearly in the work of Erving Goffman and Kenneth Burke. Goffman captured and popularized the essentials of the performance imperative and its corollary concepts of roles and expectations.[13] In a more diffuse way, rhetorical critic Kenneth Burke used the language of "dramatism" (with terms such as *act*, *agent*, and *scene*) to build a complete analytic and critical system.[14] With others, Goffman and Burke provided a compelling and coherent case for understanding human action as the natural outcome of the need to "sustain" and "manage impressions."[15]

THE MEDIA FRAME

What we know about the world has been told to us or performed for us by others at the distant end of a long organizational chain. The United States is awash in media outlets that make up these links. No society comes close to matching its expressive and informational infrastructure. There are nearly 1,500 daily newspapers published in the fifty states, reaching nearly half of all households.[16] More than 13,000 radio stations are on the air, and nearly 1,700 individual television stations. Almost 12,000 cable systems operating in 34,000 individual communities[17] offer television choices that place TV entertainment and absurdities just one click away.

In these electronic and print forums, politics is a common subject of discussion and ridicule. Radio talk show host Rush Limbaugh, for example, has an audience of fifteen million listeners. He and his pretenders in virtually every radio market fill the airwaves with Limbaugh's signature blend of right-wing machismo, anger, and satire.[18] Bloggers on the Internet do much the same, a topic we will return to in a later chapter. But television holds a special place in the organization of our perceptual world. "We are now a culture whose information, ideas and epistemology are given form" by its presence, notes Neil Postman.[19] Perhaps no other piece of technology has captured—or perhaps enfeebled—the human imagination. Americans spend almost as much time watching television as they do sleeping. The average home has a set turned on almost eight hours a day. And in spite of the fact that there are literally dozens of impoverished but politically sophisticated magazines in circulation in the United States,[20] nearly 70 percent of Americans report getting most of their news from television.[21]

Key to the media frame is the idea that media generally guide us to certain issues and away from others. This is the core prediction of agenda-setting theory, which accounts for the diffusion of political information throughout society.[22] In the words of one of its early researchers, agenda setting "captures the idea so long cherished by social scientists that the mass media have a significant impact on our focus of attention and what we think about."[23] In one early study, for instance, Maxwell McCombs and D. L. Shaw found that newspapers in North Carolina were "the prime movers" in defining the issues voters would focus on in the 1972 presidential campaign. "Issues emphasized by the newspaper in the late spring and early summer exerted a major influence on what voters regarded as the major issues during the fall campaign."[24] Television, they found, played a similar role in highlighting other issues as election day approached.

Consider the process of agenda setting on the single issue of abused children. As Barbara Nelson notes, the problem of battered children has been known and discussed by a wide range of social welfare groups over the last hundred years. But public awareness of the problem surfaced only after specialists writing for professional journals were able to comment on the problem in general interest media, such as *Newsweek* and *Life* magazine. She notes that these accounts (starting, largely, in the 1960s) then triggered more news reports of the crime of child abuse, creating an upward curve of public awareness. "Once child abuse was rediscovered as a social problem, newspapers began to cover cases more frequently and intensively."[25] Such coverage then provided a level of public awareness that would enhance the likelihood of future reporting on the issue.

On "normal" news days, important print sources such as the Associated Press, *New York Times*, *Wall Street Journal*, and *Washington Post* act as de facto brokers of political news for other media. In times of a man-made or natural catastrophe, however, the pattern tends to reverse. Power migrates *to* cable news organizations as millions of Americans look for extended coverage. With a major story or crisis such as the events of 9/11 or Hurricane Katrina in 2005, cable news tends to go into a single-event mode. Its repetitious fugue of related stories finally burns into the consciousness of most Americans.

In political campaigns, the essential features of agenda setting seem especially dramatic. The importance the American public attaches to certain issues or individuals is largely a function of news coverage. In political campaigns, as Roger Simon has observed, candidates no longer "count the house" to estimate their prospects on election day. "Today, they count the cameras."[26] In the early stages of presidential campaigns, for example, the success of candidates is likely to be tied to the decisions of the local and national media to feature or ignore them. Media writer Tom Rosenstiel has called this the "invisible primary." Reflecting a widely held view among reporters and candidates, he notes that the first presidential primary is preceded by an invisible one "conducted by a closed circle of journalists and Washington insiders that decides which candidates could raise money, build an organization, and win party support."[27]

Agenda-setting theory has been refined in recent years by researchers such as Shanto Iyengar and Donald Kinder, who have noted that television shapes not only our awareness of events but also the very standards by which we come to judge the performance of specific public figures, such as the president. Through what Iyengar and Kinder call the "priming effect" of television, they note that we are inclined to judge the agents that appear in stories based on the context the story places them in. For example, "when primed by television news stories that focus on national defense, people judge the president largely by how well he has provided, as they see it, for the nation's defense; when primed by stories about inflation, people evaluate the president by how he has managed, in their view, to keep prices down."[28] By experimentally altering different video news segments in which the president and others were viewed, Iyengar and Kinder were able to assess how individuals altered their judgments. "By calling attention to some matters while ignoring others," they note, "television news influences the standards by which governments, presidents, policies, and candidates for public office are judged."[29]

Thus, if a newscast does a package of stories covering, say, a visit of the president to Japan, priming theory would lead us to believe that how that visit is framed will affect our attitudes toward the president. Is the story introduced with a reminder that the Japanese government is indebted to the present administration for helping stabilize its own economy? Or is this package introduced with references to the president's last visit, which was marred by a major diplomatic failure? Priming theory would lead us to assume that the president would fare better in the first case than the second. In other words, "the more prominent an issue is in the national information stream, the greater . . . the weight accorded it in making political judgements."[30]

For the vast American mainstream, politics is thus what the networks, cable channels, and local television stations tell them it is. Our civil life is a series of narratives jointly constructed by political agents and their dependent observers in the information and entertainment industries. Currently ABC, NBC, Fox News, and CNN are still the most common national portals into this world. These networks represent a declining but important part of the four hours of television consumed daily by the typical American. The networks also have their regional counterparts in television markets across the nation. Some are journalistically as strong as KCRA in Sacramento, with its emphasis on serious investigative reporting, or as weak as all three network affiliates in Albuquerque.[31]

Only a minority of Americans seek out more. Smaller numbers see an impressive range of campaign events, public forums, and congressional work on the cable industry's authentic gift to the nation's civic life, C-SPAN. Its coverage shuns the slice-and-dice editing common to the networks, giving most Americans their only chance for direct observation of political work and performance. National Public Radio's *Morning Edition* offers its weekly audience of thirteen million listeners a combination of headlines and deeper national and international reporting.[32] Many also read about politics in the daily press. Some of the richest political coverage exists in the nation's leading newsweeklies and newspapers represented by the *New York Times*, *Washington Post*, *Wall Street Journal*, *The Economist*, and others. Americans also seek out-of-the-mainstream political opinions on the Internet or in a spectrum of opinion magazines. But the national norm in terms of the primary sources of political consciousness lies in television news and its entertainment variants (i.e., *ABC World News Tonight*, *NBC Nightly News*, *60 Minutes*, *Dateline*, and their cable counterparts).

This dominance of television as a vehicle for political information has been apparent for years, but it needs several important caveats and clarifications. First, *dominance* is a relative term. In the last decade, traditional network news shows have not been able to hold on to their audiences. The pool of available viewers for any single program is shrinking because of more channel choices and more competition from the Internet. Only about 22 percent of Americans between the ages of thirty-five and fifty "regularly" watch a network newscast.[33] And the percentages are even lower for younger Americans, who now spend as much time on the Internet as they do watching television.[34] Second, most forms of television news represent a relatively low and distant form of political consciousness. A half-hour "news hole" represents about twenty minutes of actual story content (see table 2.2 in chapter 2). And the kinds of stories that get told have changed over the last thirty years. As table 1.1 illustrates, less time is spent on government and international news. More time goes to crime and health news reporting. And within that space there must also be room for stories about scandals, celebrities, and less-than-urgent events.[35] Because television wants to hold our attention, it keeps its segments short and firmly in control of the reporter-narrator. Those whom the stories are ostensibly about—ranging from economists to presidents—are given mere seconds to make their own points.[36]

To be sure, "crisis coverage" of events such as a terrorist attack can change all of these patterns. On September 11, 2001, the average American watched more than eight hours of news coverage.[37] Virtually nothing the news business had planned for that day remained in place. The nation was under attack from the air. Victims were lost, and heroes were about to be discovered. The president promised revenge, and some news narratives indirectly nursed fantasies of an invasion that would reach into the farthest corners of the conti-

Table 1.1. Top Story Categories for Newscasts at ABC, CBS, and NBC, 2004*

Category	Number
Iraq	2,567
Presidential campaign	1,688
Economy/business	1,108
Terrorism	917
Crime	691
Natural disasters	679
Health issues	667
Sports	331

Source: Adapted from Media Monitor, January/February 2005, "Year in Review," http://www.cmpa.co/mediaMonitor/documents/05.03.28.Jan.Feb.pdf (accessed April 28, 2005).
*Several topics featured in some stories.

nent. But as Robert Putnam has noted, "Scandals and war can still rouse our attention, but generally speaking, fewer Americans follow public affairs now than did a quarter century ago."[38]

A third key conclusion about television news is that we frequently underestimate the importance of its local forms in individual markets. Some 60 percent of Americans claim to be regular viewers of news at the local level, significantly higher than the audiences for national news programs.[39] These viewers are older, sometimes isolated, and more loyal to their choices of programs. They are also rewarded with what is perhaps television's most significant psychological effect: its ability to manufacture a sense of familiarity and identification with its recurring personalities. This process of "parasocial interaction" can allow television "personalities" to function as surrogates for limited or nonexistent interpersonal relationships, providing sources of continuity in an age of discontinuities.[40] Reporters may come and go. But an anchor departing the *Six O'clock News* for the rewards of a bigger market may be missed by viewers like a lost child. As many have noted, the "information" of television is as much about the personal details of its recurring characters as their ideas or acts.[41]

Indeed, at the local level, high-quality news may hardly be the point. A Project for Excellence in Journalism study in 2001 found that a typical newscast has little room to engage the viewer on significant political issues. Its sample of many large and small market stations found a number of common but superficial features, including the disturbing fact that most virtually ignore poverty, welfare, and homelessness in their coverage. Researchers observed a number of patterns indicative of the pressure to complete for the limited interests of most viewers:

- Forty percent of the stories last 30 seconds or less.
- One in four stories is about crime, law, or courts.
- Less than 1 percent of stories could be called "investigative."
- Health stories outnumber all other social issues by 32 percent.
- There are as many stories about the bizarre (8 percent) as there are about civic institutions.[42]

The old cliché that television functions as a "headline" service is confirmed in these findings. While it is obviously true that richer and more detailed sources of information exist, far fewer Americans seek them out (table 1.2). What remains most troubling with the weakest of television "shows" that masquerade as "news" is that we take them seriously at all. As Postman has noted, television "is at its most trivial and, therefore, most dangerous when . . . it presents itself as a carrier of important cultural conversations."[43]

Table 1.2. Sources of Campaign News, 1992–2004: First Medium Mentioned (%)

	February 1992	*February 1996*	*January 2000*	*January 2004*
Television	68	73	68	68
Newspaper	20	15	15	15
Radio	8	8	8	7
Internet	—	1	4	6
Magazines	2	1	2	1
Other	1	1	2	1
Don't know	1	1	1	2

Source: Adapted from Pew Research Center for the People and the Press, "Cable and Internet Loom Large . . . ," January 11, 2004, http://people-press.org/reports/display.php3?ReportID=200 (accessed May 25, 2006).

EXPANDING THE RANGE OF THE MEDIA FRAME

Although the formulas and constraints of television define the political world for many, it would be a mistake to look only at traditional settings such as newscasts for political content. A number of productive pathways are open to us to illuminate how forms of political "spin" and "image management" invite analysis. Consider three methodological starting points.

First, "texts" can take many forms. Only two generations ago, a political message was usually defined as a speech. Now, however, we understand that political messages exist at several levels: as traditional messages in the form of ads, speeches, campaign websites, and so on, or as the subtext to ostensibly nonpolitical information (i.e., a Smithsonian exhibit of the World War II bomber *Enola Gay*, Ken Burns's 1990 television series *The Civil War*, or Oliver Stone's 1991 film *J.F.K.*). Moreover, the possibilities for innovative dramatization of political choices are represented by endless examples of diverse texts: Tony Kushner's expansive portrait of the United States' early responses to HIV/AIDS in *Angels in America* (2003), the rhetoric of the "Truth and Reconciliation" movement that blossomed in Africa and Latin America and bore fruit in postapartheid South Africa,[44] the steady efforts of a small Seattle-based "journal of positive futures" to redefine political action in terms of community-level problem solving,[45] or even the decision of conductor Daniel Barenboim and author Edward Said to organize an orchestra made up of young Israeli and Palestinian musicians.[46] Political attitudes and values are embedded in the rhetorical choices of virtually every message form. And in cases like those just cited, they can break through the dry crust of conventional he said/she said reporting.

Second, it is the nature of humans and institutions to be rhetorical and dramatic. Individuals have expressive needs: ways to represent feelings and passions, with or without information to induce action from someone else. Communication is not just an ancillary to a more authentic political reality. It is frequently *the* dominant reality. What did it mean, for example, that the Pentagon hired a noted scene designer to build a $250,000 television set in Qatar for military briefings during the 2003 invasion of Iraq?[47] A conventional approach might be to conclude that they had resorted to "theatrics" far removed from the business of military affairs. But more than a few writers have noted that Hollywood and the Pentagon increasingly seem to be in the same business of dramatizing and portraying the effects of military missions.[48] The deeper lesson is that it is sometimes an error to see "representations"—dramatic or symbolic—as reductions of something else that must be understood in noncommunicative terms. To be sure, in the literal world of the theater, it makes sense to note that scenery, props, and actors are stand-ins meant to replicate a reality we perhaps already "know." But even in this world a play gains force by revealing plausible and deeper truths through character and conduct. As Hugh Duncan has noted, theater is "the means by which we become objects to ourselves."[49] The Department of Defense does not merely "reflect" its work in its rhetoric and public relations activities. Communication *is* its work or at least a significant part of it. The business of managing public opinion is inexorably woven into its essence and structure.

Hardened White House operatives know this, though their inflated claims of power can seriously underestimate the essential importance of truth in drama. A writer preparing a long essay on the 2004 campaign recalls with some chagrin what an aide to President George W. Bush described to him as the place of journalism:

> Guys like you are "in what we call the reality-based community," which he defined as people who "believe that solutions emerge from your judicious study of discernible reality." I nodded and murmured something about enlightenment principles and empiricism. He cut me off. "That's not the way the world really works anymore," he continued. "We're an empire now, and when we act, we create our own reality. And while you're studying that reality—judiciously, as you will—we'll act again, creating other new realities, which you can study too, and that's how things will sort out. We're history's actors . . . and you, all of you, will be left to just study what we do."[50]

The aide's statement may have been stunningly arrogant. But it is also true.

Third, we increasingly approach many of life's texts from a "side stage" rather than "front-of-stage" view. As Joshua Meyrowitz describes it, a side-stage view of life lets us see performers shift from one role to another.[51] When we see a performance from the wings of the stage, we glimpse not just the actors in character but all of the apparatus that supports the performance, as well as all of its artifices. A simple view of the theatrical metaphor invites us to constitute "performances" as what is—at least figuratively—"onstage" at any given moment. All of us have onstage moments when we move through the public parts of our lives at work and other venues where a performance is partly the product of others' expectations. But we increasingly live in an age that has as much interest in what goes on *behind* the curtain as in front: what constitutes our private lives as well as our public selves. To be sure, the novel and the film have always explored these "back regions." The backstage drama was as much a staple of Hollywood in the last millennium as it was in the new. Television has simply taken the process further.

This interest in the side-stage view obviously applies to professional performers but also to the rest of us as we negotiate the changing requirements of various audience/scene combinations. We have essentially become judges of the ways others manage their role repertoires as the environments of their daily lives change. This is primarily the source of fascination in television's glut of reality shows, with their voyeuristic fascination with teams, strategies, and "makeover" surprises. In this last genre, a show focuses on the laborious back-region preparations to transform a person or a house. Only the last act is a front-region event, where the transformation of the actor or a home is fulfilled in a front-region "coming out," to the evident delight of all. Like campaigns leading to elections, the strategies of design and execution *are* the story. As natural decoders of motives, we want to observe and "read" the attempts of all involved to manage new scene/act adjustments.

ALTERNATIVE SOURCES OF POLITICAL CONSCIOUSNESS

This book is primarily about the production of meaning through journalism, narrative, and television news. It observes a mostly passive polis reacting to a continuing parade of events staged to confirm or challenge governmental power. But if television remains as the primary shaper of political consciousness, what are its alternatives? What other kinds of experience can awaken or intensify interest in our national life?

In an era when most writers lament low levels of civic engagement, Michael Schudson's work offers an optimistic contrast. His expansive list of the ways modern Americans participate in public life covers a range of activities beyond passive spectatorship. Americans, he notes, are citizens not only at the polls.

> They are citizens in their homes, schools, and places of employment. Women and minorities self-consciously do politics just by turning up, so long as they turn up in positions of authority and responsibility in institutions where women and minorities were once rarely seen. They do politics when they walk into a room, anyone's moral equals, and expect to be treated accordingly. The gay and

> lesbian couples in Hawaii in 1991 or Vermont in 1997 are political when they try to be legally married. . . . Others do politics when they wear a "Thank You for Not Smoking" button or when they teach their children nutritional labeling at the supermarket or when they join in class action suits against producers of silicone breast implants, Dalkon shields, or asbestos insulation.[52]

Indeed, many actions that we take serve as a reminder that the "personal is political." But an expansive view of citizen participation must include more, a view Schudson acknowledges. For starters, it might encompass the kinds of concerns taken up by progressives at the turn of the twentieth century to assure at least a limited form of social justice for vulnerable groups like children and the poor. For example, Robert Putnam notes that activists of the progressive era "devoted their intellectual, organizational, and financial energies to blazing constructive new paths for youth," setting up organizations, parks, and clubs.[53] In that remarkable age, scores of commentators and organizations became committed to reforming what William Allen White describes as a government that "had fallen into the hands of self-seekers" and widened the gap between "the haves and have nots."[54]

Putnam's reformers were moved to active work and financial support. They did more than show up. Presumably, they also became committed for reasons larger than their own self-interests. Therein lies the great divide in the meaning of citizenship. "Gaming the system" for oneself or family is easy. Voting one's interest takes little effort and no sense that one is living for others as well as oneself. Millions are more or less engaged at these levels. But only a tiny fraction use their energies or experience to enter into national or community conversations about issues and ideas for which they have no immediate personal or financial stake.

Consider several examples of heightened forms of consciousness where it is possible to imagine motives larger than personal self-interest. In the realm of political advocacy on the left, Moveon.org began as an effort to organize opposition to a congressional steamroller determined to impeach Bill Clinton. The work of a California couple working out of their Berkeley home, Moveon.org slowly evolved into a huge Internet-based campaign to organize the Democratic Party for a whole series of legislative and campaign activities. A portion of its 2.9 million members in every state increased voter registration and turnout in the 2004 election. As a "527" organization under new 2002 campaign finance laws, it also raised $15 million for issue ads against administration policies that, in its members' opinion, would impair the futures of generations yet born.[55]

On the right in the same period was the hierarchy of the American Catholic Church. Faith-based political consciousness has always been part of American life, a kind of wild card that lays down "values" that, for many of those who hold them, are not open to normal processes of debate and compromise. It was perhaps never a greater factor in a modern campaign than in 2004.[56] In that tradition, the church issued a voter's guide to millions of American churchgoers, urging them to vote "to promote the common good." It also listed five "nonnegotiable issues" that—strictly interpreted—would prohibit voting for Democratic candidate John Kerry. The five "serious sins" were abortion, euthanasia, stem cell research, cloning, and homosexual marriage.[57] Members of churches rarely vote as blocs, but more Catholics voted for Methodist George Bush, who agreed with most of the church's positions, than for the Catholic Kerry, who did not.[58]

A deeper level of consciousness can be gleaned from experiences that transform a person's understanding of the political forces operating within the culture. Julie Lindquist's story about her experiences struggling to make ends meet as a bartender offers a prosaic example. Her book is a straightforward ethnographic study of argument in a "safe" public place. But it is also a microscopic survey of how her persona and political ideas were absorbed by customers, who largely rejected her outspoken defenses of "welfare government."[59] She recalls growing up with a dawning awareness of the deprivations of her working-class roots, noting that it slowly fed an appreciation for how governmental efforts can help the poor "escape" the limitations of class.[60] She writes about her uncertain place in the male sanctuary of a bar, where her evocative appearance is one of the commodities that the owner is selling. Lindquist's budding social conscience, and the knowledge of the "regulars" that she was also a graduate student at the local university, gave her a very different identity from that of the truck drivers who made up most of her clientele. She remembers her first "discovery" of class theory and her sense of vindication and regret that others still "didn't get it."[61]

Former seminarian and political reporter Chris Hedges learned harder lessons as a war correspondent for the *New York Times*. He is no stranger to civil and international conflicts, having spent time in the Persian Gulf, Bosnia, and El Salvador. And like other journalists and military personnel who have seen too much war, he has little interest in romanticizing its bloodshed.

Hedges distinguished himself in 1993 during the first Gulf War. He was one of the few American journalists able to function on his own, partly because he could speak Arabic. But a recent book entitled *War Is a Force That Gives Us Meaning* offers anything but a heroic account of modern warfare or the incipient nationalism that fuels it. Informed by the tribal conflicts of Bosnia and the uses of war to maintain national myths, Hedges concludes that we have turned conflict into a "spectacle," a form of "entertainment" and hero making that gives us "a heady pride in our military superiority."[62] He understands that the enterprise of war reporting will be obliged to sustain "civilian and army morale." But he is not willing to forget its human costs:

> I saw high explosives fired from huge distances in the Gulf War reduce battalions of Iraqis to scattered corpses. Iraqi soldiers were nothing more on the screens of sophisticated artillery pieces than little dots scurrying around like ants—that is, until they were blasted away. Bombers dumped tons of iron fragmentation bombs on them. Our tanks, which could outdistance their Soviet-built counterparts, blew Iraqi armored units to a standstill. . . . Here there was no pillage, no warlords, no collapse of unit discipline, but the cold and brutal efficiency of industrial warfare waged by well-trained and highly organized professional soldiers.[63]

The most profound forms of political consciousness come from such unmediated experiences. We have romanticized this idea in cinematic fables of commitment that range from Michael Curtiz's *Casablanca* (1942) to Neil Jordan's *Michael Collins* (1996). Yet there is power in the idea that political renewal flows from hard experience. To borrow from Tagore's song poem that opens this book, such experience can communicate "truths" that the "dreary sands of dead habit" can never match.

THE DECISION TO OPT OUT

The United States is one of the world's great open societies. But it is also a nation with relatively low levels of political interest and participation. Millions of Americans simply opt out of participating or even observing the political process. We declare "landslides" when less than 30 percent of eligible voters bother to cast their ballots. And party identification and activism is at an all-time low, replaced in part by relatively small cores of activists and others motivated by single issues, such as abortion, tax reduction, or gun control. Even with relatively high levels of grassroots activism in the intensely fought election of 2004, just under 60 percent of eligible citizens showed up to vote.[64] As Murray Edelman has noted, "nonvoters constitute a larger political grouping in America than the adherents of any political party."[65]

A study by the Pew Research Center at the start of the 2004 campaign season provided some sobering conclusions about the state of the nation's polis. Focusing specifically on news usage by a cross section of Americans, the center's findings confirmed a stark level of disengagement:

- For Americans under thirty, *comedy shows* were mentioned nearly as often as newspapers and television newscasts as a source of election news.
- Only 15 percent cited newspapers—traditionally a rich source of information—as their "main source" of news; 68 percent cited television.[66]

- During the intensely covered Iowa caucuses in January 2004, only a quarter of the sample could correctly identify the candidate who was the long-serving majority leader in the House.
- Sixty-four percent of respondents under thirty indicated that they are "not even somewhat interested" in campaign primaries.
- Only about 7 percent of the sample said they were following election events "closely."[67]

There are many explanations to account for this paradox of low interest in a time of informational richness. The parties themselves may be reluctant to expand the voter base beyond specific target groups.[68] But the most frequently cited reason is that Americans feel unempowered. With politics a distant mediated reality, many citizens seem to feel like spectators curtained behind a glass wall. By defining politics as conflict among parties, professional politicians, and "special interests," we have seemingly stripped away a sense of direct membership in a larger community. We are not citizens but "targets" to be motivated with self-serving political ads and direct mail appeals. Our vote is often understood as simply a confirmation of prior polling. And, depending on which member of television's "chattering classes" is talking, we have been either "duped" or "educated" on the issues. With voting treated as just another form of manipulated consumer behavior, it is little wonder that many do not find it rewarding. As Don Slater notes, "The political sphere, it is frequently argued, has given ground to the private sphere as the place in which questions of purpose and meaning are pursued, and this private sphere is in turn dominated by an essentially consumerist self-understanding: We come to relate self to society through notions of private choice among needs-satisfying commodities."[69]

From this perspective, questions of the "public good"—what is useful for the larger society—are often ignored in favor of materialist and personal standards. Needs tend to trump social "goods" as determinants of attention or inattention, involvement, or disinterest. In a political campaign, relevant appeals are based on what a politician can do for the voter, *not* for the society. Hence, the stock query issued by a challenger in a political campaign "Are *you* better off now than you were four years ago?" assumes that self-interest is the primary measure of civic virtue. Such political narcissism accounts for the near-exclusion of issues from our public discourse that are not directly anchored to the holy grail of tax reduction.[70] Tax policy is especially governed by a ruthless vehemence that makes even the most cash-starved governor the Antichrist for even suggesting new forms of "revenue enhancement."[71]

We are cynical for other reasons. In 2000, a muddled electoral system in Florida and elsewhere failed to yield a clear presidential victor. The anomaly of the Electoral College system gave the second-highest vote getter the White House, sending the candidate with the largest plurality home. In addition, increasingly rapid cycles of governmental activism and inaction, accompanied by their corresponding rhetorics of hope or despair, have left a majority of Americans with doubts about the abilities of civil institutions in general and the federal government in particular "to do what is right."[72] Jimmy Carter campaigned in 1976 on the hopeful theme that he would produce "a government as good as its people." Ronald Reagan defeated him four years later by noting that government itself was the problem.[73] And, although that was not the view of Bill Clinton, Reagan's distrust of government again became the official norm after 2000.

This distrust of government is fueled by the common idea that organizational units—ranging from governments to corporations—are fundamentally flawed. It is an article of faith today that organizations in postindustrial society are usually inadequate to the task of addressing problems that are subtle and complex. When was the last time you saw a film or television program that featured solutions to life's problems managed by an organization? As noted in the final chapter, characters in prime-time melodrama must typically be the agents of their own salvation.

Similarly, governmental and corporate bureaucracies have been analyzed, deconstructed, and dismissed as necessary but imperfect vestiges of advanced societies.[74] They are the ones held responsible for voting tally miscounts, corrupt investment funds, and $100 screws built into $25 million airplanes. Exceptions are made for innovators and groups that have bucked the tide: the federal government's Head Start program; Internet giants eBay, Google, and Amazon. But few Americans are willing to be counted as defenders of organizational life—a fact that feeds an antigovernmental bias and undermines the credibility of most political discourse (see table 1.3).

Journalists in particular are perceived to have their own problems. Most studies of American confidence in key institutions place national journalists in the cellar with lawyers, behind even Congress and state government.[75] Low levels of credibility are reflected in what appears to be an endless and largely futile debate about the alleged political biases of specific outlets. The titles of recent best sellers indicate this trend, ranging from Bernard Goldberg's *Bias: A CBS Insider Exposes How the Media Distorts the News*[76] to Eric Alterman's *What Liberal Media? The Truth about Bias and the News*.[77] Many Americans probably also sense that most popular television outlets have placed their news operations in the uncomfortable position of pandering for audience ratings while trying to address the nation's informational needs. Every time a morning news show "shills" for its own network's latest reality series, the message is received.[78]

Table 1.3. Citizen Confidence in Selected American Institutions (%)

	"A Great Deal"	*"Some"*	*"Very Little"*
U.S. military	68	26	4
Churches	44	30	9
Presidency	28	41	20
Health care providers	26	49	19
Local news media	16	55	20
U.S. Congress	12	57	22
National news media	10	49	27
Lawyers	9	49	26
Large corporations	9	46	32

Source: Adapted from "Public Opinion on Higher Education," *Chronicle of Higher Education*, August 27, 2004, 35.
Note: Categories of "None" and "No opinion" not included.

For the restless viewer, all content tends to be measured by its ability to conform to its imperatives for visual stimulation and amusement. Postman has noted that "entertainment is the supra-ideology of all discourse on television."[79] Americans are "the best entertained and quite likely the least well-informed people in the Western world."[80] Anyone who has observed an otherwise thoughtful politician trying to form a thirty-second campaign message or seven-second sound bite senses the problem. In the world of television, political agents must compete with a funhouse of clowns, fools, singers, aliens, and talk show confessors. An earnest discourse of ideas is easily ignored by distracted viewers used to entertainment that alternately rewards the trivial and punishes introspection.

There are no easy remedies for the decline of confidence in American political institutions. Influential observers such as Schudson see some compensating advances, such as less dependence on political parties in favor of activists motivated by specific issues.[81] But as these pages document, a number of patterns that contribute to public suspicions are firmly entrenched, including the deep partisanship of Congress and the tendency by the press to report political messages in terms of their strategic objectives rather than their substance.[82]

SUMMARY

Let us conclude on a hopeful note. Communication as performance *can* carry its own claim to authenticity. The idea of "staging" an event to enact and symbolize a group's efforts is not inherently demeaning or limiting. The challenge of our age is to harness the resources of the imagination that lie mostly dor-

"We've been taking a little harder look at journalists lately."

mant in spectators. The effective dramatization of politics can heighten political consciousness, moving many to go beyond the tired media-driven formulas documented in the chapters that follow. Like all forms of communication, the requirements of dramatization can be handled well or badly, with vision or carelessness.

NOTES

1. Murray Edelman, *Constructing the Political Spectacle* (Chicago: University of Chicago, 1988), 102.
2. The view builds on the long-term connections presidents, cabinet members, and many members of Congress have established with the nation's power elite. For a typical view of these links, see Michael Moore, *Dude, Where's My Country?* (New York: Warner Books, 2003), 1–33.

3. Ed Reilly quoted in Matt Bai, "Going Deep: With Iowa's Meta-Voters," *New York Times Magazine*, January 18, 2004, 36.

4. Most members of the United States Senate are millionaires, and many have used part of their own fortunes to win their seats. The same could be said of some recent presidents, including George Bush Sr. and his son, John F. Kennedy, and Lyndon Johnson, who acquired wealth through marriage. Presidents Nixon, Carter, Reagan, and Clinton had more humble middle-class origins, husbanding power and connections before running for president.

5. Dana Milbank, "The Military Is the Message," *Washington Post*, May 2, 2003, A24.

6. Milbank, "The Military Is the Message."

7. Frank Rich, "Top Gun vs. Total Recall," *New York Times*, September 14, 2003, sec. 2, 7.

8. Milbank, "The Military Is the Message."

9. Quoted in Richard Stevenson, "White House Clarifies Bush's Carrier Landing," *Washington Post*, May 6, 2003, A20.

10. Stevenson, "White House Clarifies."

11. Elisabeth Bumiller, "A Proclamation of Victory That No Author Will Claim," *Washington Post*, November 3, 2003, A16.

12. Ken Auletta, "Fortress Bush," *New Yorker*, January 19, 2004, 64.

13. Erving Goffman, *The Presentation of Self in Everyday Life* (New York: Anchor, 1959), 1–66.

14. Kenneth Burke's dramatism is not easily represented in one source. A good start, however, is his *A Rhetoric of Motives* (New York: Prentice Hall, 1953), 43–110.

15. Goffman, *The Presentation of Self*, 15.

16. Jean Folkerts and Stephen Lacy, *The Media in Your Life*, 3rd ed. (Boston: Allyn & Bacon, 2004), 146.

17. "Year in Review," in *Broadcasting and Cable Yearbook: 2002–2003* (New York: Broadcasting and Cable, 2003), xxxii.

18. "Kathleen Hall Jamieson on Talk Radio's History and Impact," *NOW with Bill Moyers*, December 20, 2004, http://www.pbs.org/now/politics/talkradiohistory.html.

19. Neil Postman, *Amusing Ourselves to Death* (New York: Penguin, 1985), 28.

20. To cite two examples from the ideological left and center, both *Mother Jones* and the *Washington Monthly* actively seek contributions from their subscribers to keep them marginally solvent. In-depth opinion magazines, like other nonprofits, often need wealthy patrons to keep them afloat.

21. "Year in Review."

22. See Everett Rogers and James Dearing, "Agenda Setting Research: Where Has It Been and Where Is It Going?" in *Communication Yearbook*, vol. 11 (Beverly Hills, Calif.: Sage: 1988), 555–94.

23. Maxwell McCombs, "The Agenda Setting Approach," in the *Handbook of Political Communication*, ed. Dan Nimmo and Keith Sanders (Beverly Hills: Sage, 1981), 121.

24. McCombs, "The Agenda Setting Approach," 127.

25. Barbara Nelson, "Making an Issue of Child Abuse," in *Agenda Setting: Readings on Media, Public Opinion, and Policy Making*, ed. David L. Protess and Maxwell McCombs (Hillsdale, N.J.: Erlbaum, 1991), 168.

26. Roger Simon, *Road Show* (New York: Simon & Schuster, 1974).

27. Tom Rosenstiel, *Strange Bedfellows* (New York: Hyperion, 1993), 47.

28. Shanto Iyengar and Donald R. Kinder, *News That Matters: Television and American Opinion* (Chicago: University of Chicago Press, 1987), 114–15.

29. Iyengar and Kinder, *News That Matters*, 63.

30. Shanto Iyengar, *Is Anyone Responsible?* (Chicago: University of Chicago Press, 1991), 133.

31. Project for Excellence in Journalism, "Who's Best in 17 Cities: Local Television News," *Columbia Journalism Review*, November–December 2002, 96, 98.

32. The growth of National Public Radio (NPR) is one of the bright spots in the coverage of public affairs. The audience for *Morning Edition* alone grew 41 percent between 1999 and 2004. NPR now reaches twenty-two million listeners a week on over 770 stations. Lynette Clemetson, "NPR Is Replacing Morning Host," *New York Times*, March 24, 2004, E1.

33. Pew Research Center for the People and the Press, "Public's News Habits Little Changed by September 11," June 9, 2002, http://people-press.org/reports/print.php3?PageID=612 (accessed May 22, 2006).

34. Janet Kornblum, "Study: Internet Tops TV in Battle for Teens' Time," *USA Today*, July 24, 2003, 8D.

35. "Changing Definitions of News," Project for Excellence in Journalism, March 6, 1998, http://www.journalism.org/resources/research/reports/definitions/default.asp (accessed May 22, 2006).

36. This is an old and continuing problem. See, for example, Sig Mickelson, *From Whistle Stop to Sound Bite* (New York: Praeger, 1989), 162–64.

37. Stacey Kanihan and Kendra Gale, "Within 3 Hours, 97 Percent Learn about 9/11 Attacks," *Newspaper Research Journal*, Winter 2003, 79.

38. Robert Putnam, *Bowling Alone: The Collapse and Revival of American Community* (New York: Simon & Schuster, 2000), 36.

39. Pew Research Center, "Public's News Habits Little Changed."

40. Joshua Meyrowitz, *No Sense of Place* (New York: Oxford University Press, 1985), 118–21.

41. See, for example, Roderick Hart, *Seducing America: How Television Charms the Modern Voter* (New York: Oxford University Press, 1994), 23–51.

42. Lee Ann Brady and Atiba Pertilla, "The Look of Local News," *Columbia Journalism Review*, November–December 2001, 11.

43. Postman, *Amusing Ourselves to Death*, 16.

44. For an overview of the objectives of these commissions, see Robert Rotberg, "Truth Commissions and the Provision of Truth, Justice, and Reconciliation," in *Truth v. Justice: The Morality of Truth Commissions*, ed. Robert Rotberg and Dennis Thompson (Princeton, N.J.: Princeton University Press, 2000), 3–8.

45. *Yes*, a quarterly journal, defines its mission as supporting "people's active engagement in creating a more just, sustainable, and compassionate world" (Winter 2004, 3).

46. Daniel Barenboim and Edward Said, *Parallels and Paradoxes* (New York: Pantheon, 2002), 6–14.

47. Frank Rich, "Iraq around the Clock," *New York Times*, March 30, 2003, sec. 2, 1.

48. Jonathan Burston, "War and the Entertainment Industries: New Research Priorities in an Era of Cyber-Patriotism," in *War and the Media: Reporting Conflict 24/7*, ed. Daya Thussu and Des Freedman (London: Sage, 2003), 163–75.

49. Hugh Duncan, *Communication and Social Order* (New York: Oxford University Press, 1962), 79.

50. Ron Suskind, "Without a Doubt," *New York Times Magazine*, October 17, 2004.

51. Meyrowitz, *No Sense of Place*, 47.

52. Michael Schudson, *The Good Citizen* (Cambridge, Mass.: Harvard University Press, 1998), 299.

53. Putnam, *Bowling Alone*, 393.

54. Quoted in Bill Moyers, "This Is Your Story—The Progressive Story of America," speech at Campaign for America's Future Conference, June 4, 2003, http://www.commondreams.org/views/03/0610.htm (accessed July 11, 2003).

55. Tera McKelvy, "Onward and Forward," *The American Prospect*, August 2004.

56. For a variety of observations on the role of religion in American life, see E. J. Dionne Jr., Jean Bethke Elshtain, and Kayla M. Drogosz, eds., *One Electorate under God? A Dialogue on Religion and American Politics* (Washington, D.C.: Brookings Institution, 2004).

57. Catholic Answers, "Voter's Guide for Serious Catholics," http://www.catholic.com/library/voters_guide.asp (accessed December 23, 2004).

58. Katharine Seelye, "Moral Values Cited as a Defining Issue of the Election," *New York Times*, November 4, 2004, P4.

59. Julie Lindquist, *A Place to Stand* (New York: Oxford University Press, 2002), 73–118.

60. Lindquist, *A Place to Stand*, v–vii.

61. Lindquist, *A Place to Stand*, vii.

62. Chris Hedges, *War Is a Force That Gives Us Meaning* (New York: Public Affairs Press, 2002), 142–43.

63. Hedges, *War Is a Force*, 84–85.

64. Committee for the Study of the American Electorate, "President Bush, Mobilization Drives Propel Turnout to Post-1968 High," November 4, 2004, http://www.fairvote.org/reports/CSAE2004electionreport.pdf (accessed May 22, 2006).

65. Edelman, *Constructing the Political Spectacle*, 7.

66. For decades, media analysts have noted with regret steady declines in newspaper circulation figures. The conventional view is that Americans have more news options than ever, preferring "easier" media for news such as television. For some caveats to this view, see Paul Farhi, "A Bright Future for Newspapers," *American Journalism Review*, June–July 2005, http://www.ajr.org/article_printable.asp?id=3885 (accessed May 22, 2006).

67. Based on a national sample of 1,506 respondents. Pew Research Center for the People and the Press, "Cable and Internet Loom Large in Fragmented Political New Universe," January 11, 2004, http://people-press.org/reports/print.php3?PageID=774 (accessed May 22, 2006).

68. Frances Piven and Richard Cloward, *Why Americans Still Don't Vote* (Boston: Beacon, 2000), 23–44.

69. Don Slater, "Political Discourse and the Politics of Need," *Mediated Politics: Communication in the Future of Democracy*, ed. W. Lance Bennett and Robert Entman (New York: Cambridge University Press, 2003), 117–18.

70. This perhaps explains why the world's wealthiest country is not ranked first on the United Nations' prestigious Human Development Index. The index is a measure of the key services nations provide that contributed to health, education, and economic security. In many categories, a number of countries (Canada, Norway, Australia, and others) rank ahead of the United States. See United Nations, *Human Development Reports*, http://hdr.undp.org/reports/view_reports.cfm?type=1 (accessed May 22, 2006).

71. For a brief case study, see James Dao, "A Governor's Hard Sell: Higher Taxes in Virginia," *New York Times*, January 20, 2004, A12.

72. Sam Roberts, "In Government We Trust (as Far as We Can Throw It)," *New York Times*, January 4, 2004, Week in Review, 4.

73. See Craig Smith, "President Jimmy Carter's Inaugural Address, 1977," and David Henry, "President Ronald Reagan's First Inaugural Address, 1981," in *The Inaugural Addresses of Twentieth-Century Presidents*, ed. Halford Ryan (Westport, Conn.: Praeger, 1993), 245–70.

74. Seymour Martin Lipset and William Schneider, *The Confidence Gap: Business, Labor and Government in the Public Mind* (New York: Free Press, 1983), 13–40.

75. "Public Opinion on Higher Education," *Chronicle of Higher Education*, August 27, 2004, 35.

76. Bernard Goldberg, *Bias: A CBS Insider Exposes How the Media Distorts the News* (Washington, D.C.: Regnery, 2002).

77. Eric Alterman, *What Liberal Media? The Truth about Bias and the News* (New York: Basic Books, 2003).

78. For a fuller discussion of this bind, see Robert McChesney, *The Problem of the Media* (New York: Monthly Review Press, 2004), 58–97.

79. Postman, *Amusing Ourselves to Death*, 87.

80. Postman, *Amusing Ourselves to Death*, 106.

81. For his overview of evolving forms of American citizenship, see Schudson, *The Good Citizen*, 294–314.

82. Joseph Cappella and Kathleen Jamieson, *Spiral of Cynicism: The Press and the Public Good* (New York: Oxford University Press, 1997), 34.

Chapter Two

Forces Shaping the News Business

> We have more tools at our disposal and we are more skillful at applying them than any previous generation of journalists. But we're afraid of the competition, afraid of earning less money, afraid of losing our audience.[1]
>
> —Ted Koppel

> Because most members of the public know and care relatively little about government, they neither seek nor understand high-quality political reporting and analysis. With limited demand for first-rate journalism, most news organizations cannot afford to supply it, and because they do not supply it, most Americans have no practical source of the information necessary to become politically sophisticated.[2]
>
> —Robert Entman

Political journalism and its corollary forms are but a small part of the media environment. Even so, with some notable exceptions, journalists are subject to the same structural forces that control resources and decisions within most forms of mainstream media. This chapter considers these different business and performance forces that shape the form and content of news. The first and most obvious force is the intense profit-driven orientation within corporate news divisions. The second might be called the "story structure" imperative. The conventions of news gathering are heavily influenced by our innately human and hardwired preference for structuring information in the formulas of melodramatic narrative. This has always been so, but what has changed in the last fifty years is our increasing dependence on commercial television as the organizing structure for creating a national political consciousness. With its emphasis on entertainment, pacing, and merchandizing, television has sometimes enhanced and often undermined the American appetite and understanding of political institutions. Along with a survey of these two basic pressures, we will conclude by considering imaginative alternatives to the standard news frame.

THE NEWS BUSINESS: FROM LOSS LEADER TO CASH COW

Just before radio first emerged as a cultural force in the 1920s, there were those—including the future president of NBC's parent company—who believed the medium was too valuable to become a marketing tool for advertisers. David Sarnoff's 1916 vision for a "radio music box" did not include commercial announcements that would enter the home uninvited and intrude on the lectures and concerts he envisioned.[3] Sarnoff proposed something like the revenue system that exists for the British Broadcasting Corporation today: listeners would pay a user fee for a range of services.

He couldn't have been more wrong. He may have been a technical visionary, but he misjudged the appeal that radio would have to a nation beginning to discover all the pleasures of the Jazz Age. By 1922, commercials and program sponsorship were already fixtures in some stations and soon would be in others looking for a way to sustain their operations.[4]

Sarnoff's error is understandable. It has often been the case that inventors and innovators of new technologies have been more enamored of their machinery than ways of making money from it. Thomas Edison was slow to understand the commercial potential of the "talking machine," thinking it was perfect for office dictation.[5] Likewise, radio was first regulated by the navy, because it thought that its best use during World War I was as a transoceanic medium. And the Internet, of course, was originally designed not for home entertainment but as a way to organize reliable data links for military planners and academic researchers. While new technologies initially blossom under the work of their originators, most sooner or later face a reckoning with the forces of the investment marketplace.

The news business has followed a similar arc of innovation reined in by commercialization and consolidation. When CBS and NBC began news operations that would mature throughout World War II, these early divisions were generally not expected to make a profit. News was a "loss leader," a service the network offered and supported out of its entertainment revenues. Fast-forward to as late as 1991, and we find that NBC could still accept the idea that its considerable news operations would just break even.[6] But by 2004, as a division in a much larger company, NBC News was contributing $300 million in operating profits to General Electric.[7] In the decades-long conversion to news as an awkward hybrid of information and entertainment, the division reduced its reporting staff, shifted resources away from news gathering to *reporting of what others had gathered*, and changed its content so it would make fewer demands on somnambulistic viewers.[8] Competition from cable and other news and entertainment options combined with the imperative for every unit of GE to contribute healthy profits.

Some of NBC's journalists were embarrassed by what had happened.[9] But the company's managers seemed pleased that it had figured out a way to get more milk out of a smaller cow.

Fewer Owners

Since at least the 1950s, the number of separate owners of newspapers and radio and television stations has steadily declined. To the increasing alarm of media observers, a small number of corporations dominate the most popular media outlets in the largest American cities. When Ben Bagdikian wrote the first and definitive jeremiad about the evils of "monopoly" ownership, he identified fifty major corporations and expressed concern that public discussion of significant issues would be reduced by so few owners.[10] In the first years of the new century, the list plummeted to fewer than ten (Time Warner, Disney, News Corporation, NBC Universal, Viacom, Bertelsmann, and a few others), intensifying concern that news was becoming an "industrial byproduct" of the entertainment industry.[11] His analysis describes the rush of these firms to create vertically integrated entertainment giants and assesses how just a few dominant owners restricts political diversity:

> They have been able to promote new laws that increase their corporate domination and that permit them to abolish regulations that inhibit their control. Their major accomplishment is the 1996 Telecommunications Act. In the process, power of media forms, along with all corporate power in general, has diminished the place of individual citizens. In the history of the United States and in its Constitution, citizens are presumed to have the sole right to determine the shape of their democracy. But concentrated media power in news and commentary, together with corporate political contributions in general, have diminished the influence of voters over which issues and candidates will be offered on Election Day.[12]

In addition to Bagdikian, others, such as Robert McChesney,[13] have contributed to a growing awareness that the modern pattern of many outlets owned by a few companies does not necessarily assure the full and free public debate the nation's founders had in mind.

Consider the rise and fall of CBS. In its heyday, CBS nurtured the careers of Edward R. Murrow, Walter Cronkite, Fred Friendly, and others. The news operation was considered a special division to be insulated from the entertainment and profit imperatives that remained for other parts of the company. CBS News produced prime-time documentaries on the exploitation of migrants in America, the scourge of McCarthyism, and the consequences of the United States' Vietnam policy.[14] And though it had fewer television rivals when it was under the control of William Paley, CBS competed against hundreds of independently owned newspapers, radio stations, and magazines.

Trouble for CBS began in 1984 when a group of political conservatives, including North Carolina senator Jesse Helms, announced their intention to purchase sufficient shares of the company to be able to control what they felt were its left-leaning news staff. It was doubtful they could ever achieve their goal, but the takeover attempt was enough to put the company into play as a takeover target. The following year Atlanta media mogul Ted Turner made a more serious attempt to purchase CBS by using a byzantine arrangement involving the use of junk bonds. He, too, had little chance of success, but the CBS board took defensive action by purchasing back much of its stock, cutting staff, and selling profitable operations such as its St. Louis affiliate, KMOX-TV.[15]

At the same time, the shrewd chief financier of the Loews Corporation, Larry Tisch, began to buy large blocks of CBS stock and was soon invited to join CBS's board of directors. One reason the invitation was extended was the fear that Tisch, too, had his eye on the company. The board figured that it was better to have him as an ally than as the engineer of a hostile takeover. After a failed attempt to convince its members to accept a friendly takeover by the Coca-Cola Company, CEO Tom Wyman was forced to resign, and Tisch was asked to take his place.

Tisch was known as a generous benefactor to many New York cultural institutions, but he was notably stingy in his stewardship of CBS. He admitted that he knew little about the entertainment business, a fact that became evident when he sold off the very profitable CBS Records Division to the Sony Corporation. The removal of that jewel from the company crown was followed by further liquidations of the research division, most of its book publishing arm, and its music businesses. Decisions to downsize the news and entertainment divisions followed, and the *CBS Evening News* lost its reputation as the "newscast of record" to the more ably managed ABC and cost-efficient CNN. As Peter Boyer notes, by the end of the 1980s, CBS was no longer a media giant "but a relatively small broadcasting company with a lot of cash."[16]

The company was now ripe to be consolidated with other companies. It was sold to Westinghouse in 1995 and then to Viacom in 1999. And with sudden speed, the formerly proud news division found itself competing for scarce resources within a sprawling media empire.

CBS News staffers also came to understand the hard commercial realities of functioning in an entertainment-centered environment. In 2004, a producer was fired for daring to interrupt a prime-time drama with an announcement of the death of Yasser Arafat, who had led the Palestinian cause for nearly forty years. The network actually apologized for interrupting the flow of entertainment for breaking news.[17] Early in the next year, *Evening News* anchor Dan Rather felt compelled to move up the date of his planned retirement after he defended a campaign story about President Bush that was later shown to be inaccurate. And, more ominously, others came to understand that if they pushed for more "hard" news stories from foreign capitals, they would be reminded that they jeopardized the division's $150 million annual profits by being out of step with other high-rating newscasts.[18] As CBS chief Leslie Moonves observed about the *Evening News* in the fall of 2005, "we're trying to change it, make it more user-friendly, obviously to skew it a bit younger."[19]

What was lost at CBS? The answer gets to the heart of what is at stake with the intense competition to maximize a return to shareholders of all media companies. Henry Giroux has posed the problem as a battle between "unfettered consumerism," on one hand, and recognition of less commercial but vital social values, on the other, including "a respect for freedom, equality, liberty, cultural differences, constitutional rights and economic justice."[20] Such idealism is not far-fetched, especially given the long-standing doctrine that officially makes broadcasters licensees using the *public* resource of the airwaves.[21]

In terms of journalistic excellence, there are many potential standards by which an outlet might be judged. Certainly the closing of CBS foreign bureaus in Paris, Frankfurt, Rome, and Johannesburg, among other capitals, offers less to audiences of the *CBS Evening News*.[22] More significantly, a number of key principles of sound journalism are at risk when news is forced to compete as a profit center within an entertainment medium:

- Protection of journalists from the commercial interests of parent companies and advertisers
- Recognition that journalistic values are not the same as entertainment values
- Management support for sufficient time or space to put events in historical, international, and social contexts
- A willingness to commit resources to difficult but important "need to know" stories
- A commitment to news gathering and "enterprise" (investigative) reporting
- A recognition that news has a civic function that may sometimes be at odds with the quest for time period dominance

As early as 1959, the political sage Walter Lippmann worried that broadcasting had already "become the creature, the servant and indeed the prostitute of merchandising."[23] The challenge to see the difference between entertainment and genuine public discussion is even more difficult now than it was in the 1950s, when it first became clear that the television networks owned revenue goldmines.

Even so, the need to honor that difference remains. When Hurricane Katrina devastated much of the Gulf Coast and forced the evacuation of virtually the entire city of New Orleans, it is instructive to note that—along with a few diehard bars in the French Quarter—only one kind of enterprise continued operations. No modern American city had ever been shut down before. And yet the seven television stations of Greater New Orleans, as well as its newspaper, remained open and provided vital information to residents preparing to flee and to those who for various reasons stayed. If we needed proof of the special status of broadcasting and journalism, it was in the fact that these services were essential to residents of the region, even though there was virtually no commerce to promote or advertising to sell.[24]

The Enduring Giants

The list is constantly shifting, but currently about ten media giants control most of the nation's information and entertainment resources.[25] Those especially relevant to continued access to diverse news and public discourse include the following:

- *Viacom*: CBS, MTV, VH1, UPN, Showtime, thirty-nine owned and operated TV stations, Blockbuster Entertainment, Paramount Pictures, book publishers, King World (TV syndication), and other television assets. Recently CBS has come under fire from media analysts and journalists for making programming and news decisions based on political and commercial pressures.[26]
- *General Electric* (and subsidiary NBC Universal): NBC, CNBC, MSNBC (with Microsoft), more than a dozen television stations, various cable channels, and Universal Studios. In addition, the company has divisions in insurance, financial services, and industrial products. GE has a reputation of an efficiently managed company but also one that expects NBC News to remember the effects its stories have on the fortunes of its industrial parent.[27]
- *News Corporation*: Fox TV, nearly thirty television stations, many newspapers, publishers, Fox News, various cable channels, sports teams, HarperCollins publishers, and the world's largest satellite TV systems (Sky TV and Direct TV). The company is known for the conservative political slant

of its newspapers and for the introduction of a conservative talk-radio style to cable news.[28]

- *Disney*: ABC, ESPN, Disney Channel, various film production units (Miramax, Touchstone, and others), ten televisions stations, fifty radio stations, theme parks, publishers, and other cable channels. Few companies seem as effective in marketing their "brands" in diverse media at the same time (i.e., using the Disney Channel to promote Disney films and theme parks).
- *Time Warner*: CNN, HBO, TNT, TBS, Cartoon network, various film production units (Warner Bros., Castle Rock), more than sixty magazines (including *Time*, *People*, and *Sports Illustrated*), recorded music, sports teams, Netscape, and America Online. The nation's largest media organization provides a compelling example of a company whose size is as much a problem as an asset. Individual units within it are often well managed. But as its merger with Internet giant AOL clearly demonstrated, a fruit salad of different businesses may never add up to a coherent whole.
- *Clear Channel Communications*: nearly forty television stations, various radio and television production companies, and *more than 1,200* radio stations, many in the same media market (i.e., eight in both Phoenix and Denver, eleven in Los Angeles, and nine in San Diego). Clear Channel is a poster child for critics of media mergers on both the political left and right. They complain that the company inhibits the ability of individual radio stations to reflect the interests and politics of their local communities.[29]
- *Gannett*: *USA Today*, *Army Times*, and more than eighty other newspapers. Many observers see *USA Today* as a shrewd adaptation of print to a marketplace dominated by the pacing and brevity of television. The company also has a reputation for purchasing newspapers and then downsizing their reporting staffs to maintain high profit levels.
- *Tribune Company*: twenty-six television stations, the Pulitzer-winning *Los Angeles Times*, *Chicago Tribune*, many radio stations, and the WB network (part owner). This company is known for buying media properties where staff resources can be shared and, especially in the case of the *Los Angeles Times*, promoting news reporting that will please advertisers.[30]

Other key companies in this forest of giants include Bertelsmann (with eighty-two formerly independent publishing companies and other holdings), Liberty Media (Discovery Channel and its clones), Dow Jones Company (the *Wall Street Journal* and other newspapers), the Washington Post Company (the *Post* and other newspapers and magazines), and the New York Times Company (the *Times*, other newspapers, and radio stations).

The last deserves mention as the owner of what is arguably the gold standard for journalistic excellence in reporting national problems and issues. In the realm of big-city newspapers, the *Times* has few journalistic rivals. It is neither the nation's largest-circulation paper nor owned by one of the largest conglomerates. But it is unmatched in its depth of general news coverage and is probably the most influential newspaper in the world. The "newspaper of record" has been around so long, it is easy to forget what it does so well: dedicating staff resources and page space to little-observed but important trends, challenging American insularity by publishing pages of foreign news, supporting Pulitzer-standard reporting,[31] engaging in fearless editorial writing even against the interests of its supposed "liberal" readers, and insulating reporters from the business and advertising sides of the paper. Media journalist Ken Auletta recalls attending a 1997 conference of Wall Street investors where newspaper executives touted the performance of their companies. Amid the talk of "brands," "content," and "products," Auletta noted that only one publisher—the *Times*'s Arthur Sulzberger Jr.—actually talked about "journalism" at the company and how its "core purpose" was to "enhance society."[32]

The paper certainly has its detractors who dislike its daily "features" sections, its sometimes minimal regional coverage beyond Manhattan, or its inevitable management and reporting gaffes.[33] But virtually every issue of the *New York Times* dramatizes aspects of the nation's civic fault lines—whether it is a full two-page, ten-column spread on a program that matches volunteers with terminally ill elderly patients who would otherwise die alone, or detailed analyses of Canadian and British health care systems.

Perhaps in its current form, the paper could only exist in the intellectual and economic milieu of the nation's largest city. But part of what makes the *Times* unique could happen anywhere—namely, its status as essentially a family-owned company with a strong sense of its value as a broker of trends and ideas. The heirs to the company are content to be profitable somewhere below the brutal industry standard of 20 percent. At the same time, its management is able to see the paper as a kind of national trust, a resource with a mandate to inform rather than pander to readers.[34]

On the broadcasting side, there is no American news organization that matches the journalistic stature of the *Times*. Perhaps the closest equivalent is the British Broadcasting Corporation (BBC), an autonomous but publicly funded institution that has been an important pillar of British culture for more than eighty years. The BBC maintains forty-one foreign news bureaus and a workforce of two thousand fiercely independent journalists. By comparison, rival CNN maintains twenty-eight foreign bureaus, and Fox News maintains just six.[35] The BBC is perhaps the only major broadcast news organization to publish and regularly discuss its principles for reporting and news gathering—a policy that reflects the fact that part of its budget is paid by its UK users.[36]

It is occasionally challenged for its accuracy.[37] But its impressive internal and overseas news services carried in forty-three languages are unmatched by any other journalistic organization, and they are often preferred by foreigners over their own local broadcasters.

The Business Model for News

All things being equal, the larger the owner of a media outlet, the more the outlet *could* afford take financial risks with ideas that might appeal to a distinct minority or verge from the center of mainstream opinion. The deeper pockets of a large corporation can support such adventures, and democracy thrives on such risk taking. For example, as a new unit within the Time Warner empire, Netscape has gained some financial protection from its larger and predatory competitor, Microsoft. Even so, most of those who have studied the effects of the consolidation of American media holdings into fewer corporate hands believe the reverse is true. With their own cultures, investment expectations, and political friends and enemies, media giants throw shadows that news units and individuals cannot easily ignore. Indeed, the biggest of the media giants are so large that it has become nearly impossible to turn a camera on a news story without also getting a corporate sibling in the viewfinder. For these reasons, most journalists know that certain subjects and story ideas are off-limits because of the commercial or ideological sensitivities of their parent companies.[38] In addition, most networks fail to alert viewers when they interview authors or entertainers employed by another part of the same corporation.[39]

The effects of media gigantism have certain identifiable features that are causes of concern. Briefly, they include the following.

Hypercommercialization

As Robert McChesney has noted, "Concentrated media control permits the largest media firms to increasingly commercialize their output with less and less fear of consumer reprisal."[40] More commercial minutes within television newscasts is one sign of this,[41] as are the decisions of most television news units to "soften" content to pick up restless eyes searching for more titillation. In a more general sense, hypercommercialism denies a place for content that cannot find advertisers or falls outside the narrow center of popular culture. Documentary film producer Bernard Stone notes that even ostensibly friendly venues such as PBS and the History Channel are a tough sell for independent producers, especially if a program deals with political issues that might discomfort advertisers or challenge viewers.[42] In traditional news, the losers in this process have been the old and not very glamorous journalistic beats of

Congress, the State Department, federal agencies, and foreign capitals. The winners have been reporters and producers who specialize in covering "lifestyles," sports, health, and celebrities.

Vertical Integration

The alleged "synergy" of vertical ownership means that a conglomerate with both production and distribution arms (i.e., Time Warner, News Corporation, or Disney) can require one division to "sell" content to another. ABC's *Good Morning America* thus promotes its corporate cousin, Disney World, by choosing segments that evoke the pleasures of the Magic Kingdom.

Or consider the case of Viacom. When CBS won the rights to broadcast the Super Bowl game in 2004, it raised few eyebrows when it also announced that its gaudy halftime show would be produced by another Viacom brand, MTV. It was only when singer Janet Jackson exposed more flesh than expected that Americans became aware of how much of the broadcast was the product of one media giant. Congress rushed to hold hearings to reassure Americans that the Republic would survive the momentary exposure of Ms. Jackson's right breast. Fewer wondered about the more interesting issue: how much embarrassing news about its parent company CBS was willing to broadcast.[43]

To be sure, cost-saving efficiencies can seem harmless, as when NBC shares content from its sister cable operations of CNBC and MSNBC. But even here there can be a hidden cost. When three news networks share the same staffs (and just eleven foreign bureaus), there is an illusion of more diversity and unanimity than actually exist.

Centralized Control of Content and Perspective

Corporations have their own cultures and styles. And in some cases, managers and owners communicate values that are ignored by individual employees at their peril. At its worst, government agencies and corporations can seek to thwart the dissemination of news and opinions the public has a right to see or hear. At its best, uniformity of content or ideology ignores unpleasant truths and trumps local needs. A newspaper or television station that appears to be engaged in the business of serving a community is also less obviously a carrier of attitudes or preferences sanctioned by the parent corporation.

Exhibit A for this tendency is usually the News Corporation. Many of its operations, ranging from Fox News to the *New York Post*, carry the politically conservative imprimatur of its CEO, Rupert Murdoch.[44] While the company is not quite an ideological monolith, its news outlets often reflect the Murdoch trademark of faux populism and right-wing indignation.

Loss of Competition

Virtually every news organization wishes that it had a near monopoly on readers or viewers. But most journalists will concede that the public benefits from true competition among outlets owned by different parent firms. New York's *Newsday* makes the *New York Times* a better newspaper. And the quality of the *CBS Evening News* benefits from its competitors at ABC and NBC. To be sure, competition is no guarantee of quality. Lately all of the cable news channels—CNN, MSNBC, and CNBC—have been following the lead of the popular Fox News in a downward spiral of journalistic bottom-feeding. The search for dominance includes everything from pontificating anchors to irrelevant sound effects. But vigorous competition remains the best insurance against the monopolization of public opinion.

Consider, for example, the single-owner media bubble that exists for Americans in even larger cities. In cosmopolitan New York, a citizen can live almost completely within the News Corporation's ideological orbit by reading the *New York Post*, watching cable's Fox News, and tuning into local news programs on Channels 5 and 9. In addition, the company's Direct TV is a portal for thousands of viewers, including access to the FX Channel, Fox Sports, and the films of 20th Century Fox. If the mood to read strikes, the company's many trade publishers have an ample list of conservative authors, including Fox News regulars Sean Hannity, Newt Gingrich, and Bill O'Reilly.

In the end, all of these forces suggest a business model that has largely abandoned a public service philosophy in favor of generating greater returns for investors. Combine other forces that make serious journalism a difficult "sell" to the American public, and one can express the fear that television news is in a death spiral it cannot shake. The words of Ted Koppel and Robert Entman that open this chapter express the circular logic that sacrifices journalistic courage in favor of complacent advertisers and audiences. Revealingly, only about one-third of Americans trust the media to get a story right[45]—about the same level of trust that Americans have in government.[46] By contrast, in the same time period, Britons were twice as trusting of the BBC as they were of their own government.[47]

It remains to look at the second level of the storytelling imperative, which springs from both psychological and economic origins.

STORYTELLING CONVENTIONS IN THE ELECTRONIC MEDIA FRAME

News reporting is shaped by a deep human imperative for narration. The nine topics addressed in this section describe journalistic conventions in the powerful vernacular of melodrama. As Walter Lippmann noted decades ago, scenes from the political world are narrated and reconstructed for us in daily news reporting. Gradually, those scenes form a picture of the world beyond our reach,[48] creating culture-wide perceptions that will guide future choices.

The Requirement for Narrative

The word *story* is such a basic descriptor of a news event that we tend to forget that it defines a unique way for organizing ideas. To "tell a story" is to set up a general structure for organizing actors and events in ways that meet certain prior expectations. The story format defines actors moving through a sequence of events filled with victims, villains, heroes, and—sometimes—fools. Conflict generates our interest and sets up the search for a third act resolution.

The story format exists in most general news reporting because it is an efficient structure for reducing complexity to a minimum and for collapsing a long time frame into a short and interesting summary. Reuven Frank, a pioneering former executive producer of the *NBC Evening News*, once defined the format for his employees in a memo: "Every news story should, without any sacrifice of probity or responsibility, display the attributes of fiction, of drama. It should have structure and conflict, problem and denouement, rising action and falling action, a beginning, a middle and an end. These are not only the essentials of drama; they are the essentials of narrative."[49]

To be sure, storytelling is not the only way to organize events for presentation to the public. In-depth coverage occurs in venues such as cable's C-SPAN and CNN, and—more frequently—in long-form coverage of events in important newspapers and opinion magazines. We leave the framework of narration when we witness events without the benefit of a narrator and without the compression of time, or when we have unedited access to a source of information (a speech, press conference, or debate). But the basic impulse to find meaning for an event in the narration of an observer is potent. Humans seem to be hardwired to structure the organization of knowledge and information within the story frame. Even most sports enthusiasts prefer television coverage of games with the dramatizing narration of play-by-play and "color" commentators. An NBC decision in 1980 to present an NFL football game without announcers—only the sound of the crowd in the stadium—was considered a resounding failure.[50] Fans wanted the backstories of the game as much as they wanted access to the action on the field.

There are enormous consequences in the use of the story format as the primary way to organize news. Narratives typically require rising action, conflict, the transformation of a key character, and usually some sort of third act resolution. In addition, narratives have the significant effect of placing the blame or the need to change on agents rather than larger social forces. Responsibility for an individual's condition usually rests squarely on the human participants involved. To a large extent, stories tend to underestimate the hard-to-dramatize structural causes of human action. For example, the problem of decreasing employment in the manufacturing sector is often understood by professional economists as a function of changing markets and the globalization of trade. From their view, the issue is less in finding fault than identifying long-term trends beyond the control of any single political figure. But the expression of this perspective is inherently less newsworthy than a political leader's attack on the "failures" of a president to deal with job losses or the alleged crafty manipulations of foreign companies guilty of "stealing" American workers' jobs. As Paul Weaver notes, public discussion is usually framed as a contest "of figures deeply and totally embroiled in an all-out struggle."[51]

We will revisit this tendency in the last chapter, but it is important to remember the high price we may pay for the news preference for simplistic or voyeuristic stories.[52] For example, one of the nation's rising political figures in 1987 was former Colorado senator Gary Hart. His special insights and expertise on military issues and terrorism contributed to his rise as a potential president. And he retains his credibility with many analysts as a writer and thinker who can get beyond partisan boilerplate. But when the *Miami Herald* tracked him down to the apartment of actress Donna Rice, the genie for simplistic narrative was out of the bottle. A picture that soon circulated with Rice sitting on Hart's lap (in a boat appropriately called *Monkey Business*) ended his electoral career. But, as Joe Trippi notes, the nation paid dearly for its interest in this sideshow.

> Think of what it cost us, to lose a man who might have been a great president, a man who knew more twenty years ago about the world we would face than many of the candidates running now. And for what: a tittering, meaningless story about what happened between two adults. A transgression that Hart's own wife had forgiven him for. Broadcast politics was more interested in tailing Gary Hart than in reporting the farsighted positions he staked out nearly twenty years ahead of his time. In the wake of September 11, 2001, which mistake was bigger? His? Or ours?[53]

The Search for Expressive "Moments"

Whereas journalists such as Ed Murrow and Walter Lippman understood the press to be a conduit to citizens about great public issues, news producers today think more in terms of private traumas and social victims. One former CBS News chief, for example, concluded that the best events for news are those that have "moments" of high emotional intensity. Vivid images of people experiencing the anguish of their lives generally fits in well with television's commercial imperative to capture large audiences for it's advertisers. "What the moments doctrine amounted to," notes Peter J. Boyer, "was a deftly designed cover for the infiltration of entertainment values into the news."

> It completely changed the way CBS reported the day's news because it completely changed what news was. There were no moments to be found in a minute-fifteen report on unemployment told by a CBS News correspondent standing outside the Department of Labor in Washington, D.C. There was, however, a moment of the highest sort if the CBS News camera studied the strained and expectant face of a young Pittsburgh mother as she stood (babe in arms) beside an employment line as her husband asked for a job.[54]

In a basic sense, the "information" communicated in the face of an impoverished mother is less about government employment programs than it is the universal experience of sharing another person's misery.

Television privileges expressive content. It saturates us with opportunities to witness other people's feelings and attitudes. Seeing people react to the events around them is one of the primary pleasures of watching television. As Joshua Meyrowitz notes, the archetypical television game show is not really about facts or information. The questions and answers of these programs are often secondary to the experience of watching how other people cope with the pressures and opportunities of winning and losing.[55] In a very basic sense, television content saturates us with people engaged in the process of communicating feelings of elation, grief, anger, and reassurance.

Consider the content of the popular magazine-style TV shows that narrow the boundary dividing personal and societal problems (see table 2.1). All—especially *60 Minutes*—have done significant investigative reports. And some routinely offer touching first-person observations from individuals dealing with sexual abuse, stresses on the contemporary family, and predatory corporate policies. But more segments seem to have drifted into a chaotic world of confrontation and emotional exploitation, merging issues with entertainment, fact with fiction, and a genuine urge to be informed with an irrepressible desire to peer into the abyss of other people's dysfunctional lives. Tallies reveal how little time these newsmagazines spend on politics, public issues, or America's place in the world.

Synoptic and Decontextualized Coverage

Television thrives on a rapid diversity of content, ranging from the number of individual shots a TV commercial director may use in one thirty-second ad

Table 2.1. Percentages of Story Categories in Prime-Time Newsmagazine Programs

	20/20 *ABC*	60 Minutes *CBS*	Dateline *NBC*
Government	0	0	1.4
Military/national security	0	5.6	0
Foreign affairs	3.3	0	0
Law/justice	6.7	16.7	12.3
Entertainment/celebrities	3.3	5.6	5.5
Human interest	10.0	0	4.1
Personality/profile	3.3	22.2	19.2
Consumer business	16.7	5.6	15.1
Health/ medicine	26.7	5.6	12.3
Crime	10.0	11.1	13.7
Education	0	5.6	0
Social welfare	10.0	5.6	4.1
Economy	0	0	0
Science/technology	0	5.6	1.4
Religion	6.7	5.6	1.4
Arts	0	5.6	0
Weather/disaster	0	0	9.6
Sports	3.3	0	0
Total	100	100	100

Source: Sample from 1997 is adapted from "Changing Definitions of News," Journalism.org, www.journalism.org/resources/research/reports/definitions/primetime.asp (accessed May 25, 2006).

(twenty is not unusual), to the decision of a news producer to cover a variety of topics and stories in a short period of time. By nearly any measure, commercial television alters its content at a frenetic pace. Continuous and rapid change of subject and perspective is both the ersatz aesthetic of our distracted age and a response to the limited interests and attention spans of television viewers.

Television news moves us from place to place, event to event, at a speed that leaves us with little time or opportunity to grasp the significance of what we are seeing. Even the venerable Walter Cronkite, who anchored the *CBS Evening News* for many years, readily conceded that he could do little more than introduce the basic elements of a significant story.[56] He termed this vexing problem "distortion through overcompression."[57] In a typical newscast, a viewer may see a story about American casualties in Afghanistan that must coexist in the same time frame with a commercial for a plant food and a report on credit card theft. A single story of major importance is never allowed to saturate our attention. Not enough relevant details are allowed to burn into an individual's consciousness to make it possible for her to have much more than a passing familiarity with the most superficial symbolic representations of the problem (see textbox 2.1).

Textbox 2.1. Topics and Timings for a Typical Half-Hour Network Newscast

NBC Evening News **for Tuesday, June 28, 2005**
Total Time: Approx. 28 min, 30 sec
News Hole: 18 min, 40 sec
Previews and Ads: 9 min, 50 sec

5:30 P.M.: Preview/Introduction Brian Williams (New York) 50 sec
Iraq/Bush Address 5 min
(Studio: Brian Williams) President Bush's speech about the war in Iraq is noted.
(Ft. Bragg: Kelly O'Donnell) What Bush is expected to say about the strategy and stakes in Iraq previewed; scenes shown of Bush arriving at Ft. Bragg, where he will meet privately with the families of fallen soldiers; speech excerpts quoted; MoveOn.org ad shown. Senator John Kerry—says our troops deserve leadership that is equal to their sacrifice.
(Studio) Brian Williams and Tim Russert discuss the high stakes for Bush, as well as criticism from Representative John Murtha, and the president's choice of venue.

Afghanistan/Helicopter Crash 1 min, 40 sec
(Studio: Brian Williams) Report introduced. Jim Miklaszewski describes the crash in Afghanistan of a U.S. Chinook helicopter, which may have been shot down. Details are given of the Taliban's claim of responsibility for the shoot-down and execution of crewmembers.

Marines/Boot Camp Death 30 sec
(Studio: Brian Williams) Discusses a hearing for a marine swimming instructor on possible criminal negligence charges in the drowning death of recruit Jason Tharp.

Iraq/Operation Sword 2 min
(Studio: Brian Williams) Report introduced. Videophone report from Richard Engel on Operation Sword, the latest crackdown on insurgents in western Iraq, presented; scenes and photos shown of U.S. troops on the move and in a night battle. Details are given about the problem of attracting attention by the movement of troops and equipment.
Upcoming Items 30 sec
(Studio: Brian Williams)

Commercials: SC Johnson; Gas-X; Aleve; Gold Bond; Quiznos; *Today*; *The Situation with Tucker Carlson* 2 min, 30 sec
In Depth (Autism and Vaccines) 3 min, 40 sec
(Studio: Brian Williams) Statistics on children with autism cited. (Washington: Tom Costello) The ongoing debate over a possible link between thimerosal in children's vaccines and autism examined; map shown of states with or considering a thimerosal ban. Autistic child's mother Katherine Labarre describes her son's symptoms. Radio host Don Imus says these parents are going to get an answer.

Author/activist Robert F. Kennedy Jr. claims the government is suppressing evidence. Center for Disease Control's Dr. Tanja Popovic says the evidence does not support the link. Senator Joseph Lieberman calls for a study by independent researchers. Immunization expert Kristin Ehresman says we need to make decisions based on science.
Upcoming Items 10 sec
(Studio: Brian Williams)

Commercials: AFLAC; Dr. Scholl's; Beneful; Nexium; *Tom Brokaw Reports* 2 min, 50 sec
Homeland Security/Information Sharing 2 min, 20 sec
(Studio: Brian Williams) Report introduced. (Washington: Lisa Myers) An alarming GAO report states that fugitives and terror suspects can still get U.S. passports four years after 9/11 because of ongoing problems with information-sharing among intelligence agencies. Examples are cited, including fugitives Donald Webb and James Eberhart, whose names are not on the State Department's lookout list. Senator Susan Collins says these problems are inexcusable. Former 9/11 Commission member John Lehman says this is a good insight into what has not been changed. Assistant Secretary of State Maura Harty claims improvement since 9/11.
Corporate Fraud/Scrushy Trial 30 sec
(Studio: Brian Williams) The acquittal of former HealthSouth CEO Richard Scrushy in his corporate fraud trial is noted. Scenes are shown from Birmingham, Alabama.
Stock Market Report 10 sec
(Studio: Brian Williams)
Foote Death 20 sec
(Studio: Brian Williams) The death of historian/author Shelby Foote is reported.
Upcoming Items 10 sec
(Studio: Brian Williams)

Commercials: GoLean Crunch; Sea-Bond; Miracle-Gro; Ascensia; Maalox; Channel 4 News 2 min, 50 sec
Swiped: Identity Theft in America (Credit Cards) 2 min, 30 sec
(Studio: Brian Williams) Special series on identity theft introduced. (New York: Ron Mott) Credit card companies' are downplaying the identity theft problem despite reports of massive security breaches. Privacy Rights Clearinghouse Beth Givens comments on consumers' worries. Two consumers comment. MSNBC technology analyst Bob Sullivan says banks don't want to inform people when their account information has been stolen because it's costly. FDIC Sandra Thompson comments on federal guidelines. The National Australia Bank's decision to close at-risk accounts and issue new cards is noted.
(Studio: Brian Williams) Tomorrow night's segment previewed.
Good Night 5:58:10 P.M.

Source: Adapted from an abstract of the NBC Evening News, June 28, 2005, Vanderbilt Television News Archive, http://tvnews.vanderbilt.edu/TVN-displayfullbroadcast.pl?SID=20051109897033691&UID=&CID=18781&auth=&code=TVN&getmonth=6&getdate=28&getyear=2005&Network=NBC&HeaderLink=794707&source=BroadcastSelect&action=getfullbroadcast (accessed May 25, 2006).

It would be unfair to lay the blame for this superficiality only on television. The rising tide of information must compete with work and life's other routine distractions for a finite amount of time. But our tendency to consume a high diet of synoptic news has no doubt contributed to a vague recognition of many topics, without much understanding of any particular one.

A Focus on Celebrity and Megatrials

In high-visibility trials, cable and broadcast programmers know they have tapped a lucrative vein that will increase their audiences and their revenues. We will discuss publicity strategies in high-profile trials in chapter 5. But it is worth remembering here that our recent history is replete with examples of news saturation focused on crime. In 1984, a trial of six Portuguese immigrants accused of the gang rape of a woman in a New Bedford, Massachusetts, bar was carried live by CNN for several hours a day. CNN sometimes cut away for other news segments, but it was usually careful to return to live coverage when the testimony was particularly lurid. Noted one of the network's writers, "Lets face it, they are running the trial because of its sexy nature. . . . And ratings are up."[58] In the same decade, the retrial of the Rhode Island socialite Claus von Bulow for the attempted murder of his wealthy wife became something of a national obsession. Even the most prestigious news outlets were caught in the frenzy, with interviews and dramatizations appearing on *Nightline*, *60 Minutes*, CNN, and the weekly newsmagazines.

In 2005, the nineteen-week trial of singer Michael Jackson on charges of pedophilia fed off the nation's twin appetites for gossip and celebrity schadenfreude. Assertions of strange occurrences at the Neverland Ranch became a constant in the national news mix. The denial of cameras to the actual courtroom turned most of the video coverage into little more than sidewalk speculation on the meaning of Jackson's ever more puzzling appearance. Conscious of charges of feeding into a news culture of tabloidization, the networks avoided the excesses of other cases, such as the 1995 O. J. Simpson trial. Even so, the announcement of his acquittal was the top news story for the week ending June 17.[59]

Television news struggles to control its gluttony for the same sensational story. Networks that operate 24/7 in particular know that sustained coverage fosters its own kind of addiction. A story with "legs"—meaning an event with "new" developments to report every hour or every day—creates a self-contained universe. It surfaces in the common realm of public discussion. And it feeds its own microuniverse of experts, advocates, and speculators.

Some news executives and journalists are aware of its costs, especially the tendency to stop the clock on other stories that the American public may need to know. After the Jackson verdict was announced, CNN president Jonathan Klein noted that he regretted the "endless parade" of his own network's stories featuring "Michael dressed like Captain Crunch, walking out of the limousine." Somewhat ruefully he acknowledged the price the network had paid for focusing too much on a story about too little: "We could have done 60 stories during that time."[60]

The Primacy of the Narrator

The traditional format for an electronic news story has the effect of putting the actual reporter in the middle of events as both narrator and interpreter. Whereas print journalists remain unseen and largely unknown, their video counterparts are a strong presence. Because most broadcast journalists assume that they provide the only sense of continuity in otherwise disjointed reports, comments from actual news sources are likely to occupy less time than the running narrative of the journalist. The story is given meaning largely through the frame of reference he or she establishes.

Consider a typical report describing a December 2003 appearance in Pittsburgh by President George Bush. ABC News anchor Peter Jennings set up the context of the visit, noting that Bush was in town to raise money for his campaign and observing that the president "could not escape a very difficult political dilemma he is in over the issue of steel tariffs." Against shots of protesters chanting, "Save our steel," and "Keep your promise," correspondent Terry Moran picked up the story and narrated the president's visit, explaining the political dynamics of removing protective tariffs on foreign steel in a state the president hoped to win in the next election. Quoting a man who mentioned that he voted for Bush the first time but would not again, Moran identified a familiar political calculus in presidential politics:

> The sentiment stems from concern here that Mr. Bush is about to reverse course and repeal the stiff, protectionist tariffs he imposed on steel imports last year in order to help ailing U.S. steelmakers. White House officials say the president has not made up his mind on whether to repeal the steel tariffs, though his economic team is urging him to do so. Today, at a fundraiser for his campaign, Mr. Bush did not even mention the steel issue.[61]

Moran went on to explain some of the pros and cons of tariffs, giving himself in a total of more than three hundred words against a mere ten from the president. While he was correct that steel tariffs were not mentioned by name, he brushed off the forty-minute, 3,300-word speech Bush had given that day,[62] including a spirited description and defense of the U.S. economy. In short, the ostensible reason for the trip—the speech—was mostly ignored.

The reasons for the primacy of the narrator are both obvious and subtle. It is clear, for example, that a long meeting of a deliberative body such as a city council cannot be easily presented in its "raw" form. The reporter's most basic job is to tell news consumers what happened and to achieve this objective quickly and fairly. But a more subtle motivation is also at work. Television journalists believe that their careers thrive or wither by how much "airtime" they are able to get. They covet "face time" when they can be seen and airtime when they are heard—two professional imperatives that increase the likelihood that stories will feature "stand uppers" that give them the opportunity to demonstrate their competence. This need to be noticed also means that viewers are often left with the irony of watching reporters in the foreground of a camera shot paraphrasing the words of the news makers barely seen in the background.

Increasing Emphasis on Anchor-Driven "News"

Narrators compete with anchors for the same coveted airtime. At the level of the *traditional networks*, anchors provide specific broadcasts with continuity, credibility, and unity. Anchors tame the unruly world by allowing its problems to only emerge from the same reassuring source. The sober tone and delivery of the anchor ought to be what CBS chairman Leslie Moonves compares with the "voice of god."[63] By contrast, most *cable* news outlets use a vast amount of their prime time for a hybrid form of "newstalk," where the anchor takes on the role of a clear-eyed oracle and debunker. Reporters from the field may offer their information but find that the anchor is either not listening or not interested in what he or she is being told. Even so, this recipe apparently works so well that many viewers seem hardly to notice the absence of more forms of traditional news gathering. All of the networks seem to nurture clusters of mostly acerbic men ready to raise an eyebrow at the ironies and offenses of public life. Though their theatrical talents vary, the emphasis of most of these anchors is on commentary and instant indignation. Among the current crop as this is written are Anderson Cooper at CNN and Keith Olbermann and Chris Matthews at MSNBC.

Indignation is especially a Fox News specialty. Although it does some straight reporting, the network's model owes less to news gathering than news commentary, reflected in the bluster of Bill O'Reilly, Sean Hannity, and John Gibson. For Fox News, France was thus not just a country with a different attitude on the 2003 U.S. invasion of Iraq but, for one of its anchors, part of the "axis of weasels." Protesters in Switzerland against the same war were, according to another, "hundreds of knuckleheads."[64] Such withering rebukes are provisional shelters from complexity, serving to protect languid consumers from potentially ambiguous and discomforting realities. In the rhetorical framework described by Ernest Bormann, these interpretive riffs use a few facts to "chain out" fantasies that confirm what most want to believe.[65] The process is psychologically comforting for those who must find simple "truths" in complex events.

A Preference for Pictures Rather Than Ideas

To assert that television news needs interesting pictures is to state the obvious. Video news grew out of the riveting photojournalism that for decades captivated readers of *Life* magazine and, even earlier, movie audiences addicted to the weekly newsreels of 20th Century Fox and others. "In television," ABC's Peter Jennings once stated, "you're obligated to write to the pictures."[66]

News as a visual form is as much an imperative for news makers as broadcast journalists. We need only recall the largely successful efforts of the White House staff to "sell" the leadership of Ronald Reagan to the American public. White House public relations expert Michael Deaver helped execute a string of photogenic presidential visits in Reagan's first term. The point was to find interesting images that could substitute for substantive discussion or press questioning. Carefully planned visits to the demilitarized zone between North and South Korea, to an Irish pub (to demonstrate Reagan's solidarity with working men and women), and to a defense plant building the B-1 bomber were among the scores of appearances that helped orchestrate favorable public attitudes. ABC's Sam Donaldson noted that Deaver understood "a simple truism about television: the eye always predominates over the ear."[67] Even reporter commentary that communicated doubts about Reagan's "disengaged" style had little negative effect on viewer attitudes *if* it was accompanied by pictures featuring Reagan's affability under full sail.[68]

One consequence of the primacy of pictures in shaping the content of television news is that our attention is drawn to the observation of emotions and behaviors as much as the *substance* of news. A news producer who decides to devote significant amounts of airtime to nonvisual stories—on tax reform, the validity of college entrance exams, ethics codes for public officials, or the mental illnesses of defendants in trials—faces some difficult choices. These subjects involve abstract concepts such as justice, fairness, intelligence, and compassion. All are significant, but they are not easy to portray without resorting to "talking heads." Concern for lost viewers will often force a producer to choose a very short segment of discussion or a pattern of narration-over-video, in which crude behavioral approximations are found (B-roll footage of people completing tax forms, elderly patients receiving medical treatment, students in a classroom, etc.) to give the unengaged viewer something to watch.

The price we have paid in our recent history for news driven by events rather than ideas is quite high. For example, scandals involving excessive executive pay, unethical trading of stocks "after hours," and other forms of corporate malfeasance have generally been discovered by governmental agents, such as New York's attorney general Elliot Spitzer, rather than the media's own investigative reporters. Because white-collar crime carries few interesting pictures, it gets significantly less attention.

A classic example was the savings and loan crisis in the 1980s. During this period, many financial institutions became insolvent by extending credit to poor risks. When the economy faltered, thousands of commercial loan clients of the banks were unable to survive and repay their debts. In the end, the federal government (through individual taxpayers) had to cover many of these federally insured transactions. As reporter Ellen Hume wrote at the time:

> It was a numbers story, not a "people" story. . . . Financial stories are particularly hard for television. A reporter or candidate competing to create the most

"Adding to the tragedy was the fact that no one caught it on tape for your amusement."

> memorable sound bite wasn't about to get one with the thrift question. When asked why TV hadn't covered the crisis much even after it made headlines in 1988, the President of NBC News, Michael Gartner, observed that the story didn't lend itself to images, and without images, "television just can't do facts."[69]

To the extent that Gartner was right, public discussion via traditional video news gathering is likely to remain as an impoverished form of discourse. A medium that has tied its fate to what people *do* rather than to what they *think* is encumbered by its own kind of overwhelming debt. When we give preference to movement (events, activities) over thought, we have handicapped our ability to understand the intellectual superstructure of our culture. A child's understanding of the American Revolution, for example, may be largely in terms of selective reconstructions tied to visual referents, such as the Boston Tea Party or the meetings of the First Continental Congress. A more mature understanding of the revolution obviously takes a broader look at the history of ideas and economic forces that shaped the period and the generative power of these ideas (particularly from English thinkers) in shaping the attitudes of Jefferson, Madison, and others. Of course, as any C-SPAN viewer knows, television does not prevent the discussion of ideas. But ideas are disadvantaged in any medium that is structured to entertain the eye.

Globalism, but from an American Point of View

Our mastery of geosynchronous satellite technology after the 1970s made it possible to have broadcast platforms hovering twenty-two thousand miles above the Earth, dependably linking its furthest corners. Among the prime users of leased transponders on these "birds" are television news services. If the result is not fully the "global village" that media theorist Marshall McLuhan predicted four decades ago, citizens of much of the world are still within easy reach of vivid reportage from most distant "hot spots" and political capitals. But there is an irony in this capability. If the pictures and events are from other cultures and places, the *point of view* of most American foreign reporting is still firmly fixed within an American frame of reference.

The best way to characterize the American pattern for presenting foreign news is perhaps in the phrase *ethnocentric globalism*. We see ourselves as very much a part of the world, but we also want to be removed from it and to judge the behavior of other nations in terms of our own national needs and values. Indeed, according to the *Tyndall Report* summary of news coverage of the three broadcast networks in 2003, the only top foreign news stories given significant amounts of network time were related to terrorism, Israel, North Korea, and Iraq. Even in the year of the Iraq war and official hand-wringing about terrorism, a bare 18 percent of American news originated

Textbox 2.2. De Facto and Lawful Constraints on Political News: A Sampler

In this study, we have focused on structural or psychological constraints on journalists. But as the examples here indicate, there are statutory and commercial limits on the flow of information as well.

1. In July 2005, journalist Judith Miller was jailed for three months for refusing to name a confidential source. It has long been a custom in American political life for journalists to promise anonymity to sources in exchange for information that may be in the public's interest to know. Corruption or malfeasance is difficult to document if sources cannot be protected. In this case, Miller refused to name her source in a story about the "outing" of CIA agent Valerie Plame by a White House official. The agent's name was passed to the columnist Robert Novak evidently as retribution against Plame's husband, who had been critical of the administration's Iraqi policy. Many states have shield laws that protect reporters from grand juries seeking their notes and sources. But there is no such federal law. "The freest and fairest societies," Miller noted after being sentenced, "are not only those with independent judiciaries, but those with an independent press that works every day to keep government accountable."[1]

2. In 2005, a federal appeals court threw out a lawsuit that would have required the Bush administration to release records about officials and industry leaders who met with Vice President Dick Cheney in meetings of the White House Energy Policy Task Force. The group proposed critical energy policies and priorities that would guide the administration through both terms. Critics suspected that policy was largely set by representatives of the petroleum industry, and they charged that the public had "a right to know whether lobbyists became de facto members of the Energy Task Force."[2] During the Clinton administration, the *same* appeals court used the open-disclosure rules of the Federal Advisory Committee Act—which is still in force—to *require* the release of names of outside participants of a White House Health Advisory Group. In a sign of how times have changed, it originally noted that the participants were "de facto members" of the group, and therefore the public had a right to know about the meetings.[3]

3. News organizations sometimes buckle under pressure from large corporations. In 1997, Jane Akre and her staff at WTVT News developed an investigative piece about the dangers of a growth hormone fed to dairy cows. The story noted that the hormone increased milk production in the cows but could also be a carcinogen for humans. The report also noted that the Food and Drug Administration (FDA) had done little research on the long-term effects of the hormone. After getting a threatening letter from Monsanto, the company producing the hormone, the sta-

from the networks' foreign news bureaus.[70] Significant political, social, and economic events in others nations and continents hardly registered.

And, of course, we don't know what we don't know. Ignorance begets more ignorance, creating a national sense of surprise and disgust with what looks like an increasingly alien world beyond our borders. The abandonment of the broadcast networks' full-time presence over entire continents like tion's parent company decided to kill the story. The threat of a lawsuit was too much. "Virtually everything Monsanto said was allowed to stand without refutation, even when we knew and documented certain claims to be flatly false," Akre noted. To make matters worse, the station owner "threatened us with our jobs every time we resisted the dozens of mandated changes that would sanitize the story, and fill it with lies and distortions."[4] The story never ran, and Akre and a coworker were eventually fired. She initially won a judgment against the station under Florida's "whistleblower" law, but a federal appeals court overturned the case. The court ruled that it is not against the law to broadcast incomplete or misleading information.

4. It was a small footnote, but an interesting one. After the massive flooding of New Orleans and the Gulf Coast in late August 2005, NBC helped organize a disaster relief "special" to raise funds for the Red Cross. Among the musicians participating in the program was the singer Kanye West, who apparently went off script, suggesting that media coverage of looters was racist and that the president cared insufficiently about black people.[5] The program was "live" on the East Coast. But NBC edited out the comments before offering the program in the West, noting that "it would be most unfortunate if the efforts of the artists who participated" was "overshadowed by one person's opinion."[6] Apparently any opinion about the slow governmental response to the disaster was too dangerous for the program.

NOTES

1. Quoted in Bay Fang, "A Murky Case Takes a Bizarre Twist," *U.S. News & World Report*, July 18, 2005.
2. David Savage, "Court Lets Cheney Keep Talks Secret," *Los Angeles Times*, May 11, 2005.
3. Savage, "Court Lets Cheney."
4. Bruce Porter, "Handling Hot Potatoes," *Columbia Journalism Review*, November/December 2002, http://www.cjr.org/issues/2002/6/books-borj.asp (accessed May 25, 2006).
5. Lisa de Moraes, "Kanye West's Torrent of Criticism, Live on NBC," *Washington Post*, September 3, 2005.
6. de Moraes, "Kanye West's Torrent of Criticism."

Africa, Asia, and Latin America leave them with little choice but to duplicate the military logic of dropping in only after a crisis unfolds. "I don't need a bureau in Africa," asserts ABC's Paul Slavin. "I am much better off with David Wright getting there for three weeks."[71] Presumably, residence of even one journalist on an entire continent is no longer necessary. Reporters can apparently catch up on the social, political, economic, and religious developments of many countries sharing the same landmass during their ten-hour flight from New York. We will consider more features of this tendency away from foreign coverage in chapter 6.

Narrational Authority: A Preference for Official Voices

In their analysis of television coverage of the near meltdown of the nuclear reactor at Three Mile Island in 1979, Dan Nimmo and James Combs were surprised to discover that a story with implications of regulatory and corporate failure was largely told from the point of view of officials from those two groups. "For CBS," they noted, "TMI was primarily a Washington story, not a localized one."[72] It is a paradox of American journalism that, while many reporters privately express their suspicions of official sources and high-level corporate leaders, their broadcast narratives usually quote those leaders' words to frame the story.

The agenda-setting and gatekeeping functions of the electronic media favor those *in* power more than those *affected* by power. The daily news agenda of Senate hearings, presidential statements, and news conferences are easy to cover. People in official Washington and their corporate counterparts are knowledgeable, savvy to the ways of the media, and easy to locate for comments or reactions. Because they often initiate news coverage, they help create interest in the institutional views they represent. But they also contribute to what journalist Clarence Page calls the "Rolodex Syndrome," meaning a dependence on familiar names and faces as the pressure to finish a story presses in.[73] Part of Page's point is that it is easier to interview a White House official for a two-minute piece on the causes of urban unemployment than a group of individuals waiting for interviews at a state unemployment office. The latter group is less likely to give usable sound bites than the official who has the rhetorical fluency and interest to summarize the scope of the problem.

News is thus a product of the individuals and bureaucracies that are ostensibly the objects of neutral and unbiased reporting. Access to the media to influence public opinion is—at best—uneven. In many cases, the power to define and narrate a news event is shared with the public figures who have the most to lose or gain.

SUMMING UP: EXTENDING THE NARRATIVE IMAGINATION

The synoptic news coverage that dominates the time of the networks and the attention of most Americans is not likely to be transformed soon. The financial forces and limited-time story structures identified here are settled professional conventions and welcomed by most in the networks' audiences. To be sure, as we note in chapter 3, the fragmentation of leisure time into diverse Internet preoccupations will create more competition with mainstream news outlets.[74] And more thoughtful and thorough public affairs programming will continue to exist on the fringes of network prime time and during national crises originating from natural and human causes. ABC's *Nightline*; PBS's *Frontline, P.O.V.*, and *Independent Lens*; and NBC's *Meet the Press* especially remain models of public affairs programming, though the first four have somewhat tenuous commitments from their networks.[75] All are a reminder that programming does not have to be predicated on hosts with more attitude than curiosity.

Looking into the future, we see that the better opportunity for engaging citizens in the work of building a civil society probably exists in forums outside the current constrained news formats of network and cable television. These formats include traditional documentaries, as well as more overtly dramatic settings such as docudramas and long-form conferences. Some of these exist on the margins of commercial success. Others fit squarely within the entertainment structures of the networks.

Consider several examples of recent television programs that were available to most American households. Some won coveted Peabody Awards. Others were received with minimal fanfare and were produced at relatively modest costs. But all illustrate the possibilities of the narrative imagination in the exploration of political and social issues.

- *The State of the Black Union*, February 28, 2004, New Birth Baptist Church, Miami, Florida, carried by C-SPAN. Under the guidance of Tavis Smiley, this fascinating daylong forum explored the future of the black family. Participants including former surgeon general David Satcher, Princeton University professor Cornel West, Representative Sheila Jackson-Lee, Myrlie Evers-Williams of the National Association for the Advancement of Colored People (NAACP), and others engaged in a discussion of the effects of the relative importance of self-esteem, identity, racism, sports role models, and external forces shaping the African American family.
- *In Search of Shakespeare*, a four-part BBC production broadcast on PBS in February 2004. This show was an inventive and visually stunning video exploration of the life and times of Shakespeare, with an emphasis on Michael Wood's narrative of how the social and religious tenets of Elizabethan times shaped Shakespeare's marriage, plays, and players. Filmed in contemporary locations that were important to the playwright, the program captured continuities that link Shakespeare's world to our own.
- "Drug Wars," a two-part *Frontline* program in 2000 devoted to exploring national pressures and values that are frequently missed in reporting on the

"war against drugs." The real service of this documentary, produced by Martin Smith and Lowell Bergman, was to shun the standard law enforcement frame in favor of explorations of the social and economic causes of drug sales in Colombia and the United States.

- *Nightline*, ABC News. This half-hour program was started in 1979 to cover the Iranian hostage crisis. It has retained its interest in foreign news, providing stories that frequently go beyond crises and an American point of view. Originally shaped by Ted Koppel and executive producer Tom Bettag (who have since retired from the show), the program gained stature for being less about the recapitulation of familiar events and more about their causes and consequences.
- *The West Wing*, John Wells Productions/NBC. Largely avoiding momentous plot action in favor of contextual detail, the *West Wing* offered vivid glimpses of the political crosscurrents and difficult trade-offs facing presidents. The best episodes in the series illuminated the ways factions complicate the shaping of executive decisions. Using issues and events that have arisen in recent administrations, the early scripts of Aaron Sorkin were particularly good at chipping away at the counterfeit certainties of presidents and their journalistic observers.
- *The First Year*, Teachers Documentary Project, PBS. This 2001 study by Davis Guggenheim examined the successes and failures of five novice teachers newly employed in the Los Angeles Unified School District. The program showed some as instinctively resourceful problem solvers. Others seemed to flounder, often because of a lack of support from their schools and stunning levels of indifference from parents. Although the program focused on new teachers, it provided the invaluable service of reminding viewers of how much the fate of an individual classroom is tied to the human resources of a given school and the support the school receives from the community.
- "Regret to Inform," part of the *P.O.V.* series on PBS. Barbara Sonneborn's 1999 documentary explored the death of her husband, Jeff, in Que Son, Vietnam, in 1968. But its larger purpose was to forgo body count reporting in favor of a meditation on the costs of war that must be borne by the families left behind.

Although these are very different explorations of their subjects, the programs and the best elements of our current public affairs coverage have a few broad traits in common. First, each producer or filmmaker was given enough time to explore and illustrate trends and patterns, not just actions. Effective dramatization of a problem tends to deny simplistic solutions that can only be asserted when underlying social or economic causes remain unknown. Longer-form media contextualize problems by putting them back into their specific settings. In the case of Davis Guggenheim's study of new teachers, the question the program posed was not whether the schools are failing or succeeding but rather how a range of structural factors can undermine a teacher's attempts to construct a community of learners.

Second, with regard to giving over time for the public discussion of vital issues within the television industry, American television viewers must increasingly rely on the politically embattled and underfunded PBS for investigative reporting.[76] The network still occasionally attempts to do the kind of enterprise reporting that is found in larger newspapers and magazines. Conceivably, there was a time in the 1960s or 1970s when something like "Regret to Inform" might have made it on the air at a commercial network. Perhaps *CBS Reports* or *NBC Whitepapers* where not as innovative or daring as broadcast historians remember them to be. Yet they did take risks by asking Americans to spend one hour of prime time considering a range of sometimes uncomfortable but pressing national issues.[77] Beyond the limited scheduling of programs such as PBS's *Now*, *Frontline*, and *Frontline World*, it is difficult to locate regularly scheduled prime-time programming that gives priority to uncovering the contextual dimensions of an issue.

Put another way, the difference between shoutfests like Fox's *The O'Reilly Factor* or MSNBC's *Hardball* and the impressive potential of television journalism is the difference between a trip to Muncie and a trip to the moon. The first ventures no farther than comfort will allow. The second trades safety for curiosity and holds out the possibility of a transformational experience.

NOTES

1. Quoted in Ken Auletta, *Backstory: Inside the Business of News* (New York: Penguin, 2003), 98.
2. Robert Entman, *Democracy without Citizens* (New York: Oxford University Press, 1989), 17.
3. Eric Barnouw, *A Tower of Babel* (New York: Oxford University Press, 1966), 78–79.
4. Barnouw, *A Tower of Babel*, 99–114.
5. Roland Gelatt, *The Fabulous Phonograph: 1877–1977*, 2nd ed. (New York: Macmillan, 1977), 17–32.
6. Ken Auletta, *Three Blind Mice: How the TV Networks Lost their Way* (New York: Random House, 1991), 347.
7. Janice Hui and Craig LaMay, "Broadcasting and the Public Interest," in *The Business of News: A Challenge for Journalism's Next Generation*, ed. Cynthia Gorney (New York: Carnegie Corporation of New York, 2002), 47.
8. See Penn Kimball, *Downsizing the News* (Washington, D.C.: Woodrow Wilson Center Press, 1994), 23–66.

9. Tal Sanit, "The New Unreality: When TV Reporters Don't Report," *Columbia Journalism Review*, May–June 1992, 18.

10. Ben Bagdikian, *The Media Monopoly* (Boston: Beacon, 1983), chap. 1.

11. Ben Bagkidian, *The New Media Monopoly* (Boston: Beacon, 2004), 11.

12. Bagkidian, *The New Media Monopoly*, 10.

13. Robert McChesney, *The Problem of the Media: U.S. Communication Politics in the 21st Century* (New York: Monthly Review Press, 2004).

14. The struggles of the News Division to maintain access and independence throughout this period are retold by Fred Friendly in *Due to Circumstances beyond Our Control* (New York: Vintage Books, 1968), 23–265.

15. Peter Boyer, *Who Killed CBS?* (New York: Random House, 1988), 197–99.

16. Boyer, *Who Killed CBS?* 323.

17. "CBS Reportedly Fires Producer over Arafat Report," *New York Times*, November 13, 2004, A13.

18. Hui and LaMay, "Broadcasting and the Public Interest," 47, 49.

19. Quoted in Phil Rosenthal, "Moonves Ready to Play Hardball in Viacom Split," *Chicago Tribune*, September 16, 2005, http://www.chicagotribune.com/business/columnists/chi-0509160202sep16,1,2058098.column (accessed September 21, 2005).

20. Quoted in Ronald Bettig and Jeanne Hall, *Big Media, Big Money* (Lanham, Md.: Rowman & Littlefield, 2003), 26.

21. The same logic means that cable systems are not broadcasters. Cable arrives through a wire rather than over the airwaves. But cable systems usually gain monopolies in their service areas in exchange for commitments to serve the needs of the community. Presumably, those needs include more than amusement.

22. Scotti Williston, "Global News and the Vanishing American Foreign Correspondent," *Transnational Broadcasting Studies*, Spring/Summer 2001, http://www.tbsjournal.com/Archives/Spring01/spr01.html (accessed May 22, 2006).

23. Quoted in Friendly, *Due to Circumstances*, 267.

24. Katharine Seelye, "To Publish, Not Perish," *New York Times*, September 12, 2005, C1, C3.

25. The data on media corporations were compiled from Seelye, "To Publish," 45, and "Who Owns What?" *Columbia Journalism Review*, http://www.cjr.org/tools/owners/, January 27, 2004 (accessed May 23, 2006).

26. See Alessandra Stanley, "A Flash of Flesh: CBS Again Is in Denial," *New York Times*, February 3, 2004, E1, E7.

27. Lawrence Grossman, "Regulate the Medium," *Columbia Journalism Review*, November–December 1991, 72.

28. David Kirkpatrick, "Mr. Murdoch's War," *New York Times*, April 7, 2003, C1, C7.

29. Adrian McCoy, "Protesters Urge FCC to Tune Out Monopolies," *Pittsburgh Post-Gazette*, May 30, 2003.

30. Auletta, *Backstory*, 75–118.

31. The paper won three consecutive Pulitzers for Public Service Reporting between 2002 and 2004.

32. Auletta, *Backstory*, 76–77.

33. Edwin Diamond, *Behind the Times: Inside the New York Times* (Chicago: University of Chicago, 1995), 64–167.

34. For a personal history of one of its best editors and an anecdotal history of the paper, see Max Frankel, *The Times of My Life* (New York: Random House, 1999), 357–525.

35. "Cable TV News Investment," *The State of the News Media 2004*, Project for Excellence in Journalism, 2004, www.stateofthemedia.org (accessed March 26, 2004).

36. See, for example, Mark Damazer, "Editorial Policy," http://news.bbc.co.uk/aboutbbcnews/hi/editorial_policy/newsid_3247000/3247578.stm (accessed May 23, 2006).

37. The biggest blow to the organization came in 2004, after an independent inquiry criticized the BBC for running a story claiming that British prime minister Tony Blair "sexed up" claims about Iraq's ability to wage war using weapons of mass destruction. The source of that claim later committed suicide. The 740-page report was widely discussed in Britain, partly because of the BBC's sterling reputation for editorial integrity. It is hard to imagine a questionable claim against an American president from Fox News or CNN creating a similar level of discussion. See Patrick Tyler, "Report on Iraq Case Clears Blair and Faults BBC," *New York Times*, January 29, 2004, A1, A11.

38. Bettig and Hall, *Big Media, Big Money*, 30.

39. David Bauder, "60 Minutes to Acknowledge Woodward Ties," Associated Press, April 11, 2004, http://news.yahoo.com/news?tmple=story&cid=503&u= (accessed April 12, 2004).

40. Robert McChesney, *Rich Media, Poor Democracy* (New York: New Press, 1999), 34–35.

41. McChesney, *Rich Media*, 3940.

42. Comments of Bernard Stone, "Imperial Projections" film series, the College of New Jersey, April 2, 2004.

43. A Lexis/Nexis search indicates that the first mention of the story on the *CBS Evening News* was a week later, in a 450-word story on February 8, 2004. At that time, questions were also raised about whether the network was using entertainment division contracts with flamboyant stars like Jackson and her brother, Michael, to leverage interviews for programs in its news division. See Stanley, "A Flash of Flesh."

44. For profiles of Murdoch and Fox News, see Ken Auletta, *The Highwaymen* (New York: Random House, 1987), 258–89, and Auletta, *Backstory*, 249–80.

45. Interview of Andrew Kohut, *NewsHour*, PBS, January 13, 2005, http://www.pbs.org/newshour/bb/media/jan-june05/credibility_1-13.html (accessed May 23, 2006).

46. Sam Roberts, "Keeping the Faith," *New York Times*, January 4, 2004, sec. 4, 4.

47. George Jones, Tom Leonard, and Matt Born, "Hutton a Whitewash," *Daily Telegraph* (London), January 30, 2004.

48. Walter Lippmann, *Public Opinion* (New York: Macmillan, 1930), 29.

49. Quoted in Edward Epstein, *News from Nowhere* (New York: Vintage Books, 1978), 4–5.

50. Red Smith, "Experiment: Mixed Review," *New York Times*, December 22, 1980, C8.

51. Paul Weaver, "Captives of Melodrama," *New York Times Magazine*, August 29, 1976, 57.

52. For further discussion of this point, see Neil Postman, *Amusing Ourselves to Death* (New York: Penguin, 1985), 87–98.

53. Joe Trippi, *The Revolution Will Not Be Televised* (New York: Regan Books, 2004), 44.

54. Boyer, *Who Killed CBS?* 139.

55. Joshua Meyrowitz, *No Sense of Place* (New York: Oxford University Press, 1985), 97–104.

56. Walter Chronkite, "Speech to the Radio and Television News Directors, December 13, 1976," in *Rich News, Poor News*, ed. Marvin Barrett (New York: Crowell, 1978), 191–98.

57. Cronkite, "Speech," 197.

58. William A Henry III, "When News Becomes Voyeurism," *Time*, March 26, 1984, 64.

59. *Tyndall Weekly*, June 18, 2005 (privately printed).

60. Klein quoted in Jonathan Darman, "In Jacko's Wake," *Newsweek*, June 27, 2005.

61. *World News Tonight with Peter Jennings*, ABC Television, December 2, 2003.

62. "Remarks by the President at Bush-Cheney 2004 Luncheon, December 2, 2003, Pittsburgh, Pennsylvania," White House transcript, http://www.whitehouse.gov/news/releases/2003/12/20031202-5.html (accessed May 23, 2006).

63. Jacques Steinberg, "At CBS News, Some Temporary Changes May Stick," *New York Times*, April 4, 2005, C1.

64. Quoted in Auletta, *Backstory*, 260.

65. Ernest Bormann, *The Force of Fantasy: Restoring the American Dream* (Carbondale: Southern Illinois University Press, 2001), 3.

66. Quoted in Martin Schram, *The Great American Video Game* (New York: Morrow, 1987), 58.

67. Quoted in Mark Hertsgaard, *On Bended Knee: The Press and the Reagan Presidency* (New York: Schocken Books, 1989), 25.

68. Rod Hart, *Modern Rhetorical Criticism*, 2nd ed. (Needham Heights, Mass.: Allyn & Bacon, 1997), 184.

69. Ellen Hume, "Why the Press Blew the S & L Scandal," *New York Times*, May 24, 1990, A25.

70. "Top Stories of 2003," *Tyndall Report*.

71. Quoted in Lucinda Fleeson, "Bureau of Missing Bureaus," *American Journalism Review*, October/November 2003, http://www.ajr.org/article-printable.asp?id=3409 (accessed March 25, 2004).

72. Dan Nimmo and James Combs, *Nightly Horrors: Crisis Coverage in Television Network News* (Knoxville: University of Tennessee Press, 1985), 80.

73. Martin Lee and Norman Solomon, *Unreliable Sources: A Guide to Detecting Bias in News Media* (New York: Stuart, 1990), 30.

74. Among what has traditionally been a key network demographic, men age eighteen to twenty-four, television viewing dropped 20 percent in 2003. Internet use has taken its place, with attention going mostly to sites devoted to pornography, music, auctions, sports, and games. John Schwartz, "Leisure Pursuits of Today's Young Man," *New York Times*, March 29, 2004, C1, C7.

75. The case of the documentary program *P.O.V.* is especially interesting. There are only twelve slots a year available to independent filmmakers through this series. Yet network screeners report receiving literally thousands of worthy programs.

76. This is a simplification, but not by much. In the large universe of commercial American television, there are other outlets carrying innovative documentaries, among them the Sundance Channel, the History Channel, and others. But their audiences are usually tiny compared with those of traditional network outlets.

77. For a history of CBS attempts to broadcast hard-hitting explorations of American issues and problems, see Friendly, *Due to Circumstances*.

Chapter Three

Discovery and Discourse in the New Media

There is a growing school of thought that certain technologies will inexorably produce positive political changes. Electricity, radio, and television were all supposed to lead to better communities and stronger democracy. Lately the computer in general and the Internet in particular have inspired even wilder claims. The theory is called "cyberdemocracy" and there might actually be something to it. After all, the Internet differs from television because it fosters communication between people, and that is what politics is about.[1]

—Chris Gray

The knowledge on the Internet can be compared with potential energy in physics: it is in an electronic holding pattern, hovering in unreal space where it remains suspended until it is summoned. Yet there are many reasons why this potential knowledge may just hang there and not fulfill its potential.[2]

—Sheldon Unger

Anyone coming to the World Wide Web with fresh eyes and a fast computer can marvel all over again at its speed and scope of content. For the young, the Internet is and always was a familiar portal to the sublime and obscene—and everything in between. But if one is old enough, it is easy to remember just how profoundly the pace and expectations of home and office routines have been transformed. In little more than a decade, the Internet and its wireless adjuncts have bridged the gap between our curiosity and our ability to satisfy it. From an informational perspective, almost anything is now possible. On the same screen in the same space, I can read the morning papers from London and Dublin, glance through *Grove Online*'s summaries of the musical influences of Eric Clapton and George Harrison, view unedited television footage of overnight carnage in the Middle East, look at a broadcaster's website for more background on a story, and see live pictures of the New Jersey shore or the pandas at the San Diego Zoo. Each of these capabilities has come through evolutionary stages over months and years. But the ability to do all of them in almost *any* place at *any* time is revolutionary. In a nanosecond on the human time line, we have created awesome metalibraries that are unimaginably rich, diverse, and sometimes coarse.

All media compress time and space. The very first film images of ordinary street scenes left turn-of-the-century viewers in nickelodeons awestruck over the camera's ability to re-create the world. And this writer is old enough (just) to remember the first 1951 coast-to-coast television hookup, where Edward R. Murrow and the nation stared in wonder at live split screen images of ships passing under the Golden Gate in California and the Brooklyn Bridge in New York.[3] Even then it was easy for a viewer to sense a change in the geography of ordinary life. Evenings were now spent on a river of popular culture that channeled through every corner of the nation.

In the business world—as Thomas Friedman documents in *The World Is Flat*—the Internet has made it possible to outsource to India and other rapidly developing countries an unprecedented range of "back office" functions, from the reading of stateside medical tests to customer support for everything from software problems to income tax preparation.[4] A service-oriented company's support staff is now as likely to be located in Bangalore as in Baltimore. Our communication systems make it possible to "be" almost anywhere at any time.

The idea of "virtual reality" is hopelessly inexact. But if it lacks precision, it can be retrofitted to suggest the portability of experience that started not just in the 1980s but in the 1450s with the printed page. The microchip and digital processor are just the most recent heirs to a five-hundred-year quest for ways to send our messages to distant others. This technology multiplies the forms of mediated consciousness that can be accessed at will. It also has few intrinsic favorites, at once accommodating idealists and crackpots, children and seniors, pornographers and evangelicals, entrepreneurs and politicos. For many, the Internet has become an essential and universal utility. But even as corporate interests increasingly dominate its portals, there still seems to be room for both the most staid and earnest of institutional users as well as indomitable cranks and debunkers.

The latter group seems drawn to the idea of an electronic Wild West. We are sentimental about the suggestion that people at the margins of society have a place to be heard. Largely anonymous armchair rebels thrive on their own kind of cyber nihilism, commenting on the "texts" of mainstream culture even without the standard equipment of institutional power, notably: money, credentials, or corporate sponsorship.

But the emphasis here is mostly on *dominant* rather than incidental uses of the Internet. Our goal is to focus on the connections to civil society that it foster or breaks. Two sections treat its effects on our collective consciousness. The first explores what we think we know about the Internet, based on user studies of a technology that is no longer just emerging. The second examines more speculative rhetorical and social consequences of civic life conducted at least partly through computer-mediated communication. Like the Internet itself, these conclusions suggest a range of possibilities and contradictions.

WHAT WE THINK WE KNOW

In Russell Neuman's phrase, the Internet is a "network of networks"[5] and, as such, disperses every kind of subject matter to mostly unknowable audiences spread across demographic and national boundaries. The bewildering diffusion of information has not prevented journalists and scholars from drawing big conclusions about how the new media fit into the older culture. Neuman's list of mostly untested but popular notions is instructive. He notes that many theorists have concluded that the Internet has done the following:

- Weakened political party systems
- Offered a new platform for hate speech
- Stimulated a new capacity for grassroots democracy
- Permitted the third world to leapfrog painful stages of industrialization into an information economy
- Robbed children of their childhood and everybody of their sense of place
- Sped up the process of government responses to international crises precluding appropriate deliberation
- Isolated family members from each other
- Permanently stabilized the business cycle
- Exacerbated gaps between information haves and have nots
- Limited the capacity of authoritarian regimes to control the flow of information within and outside their realm.[6]

This list is a good place to start. But it is important to heed cautions about succumbing to overly deterministic lists of effects. Mass media researchers learned early on that simple theories of behavioral effects were rarely confirmed in their studies.[7] Typically, media forms have multiple and sometimes contradictory outcomes. Not only are humans the carriers of enduring habits that resist change, but we also have the capacity to respond to media content in very different ways. To a significant extent, our responses to the symbolic world are buffered by the peculiar alchemy of our own personal histories.

The arrows flow the other way as well. If we know less than we once thought about media effects, we can also be baffled by even simpler questions of media use,[8] further confounding predictions about short- and long-term influences.[9] In the larger media community of service and content providers, there is growing skepticism about the accuracy of traditional survey research on how various media audiences spend their time.[10]

There is also the more philosophical question about the subjective measures and metaphors through which we view any new phenomenon. To what extent can we discover the essences of new media use by drawing comparisons with more established forms, such as television? In many ways our knowledge flows from our thinking about other media forms and their effects. For example, web designers in a sense "publish" their work, but often without the editorial functions and revenue streams of the book and magazine industries. They also "broadcast" to all comers, or at least those connected to the Internet and a search engine that can "tune in" their messages. But broadcasting is traditionally defined by large and often heterogeneous audiences—conditions rare for all but the most ubiquitous sites, such as Amazon.com or eBay.

Similarly, political parties are still the default templates for thinking about political structures. Fifty years ago, the parties were the prime organizing agents for most civic knowledge and action. In most counties and towns, civil life was tangibly supported by party ward healers, local grassroots workers, and sympathetic newspapers. As Jimmy Carter notes in a memoir of his first run for public office in Georgia, it was difficult to be a party outsider. Information and legitimacy flowed from and through the county's leaders, sometimes enabling even the recently deceased to return for just one more election.[11] The point is that while the Internet is still a relatively new medium, how we think about it is necessarily governed by older conceptual frames.

One additional caveat is in order, and it can be expressed in an open-ended logic that is perhaps more Eastern than Western. It is that the social and political strengths of the Internet are frequently also its weaknesses. It takes and gives at the same time. It can isolate in some settings but also extend the idea of community in others;[12] it fosters free expression but reaches many through increasingly large corporate gatekeepers; it can yield a breadth and wealth of high-quality information unimaginable a mere decade ago, yet it also contributes to the rapid dissemination of *mis*information. In short, it is like any new system for organizing and disseminating attitudes or information.

These empirical and epistemological problems should not deter fearless and thoughtful generalizing. But they suggest a need for humility in weighing assertions and causes. No conclusions are as frail as those we assert about the global effects of one medium. The heuristics of such conclusions must outweigh their usually important exceptions.

We start with a set of nine patterns of Internet use that range from the obvious to the new. All provide understanding for how the online world is burrowing its way to the center of American life.

1. *About 65 percent of adult Americans regularly use the Internet, with work applications leading those at home, and with e-mail as the most pervasive single use.*[13] In the month of May 2004, the average for a sample of the Internet population was sixty-four hours online at work and thirty-one hours at home. For many office workers, time on the Internet represents almost half of their work. For millions more, it is the most or second-most common way to spend leisure time. Interestingly, in both work and home, the amount of time devoted to using a *single web page* replicates the rapid sequencing of television content more than print (see table 3.1.) On the average, time spent was *a minute or less per page*.[14]

2. *Claims that the Internet fragments audiences are not fully borne out in usage tallies.* In spite of the millions of available sites on the World Wide Web, there is a concentration of use in the top two hundred or so websites, duplicating to some extent patterns seen in other mass media.[15] To be sure, some of these websites are portals to powerful search engines that send users to the farthest corners of cyberspace. Even so, Internet usage shows signs of clustering around top commercial sites, replicating patterns found in publishing, commercial television, and most other media.

The use (but not time) parallels to book publishing are especially apparent. Thousands of titles are published a year, but a much smaller number of best sellers (i.e., books with sales of more than fifty thousand) dominate the attention of most readers. Similarly, while forty-five million different people

Table 3.1. Average Web Usage per Week, October 2005

	Home	*Work*
Number of sessions/visits per person[a]	10	17
Number of domains visited per person[b]	25	40
PC time per person[c]	8 hr, 58 min	20 hr, 8 min
Duration of a web page viewed[d]	47 sec	54 sec

Sources: Condensed and adapted from ClickZ Network, November 7, 2005, summary of Nielsen/NetRatings; http://www.nielsen-netratings.com/reports.jsp?section=pub_reports&report=usage&period=weekly&panel_ty.

[a]The average number of computer sessions per person for the specified reporting period. A session consists of web sessions and/or any period of time spent using computer applications.

[b]An average of the total number of unique domains visited per person for the specified reporting period.

[c]Average time spent during active computer sessions per person for the specified reporting period.

[d]Average duration of time that a web page was viewed per person over the specified reporting period.

used various Amazon.com sites in December 2003,[16] only numbers from the teens to the hundreds probably find their way to sites devoted to niche sites dedicated to the likes of, say, French organ music or the exploits of Lewis and Clark. Internet usage thus seems to duplicate the "Lorenz Curve," where use of most products of the culture is concentrated asymmetrically in a relatively small number of the available options.[17]

These data contradict a prediction that was also a promise. Many have noted that where traditional political systems organize power hierarchically, the Internet naturally wants to diffuse power outward by decentralizing control of content. This is certainly possible. And there are hopeful cases in China and elsewhere where private websites have helped defy oppressive authority.[18] But the *possibilities* of a technology are not necessarily the same as its *social uses*.[19] Given the patterns noted for television in previous chapters, one would be a fool to bet against the resolve of commercial forces to dominate most Internet usage.

3. *With the exception of interactive games,*[20] *we can identify most Internet content in terms of its older media counterparts.* People converse with each other, buy products, research health and business topics, seek news about politics, purchase or download music, and surf for information and entertainment.[21] From an informational perspective, none of these activities are truly novel. And with the notable exception of the music industry,[22] most media forms have successfully used the Internet to extend their markets. It is easy to identify the adaptive parallels. Radio stations "stream" their content to listeners beyond their coverage area. Television networks advertise websites that extend an interested viewer's time with the program's content and advertisers. Motion picture studios look for the same synergies by drawing potential viewers to film-specific websites. And in content and style, many commercial and social action websites are essentially electronic pamphlets, providing the same kinds of information that are common to the standard direct mail brochure.

Even in its role as an innovator and model for online merchandizing, Amazon.com's trailblazing business model generally complements rather than undermines older media. A case in point is the company's development of an ambitious digital archive of more than 120,000 books. Publishers initially feared the plan to allow readers to search the database and extract excerpts. But since an entire book's content is not downloadable, many recognized that a digital library could encourage rather than limit book buying.[23]

Of course, the McLuhanesque point is still worth noting: every new media form is likely to transform its content and users in some ways. Instant messaging is not a phone call. It changes the phone's oral facsimile to a print analogue, with a range of apparent gains and losses. But it is still a conversation

"Something was definitely lost when we went from being hunter-gatherers to browser-purchasers."

with much of the same content. Likewise, where the traditional six-sided political pamphlet assumes a linear sequence for developing its content, its web counterpart offers links that can be opened in a more random sequence. And where the pamphlet usually ends with a response request that lists phone numbers or contact information, the Internet uses its inherent interactivity to find its readers. But in terms of content, these are evolutionary changes, often accommodating rather than undermining "competing" media.

4. *Because they often exist outside institutional settings, noninstitutional Internet "information" sources can function without central gatekeepers—roles traditionally played in organizations by superiors and, in journalism, by editors.* This is a familiar but important point. With minimal resources, anyone can offer ideas and images for consumption by other Internet users. Personal web pages, blogs, list serves, and chat rooms facilitate easy communication to self-selected niche groups (i.e., trade and professional organizations, patients seeking health advice, musicians' web pages, etc.). In many ways, this access to others without going through a central controlling authority is the most profound promise of the Internet. Given the opportunity, notes Dan Gillmor, "Outsiders of all kinds can probe more deeply into newsmaker's business and affairs. They can disseminate what they learn more widely and more quickly. And its never been easier to organize like-minded people to support or denounce a person or cause."[24]

Online blogs often serve several of these functions. Some of the most popular as this chapter is written—such as *andrewsullivan.com* or *www.wonkette.com*—range from posts of racy news cribbed from other media, to offerings of sometimes thoughtful insights on political and social issues. Matt Welch has tracked a few of the more obscure among these millions of public diaries for the *Columbia Journalism Review*, finding many to admire.

> My shortlist of favorite news commentators now includes an Air Force mechanic (Paul Palubicki of sgtstryker.com), a punk rock singer-songwriter (Dr Frank of doktorfrank.com), a twenty-four-year-old Norwegian programmer (Bjorn Saerk of http://bearstrong.net/warblog/index.html), and a cranky libertarian journalist from Alberta, Canada (Colby Cosh).[25]

Welch notes that "never before have so many passionate outsiders—hundreds and thousands, at [a] minimum—stormed the ramparts of professional journalism."[26] And in some ways he is right. It was bloggers who pursued what turned out to be suspicious evidence CBS had cited as proof that George W. Bush got special treatment as a member of the Texas Air National Guard.[27] Blogs similarly kept alive an accurate story about then majority leader Trent Lott's thoughtlessly approving comments about fellow senator Strom Thurmond's racist legacy.[28] Mainstream assertions of fact and opinion that used to go unchallenged for days or forever are now routinely vetted through a tangle of emboldened, partisan, factional, and sometimes accurate political junkies.

But it is risky to assume that a form of homemade journalism that exists without traditional checks and balances will yield more accurate stories. The evolution of the Monica Lewinsky story that immobilized the presidency of Bill Clinton and became a scandal circus is a case in point. According to the Shorenstein Center's Marvin Kalb, the infamous *Drudge Report* was—at least among younger reporters—"a popular addiction in the cubicles."[29] Matt Drudge is still best known as the self-styled reporter who would not let the Lewinsky story die. Some of his information was at least partly accurate. But without the benefit of cooler editorial heads pondering the limits of journalistic peepholes, Drudge's persistence effectively pulled *Newsweek* and then most of the journalistic establishment into a feeding frenzy at the bottom of the journalistic food chain. The Internet did its share of supporting a two-year freeze-out of harder news while the nation lined up to take a peek at the presidential tryst. Incredibly, the Lewinsky affair and the president's reaction to it comprised the *leading* television news story for most of 1998.[30]

A related feature of the web is its ability to bypass gatekeepers with peer-to-peer networks.[31] Strictly speaking, these private communication grids bypass the client–server "architecture" associated with the web in favor of direct communication between networked computers. Kazaa and Napster are well-known software applications that have facilitated this process. And, of course, there have been numerous corporate challenges to software services that facilitate the private transfer of copyrighted material such as music and films.[32] Notwithstanding the success of corporate media companies to shut down Napster for copyright infringement, the inherent decentralized structure of the Internet would seem to always guarantee communication beyond the gaze of larger corporate gatekeepers. A federal law now allows copyright holders to seek lists of people exchanging content from Internet service providers. But the numbers of infringers are so great and dispersed that enforcement is like trying to stop jaywalkers in Manhattan.

5. *The Internet radically expands an individual's capacity to find and join ideological affinity groups.* Virtual communities of affiliation represent the original promise of the Internet. Individuals isolated by geography or denied access to traditional media can use websites and related channels to share political, lifestyle, and commercial interests. Affinity groups on virtually any topic are easy to find, with the best providing links to newsgroups, chat rooms and meetings. Although ranking numbers are often disputed, Gay.com, a San Francisco–based online site, reported 1.8 million visitors even in the smaller Internet world of March 2000.[33] During the 2004 campaign, Moveon.org, the liberal activist group, claimed 1.7 million Americans on its subscriber list.[34] And presidential campaign websites can easily surpass those numbers at the peak of the campaign cycle. Viewers of *Oprah*, cribbage players, fans of British singer Sam Brown, and homebirth advocates are just a few drops in a deluge of niche interests served by websites.

Net-based campaigns are especially interesting because of their potential to identify like-minded individuals and motivate them to action. Scott Heiferman, the cofounder of Meetup.com, was instrumental in the landmark 2003 campaign of former Vermont governor Howard Dean. Meetup is a website but functions to encourage peer-to-peer communication. It helps people find others who share the same interests or concerns. The site matches people to about four thousand discrete interests ranging from owners of dachshunds to members of the Democratic Party. When campaign manager Joe Trippi discovered that the site was being used by Dean converts to find each other, he built on its potential. Trippi raised $41 million for Dean, much of it through the Internet.[35] In the process, he pointed the way to what Cass Sunstein calls the construction of a short-term political "cult":

> If you get like-minded people in constant touch with each other, then they get more energized and committed and more outraged and more extreme. The intensity of Dean's support came less from his own personal efforts than from the fact that Dean supporters were in pretty constant touch with each other, whereas geography would normally isolate them and spread them out.[36]

The Dean bloomlet eventually faded in the face of resistance from party regulars who favored the more traditional John Kerry—but not before it helped penetrate what had been an unhealthy wall of silence built around President Bush in the aftermath of 9/11. The president had successfully described terrorism as "war" and himself as a "wartime" leader. The result muted the opposition of most Democrats and the natural skepticism of the press. Yet because the Dean campaign clearly found its voice in the grass roots, it achieved the significant objective of mobilizing opposition to an administration with grandiose military ambitions. The Vermont governor's insurgent campaign remains as a lesson of the power of Internet-based organizing.[37]

The promise of connecting directly with the grass roots also has another, related side. Traditionally, the use of campaign videos and ads has had to filter through mainstream media—an enormously difficult challenge given the cost of television "buys" in even modest-sized media markets. But with the increasing use of broadband, there is now a way to distribute videos and ads virtually free. To be sure, this distribution is not broadcasting, which comes to even the most passive of consumers. But as Carol Darr, Julie Barko, and their colleagues have pointed out, many of these political websites with video downloads are effective at motivating activists.[38]

The videos coming from groups such as Moveon.org and more iconoclastic sites such as JibJab and Billionaires for Bush use satire and ridicule to take aim at the political process. JibJab's "This Land Is Your Land," for example, was unusual because it aimed at the alleged weakness of *both* candidates in the 2004 campaign. But the two-minute animated film gained an estimated audience of fifty million when parts of it surfaced on a number of television news shows.[39]

As Darr and Barko note, "spurred by the advent of inexpensive digital film equipment and widely available broadband," these edgy and partisan activists are "successors to pamphleteers of the past." Though specific data are not readily available about how often an individual filmmaker's work was seen, they argue that "influential online political citizens . . . are playing a key role in introducing and spreading this new form of partisan political content."[40]

6. *Web use among younger Americans now equals the time spent with television—a significant change, given their previously insatiable appetite for the pleasures of the small screen.* Most usage among young adults is focused on music, messaging, games, and entertainment.[41] Far fewer are interested in politics or campaigns. A Pew survey during the 2004 presidential primary season that included Dean, Wesley Clark, and Dick Gephardt found decreasing levels of political awareness with decreasing age. "Of two factual questions (which candidate served as an Army general and which served as ma-

jority leader in the House) *just 15%* of younger Americans could get either question correct (a mere *6% knew both*). By comparison 37% of people age 30–49, and half of people age 50 and older, could answer at least one of these questions."[42]

It would be a mistake to overattribute the national decline of interest in public affairs on new media. And those of us who long for the rise of another New Left in our universities can easily forget the apolitical tide of young adults. But the shift among the young from television to computer-based entertainment raises a multitude of plausible effects, including social isolation. Internet usage can pull individuals out of the broad mainstream of the culture, represented most dramatically in the declining audiences for the traditional evening network newscasts, and more generally in the replacement of the civic culture communicated in traditional media such as television news and mainstream films with a less homogenized culture of distracted amusement.[43] Younger Americans are more likely to spend time on the Internet than with television. And many use much of the same insular but interactive technology on video games, whose revenues now nearly equal those of the film industry.[44] Robert Putnam poses the pertinent question by asking whether the Internet has "become predominately a means of active, social communication or a means of passive, private entertainment."[45] Notwithstanding some evidence of increased social isolation among heavy Internet users,[46] he hopes for what since became evident in the 2004 presidential campaign: that the Internet will engage the young in vital (if virtual) communities.

7. *The Internet is phenomenologically dissimilar from its technological ancestors as a communication medium. It differs most dramatically from its related print and television precursors in its peculiar form of anonymity and interactivity.* In face-to-face communication, interactivity takes away anonymity as interlocutors become known to each other. By contrast, computer mediation usually reduces the signifiers of identity to language. At sites that invite interaction, visitors typically communicate through text, without using their names. Many more of what used to be known as "lurkers" gain access with few if any knowing who they are.

The plausible construction of an alternate role and identity has become something of a "new media" cottage industry,[47] which is discussed in greater detail later in this chapter. But, in fact, the *performance* of identity is embedded in nearly every form of human communication.

The written word offers a useful parallel. The segregation of the writer's physical self from the audience enhances the possible range of alternate identities. In writing to a stranger, an individual can obviously sustain an alternate persona. In Erving Goffman's words, every performer must have "expressive

"I'm going back to my room, where the media is a little less mainstream."

control."[48] And every layer of meaning in words and tonality must match the constructed self that is being offered.

The Internet typically shares this potential for an alternate "voice," fostering a level of anonymity that a paper trail does not always allow. Writers of all forms usually strive to create a persona through the metalanguage of style and a coherent presentation of feelings and ideas. Communication "out of character" can spoil this coherence. Another risk is a face-to-face meeting where the less well-managed physical self can convey a range of incongruent "messages." As Louis Menand wryly remarks, "Readers who meet a writer whose voice they have fallen in love with usually need to make a small adjustment afterward in order to hang onto the infatuation."[49]

But, of course, communicators via the Internet are less likely to meet. The Internet recombines the personal detail and physical distance of earlier media but increases the likelihood of permanent anonymity. It creates a "consciousness of the other" from the inferential data of their rhetoric—the kind of communication enshrined in Helen Hanff's sentimental post–World War II memoir *84 Charing Cross Road* and, more recently, in Nora Ephron's 1998 film

You've Got Mail. At the same time, it invites responses that owe something to both the reflexivity of oral conversation as well as to the extended soliloquies of the self-absorbed.

The reflexivity side of this equation makes politics and campaigns far less stable than most analysts are used to. Sources are obscure. Audiences are often unseen. And individuals can add to or reconstruct the basic materials of a message. In the words of Danielle Wiese and Bruce Gronbeck, the "Net is an unpredictable space." It "complicates and thickens the communicative scene, requiring those running for office to quickly speculate and assess how messages in an off-line world will be picked up and played out online in Web sites, message groups, and blogs."[50]

8. *Beyond routine use of large commercial sites and portals, digital media are frequently transient and consumed by fragmented and frequently unknowable audiences.*[51] The ephemeral nature of web content is one of its defining features. One recent study indicates that 40 to 50 percent of the web addresses cited in articles within two computing journals were not accessible after four years.[52] A librarian at the Internet Archive in San Francisco has similarly noted that the average life span of a web page in 2003 was estimated to be only about one hundred days.[53]

This pattern of disposability is not unknown to other popular media. But individual *issues* of magazines, newspapers, and television programs usually survive in libraries and various kinds of archives. Archiving the ephemera of the Internet, including mail, is far less common. Moreover, new versions of older media are typically around longer to establish a brand identity and find their carefully targeted audiences. The life cycle of a blog or electronic magazine may be much shorter.

With regard to the fragmented audience, it is a given that when the Internet is most clearly fulfilling its promise by connecting a specific individual to specific content, the effects of this connection are all but invisible to others. The marketing mentality that mandates tracking sites by volume falls short of offering insights on how the least visited sites fulfill individual needs. Such is the nature of a dynamic network with links that can terminate (as in file sharing or e-mail) far from the commercial centers of the culture. Since the effects of those contacts generally fly below the radar of most survey research, we have hardly begun to account for the social and psychological effects of peer-to-peer networks.

9. *Data overload on the Internet encourages "peripheral processing." People may be easily engaged, but not easily changed.* There is obviously great variability in how and why individuals come in contact with Internet content. Information and entertainment carry different expectations. In the realm of content with a persuasive objective (i.e., a political website seeking money

and volunteers, the site of an activist nongovernmental organization, or a business with products or services to sell), the Internet offers significant advantages for self-motivated users but serious obstacles for more reluctant audiences. Among other things, Internet advertising is often portrayed as more of a nuisance than a doorway to high rates of "click through."[54] But the largest problem is predicted by Richard Petty and John Cacioppo's "elaboration likelihood" model for how individuals manage their time in an overcommunicated society.

The model starts from the assumption that communication and information-seeking involve various levels of attention and commitment. The clutter of messages in daily life forces individuals into quick choices about how much time and mental effort they will put into a message. If we are strongly motivated to consume and evaluate ideas, such critical thinking—what Petty and Cacioppo call "central processing"—may produce lasting and significant effects. But most of the time we protect ourselves by processing content "peripherally," limiting our attention and time.[55] The "peripheral processor" may initially receive a message (i.e., anything from a banner ad at the top of a web page to an e-mail requesting some form of online political activism). But, as the model predicts, the pressures of time and a lower level of investment in the subject decrease the chance of fully acting on the initial impulse. A quick preliminary judgment sometimes does not stick. The idea of "information overload" in our overcommunicated society is both a reality and a cliché.

By contrast, the nominal circumstances of richer communication experiences such as film viewing are typically different. Sitting in a darkened theater for several hours and giving ourselves over to events on the screen increase the likelihood of central processing. We welcome the sensory immersion of film, which is why it can be so deeply affecting. But no such masking of competing distractions exists in the chaotic world of the Internet. It is well known, for example, that some advertisers have been disappointed by the performance of banner ads at the top of web pages.[56] The result is hardly surprising, given the brief time spent on any one site. Similarly, the flood of appeals that come to a user from spam e-mail solicitations, ubiquitous ads, and the sheer volume of "hits" to a search query clearly forces the kind of protective information processing predicted in the model.

All of the nine attributes cited here offer glimpses of key attributes and uses of the Internet. In its properties we see the same interplay between self-expression and collective consciousness that Marshall McLuhan tackled in his study of the printed word.[57] If we are still sorting out how the Internet has altered our world, McLuhan's basic point that our "sense ratios" change as media technologies change still seems secure. Like fifteenth-century institutions reshaped by the rise of typography, we feel the sting of change in ways that both diminish and empower.

RHETORICAL ATTRIBUTES OF NET-MEDIATED DISCOURSE

The remainder of this chapter uses some of these benchmark features to probe their effects on public discourse. Our focus is especially on four rhetorical and social features that seem to be supported in the structures and user routines of the Internet.

1. *In structure and practice, the Internet often fosters reactive rhetorics rather than traditional arguments. What might be called "rhetorics of attitude" affirm identity more than they address known audiences.*

Public life in the United States has always fostered its share of vituperative discourse. One can identify the corrosive atmosphere of national politics in venues as diverse as the floor of the United States Senate, where the vice president recently told a senator, "Fuck yourself,"[58] or the op-ed pages of major newspapers. We live in an era where public discussion is dominated by columnists and "journalists" who perform as indignant observers of our civic life. Shoutfests on talk radio and television's *The Capital Gang* or *The O'Reilly Factor* are emblematic of our times. Even mainstream organizations such as CBS or PBS facilitate discussion and "conversation" that are at odds with their own journalistic norms.[59]

As Lincoln Dahlberg has pointed out, the ideal of deliberative democracy should be far different. Any context, he argues should include the following:

- *Exchange and critique of reasoned . . . claims*. Deliberation involves engaging in reciprocal critique of normative positions that are provided with reasons rather than simply inserted.
- *Reflexivity.* Participants must critically examine their cultural values, assumptions and interests, as well as the larger social context.
- *Ideal role taking.* Participants must attempt to understand the argument from the other's perspective. This requires a commitment to an ongoing dialogue with difference in which interlocutors respectfully listen to each other.
- *Sincerity.* Each participant must make a sincere effort to provide all information relevant to the particular problem under consideration, including information regarding intentions, interests, needs and desires.[60]

Dahlberg mentions other traditional standards, finding at least one site in Minnesota that honors some of them.[61] But he has set the bar very high. In most nonjournalistic settings, invective and ideological inflexibility is the rule. There are perhaps few talk radio or popular television news shows that would routinely honor these standards.[62] One can easily get the impression that there are even fewer on the Internet.

Why are expressions of anger and scorn so often the norm in political blogs and other forms of discourse about public affairs? Newsgroups and chat rooms are notorious for nurturing the darker rhetorical arts of invective, ad hominem, sarcasm, and withering criticism.[63] The blogger seeking his or her way to a wide Internet readership will pay the price of neglect for being thorough, accurate, and subtle.

One can make the case that discourse generally is coarser than it was fifty years ago. In the 1950s, finding one's own version of a courtly political manner was an essential tool of access and respectability—the equivalent of a man wearing a hat to church or a woman putting on white gloves before visiting the shops downtown. That culture has changed as aspects of our private lives have eased their way into the public sphere. But the clearest reason for the web's reputation for acerbic discourse lies in its anonymity and the suspension of conventional civility for advocates concealed behind an electronic scrim. As an unidentified observer, it is easier to dismiss another person's views with a retort than a detailed argument. When one is isolated, the self-censorship common in discourse within a known community begins to yield to uncensored self-reports. All things being equal, we like to function without the burden of careful self-monitoring.

Consider several responses to the popular blogs of Mickey Kaus in the months leading up to the 2004 election pitting John Kerry against George W. Bush. "Kausfiles" is a feature in *Slate* magazine, with stream-of-consciousness thoughts, misspellings, and nonfluencies all intact. Here are two entries:

Subject: Bitter liberals wheened on rat urine
From: Mauerphquer
Date: Jun 21 2004 12:58PM
I would be angry if I were a lib myself dancing to kerrys flat tunes..I mean this guy couldnt inspire mushrooms to grow in the dark. what a BORE. . . . FACE IT LIBS YOU CAN HOLD YOUR BREATH AND COUNT TO ONE HUNDRED AND YOUR SHAR PEI WILL NEVER WIN!!!!!!

Subject: New ode to the Chickenhawk-in-Chief
From: TRACE
Date: Jun 21 2004 6:15AM
Todays poem for the faux hero who, when his chance came to serve his country, chose to have his dad get him a free pass.

Real men like Kerry volunteered for the war
Pep Squad Bush chose cheerleading at Yale
Men with balls risked their lives, did their duty and more
Bush's pom poms he'd courageously flail
Not content to let others serve for them, do their tour
Men like Kerry chose the courageous trail
Bush sent others to fight while he ran for the door
Pep squad Dubya, the cheerleading she-male[64]

These entries are not atypical of political Internet discourse, containing most of the tropes of unsigned communication. To be sure, some writers are thoughtful and sometimes empowering to readers. But the norm leans toward the sour, assertive, and exclusionary.

Arguments are better and different. A true argument includes a claim followed by evidence. It offers good and adequate reasons in support of an assertion. Sometimes these reasons are so obvious that they need no further amplification. But arguments explicitly promise to deal with the substance of an assertion in instrumental rather than just expressive terms. If we are engaged in argument, we want to know the reasons that exist for a claim. And while we can obviously dispute them, true arguments move the discussion from the motives or attributes of an advocate toward the quality of the ideas he or she is asserting.

Arguments also aspire to universal acceptance. They explicitly include reasons that the general public can potentially embrace as relevant and significant. They may be practical or idealistic, value laden or fact based, fully detailed or implied.[65] Common to all forms is the baseline assumption that arguments are constructed to find reasons that work for others as well as for ourselves.[66]

The Internet obviously carries this form of discourse in the same ways that other media do. But in a medium that almost demands peripheral processing *and* is available to unknown and unknowable readers, self-referential feelings appear to provide a larger psychological payoff. Where arguments require a greater concern for the responses and assent, pure invective is always about oneself; it defines the boundaries of one's own identity.[67] Unilateral assertion does not require the harder work of a dialogue that asks for accurate reading or listening. When ideas or feelings are set out for display but not debate, they function to assert the precincts of our accepted world: the sum of slights, experiences, and fantasies that give meaning to our lives and to events beyond our control.

2. *A corollary of "data overload" cited earlier is a huge expectation for processing information. One response to this burden might be called*

"protective ignorance," or a defensive aversion to discursive discourse. The problem is well known: the Internet can generate tons of information. But useful information is often hidden in the low-grade ore that make up the mountains of data created by searchable databases. Google identifies more than fourteen thousand hits for the Aicardi syndrome, a very rare brain disorder in girls. For the Brooklyn Dodgers, who haven't been based in New York City for decades, there are more than 150,000 hits. On millions of similar topics, the Internet promises a tidal wave of potential *data*. From what must often be a random process, we mine information on the outside chance that we can build a coherent perspective that may represent real knowledge.

Working through these stages is arduous and often debilitating. To centrally process what even a modest search can offer up can be overwhelming. By one estimate, for example, only 25 percent of surveyed medical information websites contained "adequate" or "relevant" information that would be helpful to patients.[68] Much of the rest is useless or misleading. Others have found little substantive political information in sites established by members of Congress. Only a minority even include their voting records on key pieces of legislation.[69] And, of course, the capacity to add search capabilities only makes the mountain larger. At one time, Google was reportedly adding thirty servers a day to handle the traffic created by new sites and new users.[70]

One result of this explosive growth in access to raw information is to seek protection against its bulk by finding shelter in narrow boundaries of expertise and, most provocatively, by becoming what Sheldon Unger calls "knowledge-averse." He notes, "Inundated at work, using technologies that allow this workflow to intrude readily into the rest of one's life, and encountering high entry barriers into non-specialty knowledge domains, it should not be surprising if individuals adopt a less complex and more entertainment-oriented attitude to most (non work) knowledge domains."[71] To put the matter another way, Bruce Gronbeck asks whether it possible to "run a country of soon 300 million souls with a radically fragmented citizenry—people who can use the computer's hyperlinking capabilities to run away from centers of power, action and coherent policy to more and more esoteric locations."[72] This is the old dilemma created by being exposed to enough new information to have a sense of what you still don't know. The bigger the circle of one's knowledge, the longer the circumference that marks the border of the unknown.

The urge to retreat from those borders is well known to psychologists of persuasion. In most individuals, the will to entertain new ideas is hardly robust.[73] Even so, it is disconcerting to see protective ignorance emerge as a kind of norm for users of cyberspace, even when it is not required.

Slate's "review" of former president Bill Clinton's autobiography, *My Life*, is instructive. How would this pioneering Internet magazine deal with the substantial 957-page memoir of arguably one of our brightest presidents? The book is a detailed narrative of the president's life and his astute observations about how huge economic and political changes have altered the American role in global affairs. Unfortunately, *Slate*'s decision on how to proceed would have been familiar to a cunning middle school student faced with the need to knock off a reading assignment. The online magazine assigned *three* people to divide up and read separate parts of the book, with the instructions to look only for the "juicy bits."[74] That was it. It's hard to imagine another national magazine (e.g., the *New York Times*, *New York Review of Books*, or *Harper's*) similarly dividing up the labor of a review, where each reviewer was unaware of what came before and after his or her own assigned homework. But, of course, *Slate* must offer something fresh every day. Given the choice of being either fast or thoughtful in assessing this sprawling discursive narrative, it chose the former.

3. *The Internet's anonymity and distancing of sources encourages the "performance" of attitudes.* Sometimes we use language to *show* rather than simply *say*. Julie Linquist has observed that the teasing byplay of social settings can easily encourage the *performance of arguments:* the sense that in specific settings and circumstances, *it is one's "social 'job'* . . . to enact speech in which cultural values are encoded." As was noted in the previous chapter, she frequently filled this function as the bartender and "house liberal" in a working-class restaurant.[75] In casual conversation, she and her patrons knew her role and frequently rose to take the bait of a reactionary political comment. Goffman similarly described the presentation of who we *wish* to be with careful attention to the "maintenance of expressive control."[76] He concedes that the "machinery of self production is cumbersome," yet we are strongly motivated by our desires to project an effective presentation of self that meets the expectations of others.[77]

The Internet is capable of this kind of performance, but the audience can only be inferred rather than known. In the anonymity of cyberspace, one can more freely construct a persona, even one that is little more than a random collection of incoherent attitudes. Consider reader "reviews and comments" common to popular commercial sites such as Amazon.com and the popular travel site Tripadvisor. The subject of aging described in a book by former president Jimmy Carter would seem to require a response comparable to Carter's gentle persona. Not so for an Amazon reader, who offers this shrill reply (with all of its illiteracy intact):

> **BURN THE BOOK**, October 26, 2002
> This is the worst book in the world. After just finishing Jimmy's last book An Hour Before Daylight i could say that he needs to learn how to write, this book

> was so un iteresting that i almost burnt it while reading it. I suggest that if you own this book then burn it before finishing this report.[78]

Or there are these "guest comments" from Tripadvisor about an authentic Appalachian Shangri-La: a wonderful old mountain hotel set amid 1,200 acres of protected mountain and forest land. "Very dissapointing," according to one. The food "is REALLY bad," noted another. The rooms are "extremely underwhelming" and—setting out lodging criteria that must be new to the hospitality industry—"stiff" and "uneasy."[79]

These throwaway comments certainly do little harm. A reader can gauge that they were written by fools. The point is that such hit-and-run rhetoric is common on the Internet and often supported by professional sites that are, after all, simply offering users the opportunity to exploit the net's open access. Such thoughtlessness finds a place in every media form. But the net feeds the strong impulse to use criticism as a performative gesture—a way to communicate independence and individualism against the unbroken vacuity of modern life. Assertion—even when it is silly and empty—offers its meager narcissistic rewards with no costs or obligations.

4. *The web prefers "need" appeals over traditional public arguments.* Because its content is usually consumed or created alone, it does not operate under the explicit expectations of a direct audience.

As we have noted, argumentation is constructed around the implicit expectations of an audience, with an eye on "good reasons" that aspire to universality. Need appeals are more circumstantial, functioning as a more personalized form of address. In most traditional public settings, a person would be likely to feel compelled to argue the case for, say, school vouchers by appealing to the values of the audience and community (i.e., as in an argument based on equality: "Kids in the 'wrong' neighborhoods deserve a chance to attend schools in the best parts of town"). But privately, vouchers are more likely to be discussed in terms of personal or family needs (i.e., "I don't care if vouchers weaken the city's public schools. I want the best for my children."). Put another way, in the presence of others we are less likely to discuss issues only in terms of our own interests. But leave us alone without a consciousness of audience, and we may drift in that direction.

The dispersed and mostly isolated audiences of the Internet nurture its tendency to be a private rather than public medium. We see this in the need appeals that are common to most personal and commercial websites. The home page of the AOL's struggling Netscape Network is typical. It is probably the default home page for thousands and the entry portal for many more. Predictably, it is full of "news" and features to keep users' eyes near Netscape advertisers. And, it features dozens of links that will extend the users' time with its own lineup of stories and features. On one typical day, top features on the site included "USA's Top 5 Public Restrooms," "Secrets Cleaning Companies Keep," and "How Waiters Get Us to Tip More." Information we "need to know" included "Britney's Car Accident Ordeal," "Food That Makes Men Aggressive," and tips on how to "Sharpen Your Sex Appeal Skills." "News" represented approximately one-sixth of the home page, with short stories attached to headlines such as "Martha Stewart: I Miss My Job," "Drowning Deaths a Murder-Suicide," and "Wife: GOP Leader Likes Sex Clubs." Viewers were also invited to download pictures of movie stars and women models from *Maxim* magazine, as well as the newest version of the Netscape browser.[80] All of this from a division of the largest media company in the United States.

On this day, the site had curiosities for everyone and the unmistakable features of a supermarket tabloid. Most striking is how little space on the home page was devoted to national concerns or problems, at least as it might be defined on any given day on the front page of a good newspaper. It is a challenge for our times to keep the civic engagement of the agora—the public square that nurtures community discourse—alive.

BY WAY OF CONCLUSION: QUESTIONS BEYOND WHAT WE KNOW

As Internet usage continues to diffuse through society and its primary institutions, it will surely take on many of the effects and features of established older media. It will undoubtedly be more commercial, more centrist, and widely incorporated into existing political and personal structures. Common civic functions—campaign fund-raising, consciousness-raising activities of social action groups, and journalism, to name three—have already been significantly altered.

But profound questions remain to be answered. Will relatively low levels of engagement be increased by the Internet's enormous capacity to help individuals with the same passions find one other? Will its equally staggering potential to make any user a "publisher" democratize mass society? And can the Internet facilitate meaningful forms of collective political consciousness that actually fulfill community and cultural aspirations? One hopes that political consultant Joe Trippi is right when he notes that the Internet will be the death of cynical one-way television campaigns and reporting.

> This generation of activists is being defined by what they accomplish using the Internet, just as surely as my generation of politicians and strategists was

> defined by and, eventually chained to, the television. But while TV was a medium that rendered us dumb, disengaged, and disconnected, the Internet makes us smarter, more involved, and better informed. The Internet was designed to foster cooperation; it's built on a foundation of shared innovation.[81]

And then there are the even larger questions raised by technology that further diminishes the importance of geographic and political boundaries. The increasing ability of individuals to control their own access to content from any corner of the world is its own form of time travel. Will widespread access to broadband communications undermine the nationalism and cultural identity that both feed and corrupt political engagement? Can ostensibly declining levels of civic involvement be reversed? Or will new media significantly redefine what it means to be engaged? The importation of fuzzy black-and-white images of the nation's eastern and western shores was a noteworthy precursor. The most exciting promise of the Internet is that it can carry us beyond those shores and into richer levels of political consciousness.

As Americans, we are quick to recommend the democratizing Internet to others. Yet we should not exempt ourselves. That will be a tall order for a society that mostly limits its imports to goods and prefers to see itself as a one-way exporter of political ideals.

NOTES

1. Chris Gray, *Cyborg Citizen* (New York: Routledge, 2001), 41.
2. Sheldon Unger, "Misplaced Metaphor: A Critical Analysis of the "Knowledge Society," *Canadian Review of Sociology and Anthropology*, August 2003, EBSCO Academic Premier, http://web18.epnet.com/delivery/printSave.asp?tv=1&.
3. Erik Barnouw, *Tube of Plenty: The Evolution of American Television* (New York: Oxford University Press, 1975), 171.
4. Thomas Friedman, *The World Is Flat* (New York: Farrar, Straus & Giroux, 2005), 3–159.
5. W. Russell Neuman, "The Impact of the New Media," in *Mediated Politics: Communication in the Future of Democracy*, ed. W. Lance Bennett and Robert M. Entman (New York: Cambridge University Press, 2001), 309.
6. Neuman, "The Impact of the New Media," 299.
7. For a useful overview of early research, see Melvin DeFluer and Everette Denis, *Understanding Mass Communication*, 6th ed. (Boston: Houghton Mifflin, 1998), 429–44.
8. Even relatively simple projects such as determining how much time individuals spend with specific media forms is surprisingly difficult. Diaries, phone surveys, and direct observations often reach different conclusions about the amount of time the same individuals spent with specific media. See, for example, "Study: Media Use Difficult to Measure," *Quill*, May 2004, 33.

9. See, for example, Robert Kubey, "TV and the Internet: Pitfalls in Forecasting the Future," *Knowledge, Technology, & Policy*, Summer 2000, 63–85.

10. "Study: Media Use Difficult to Measure."

11. Jimmy Carter, *Turning Point* (New York: Times Books, 1992), 74–131.

12. For a discussion of virtual communities, see Andrew Wood and Matthew Smith, *Online Communication*, 2nd ed. (Mahwah, N.J.: Erlbaum, 2005), 122–40.

13. Mary Madden, "America's Online Pursuits: The Changing Picture of Who's Online and What They Do—Summary of Findings," Pew Internet and American Life Project, December 22, 2003, http://www.pewinternet.org/pdfs/PIP_Online_Pursuits_Final.pdf (accessed May 23, 2006); and "U.S. Web Usage and Traffic, December 2003," *ClickZ.com*, January 27, 2004, http://www.clickz.com/stats/big_picture/traffic_patterns/ (accessed April 12, 2004).

14. "U.S. Web Usage."

15. James Webster and Shu-Fang Lin, "The Internet Audience: Web Use as Mass Behavior," *Journal of Broadcasting and Electronic Media*, March 2002, 6–10.

16. "U.S. Web Usage."

17. "U.S. Web Usage."

18. U.S. Department of State, "Country Reports on Human Rights Practices—2000," February 2001, http://www.state.gove/g/drl/rls/hrrpt/2000/eap/684pf.htm.

19. Not unexpectedly, most Internet users believe their lives have benefited from the experience. For a summary of survey research on use patterns and effects, see Robert J. Klotz, *The Politics of Internet Communication* (Lanham, Md.: Rowman and Littlefield, 2004), 31–44.

20. Forty-two million web users played online games in a two-month period in 2002. See Madden, "America's Online Pursuits."

21. Madden, "America's Online Pursuits."

22. See, for example, Amy Harmon, "What Price Music?" *New York Times*, October 12, 2003, sec. 2, 1.

23. Gary Wolf, "The Great Library of Amazonia," *Wired.com*, December 2003, http://www.wired.com/wired/archive/11.12/amazon_pr.html (accessed June, 8, 2004).

24. Quoted in Joe Trippi, *The Revolution Will Not Be Televised* (New York: Regan Books, 2004), 229.

25. Matt Welch, "Blogworld: The New Amateur Journalists Weigh In," *Columbia Journalism Review*, September–October 2003, http://www.cjr.org/issues/2003/5/blog-welch.asp (accessed May 23, 2006).

26. Welch, "Blogworld."

27. Corey Pein, "Blog-Gate," *Columbia Journalism Review*, January–February 2005, http://www.cjr.org/issues/2005/1/pein-blog.asp? (accessed May 23, 2006).

28. Carl Sessions Stepp, "When Everyone's a Journalist," *American Journalism Review*, December–January 2005, http://www.ajr.org/article_printable.asp?=3803 (accessed April 11, 2005).

29. Marvin Kalb, *One Scandalous Story: Clinton, Lewinsky, and 13 Days That Tarnished American Journalism* (New York: Free Press, 2001), 86.

30. "Clinton Sex Scandal Fact Sheet," *Tyndall Report*, February 13, 1999.

31. See Duncan Watts, *Six Degrees: The Science of a Connected Age* (New York: Norton, 2003), 156–61. He uses the term *peer to peer* in two senses: the obvious one

of searching and finding others who share a common interest, and a less obvious correlate that a true peer-to-peer network does not go through a central gatekeeper/server.

32. For a brief history of the issues raised by transfer of files of copyrighted information, see Klotz, *The Politics of Internet Communication*, 172–77.

33. Jon Swartz, "Net Ratings Vex Dot-coms," *USA Today*, June 20, 2000, http://www.usatody.com/money/dotcoms/dot005.html (accessed April 12, 2004).

34. Joe Garofoli, "MoveOn, a Political Force Online, Receives $5 Million Matching Gift," *San Francisco Chronicle*, November 23, 2003.

35. Todd Purdum, "So What Was That All About?" *New York Times*, February 22, 2004, sec. 4, 1.

36. Quoted in Purdum, "So What Was That All About?"

37. See, for example, Edward Cone, "The Marketing of the President," *Baseline*, December 2003, 32–55.

38. Carol Darr and Julie Barko, "Under the Radar and over the Top: Online Political Videos in the 2004 Election," Institute for Politics and Democracy & the Internet, http://www.ipdi.org/UploadedFiles/web_videos.pdf (accessed May 23, 2007).

39. Darr and Barko, "Under the Radar."

40. Darr and Barko, "Under the Radar."

41. Janet Kornblum, "Study: Internet Tops TV in Battle for Teens' Time," *USA Today*, July 24, 2003, 8D.

42. "Cable and Internet Loom Large in Fragmented Political News Universe," Pew Internet and American Life Project, January 11, 2003, http://people-press.org/reports/pdf/200.pdf; italics added (accessed May 23, 2006).

43. See chapter 2.

44. Gloria Goodale, "Video-Game Industry Mulls over the Future beyond Shoot-'Em-Ups," *Christian Science Monitor*, June 3, 2005.

45. Robert Putnam, *Bowling Alone: The Collapse and Revival of American Community* (New York: Simon & Schuster, 2000), 179.

46. Putnam, *Bowling Alone.*

47. See, for example, Stephen Chiger, "Cybersmear: Telecommunication's 200 Year Old Riddle," *Communications and the Law*, June 2002, 49–67; Sherry Turkle, "Constructions and Reconstructions of Self in Virtual Reality: Playing in the Muds," in *Culture of the Internet*, ed. Sara Kiesler (Mahwah, N.J.: Erlbaum, 1997), 143–55.

48. Erving Goffman, *The Presentation of Self in Everyday Life* (New York: Anchor Books, 1959), 51.

49. Louis Menand, "Bad Comma," *New Yorker*, June 28, 2004, 104.

50. Daniell Wiese and Bruce Gronbeck, "Campaign 2004 Developments in Cyberpolitics," in *The 2004 Presidential Campaign: A Communication Perspective*, ed. Robert E. Denton Jr. (Lanham, Md.: Rowman & Littlefield, 2005), 227.

51. User surveys indicate the owners of top websites, such as Yahoo!, MSN, eBay, and Google. See "U.S. Web Usage Traffic." But market research interested in top commercial sites conceals what is most attractive about the Internet: its ability as a highly searchable network to match a very specialized interest with a very specialized site.

52. Rick Weiss, "On the Web, Research Proves Ephemeral," *Washington Post*, November 24, 2003, A8.

53. Weiss, "On the Web."

54. "E-VOLVE: Banner Ads Are Alive—Though Not Clicking," *Marketing Week*, January 29, 2004. The exception seems to be on news sites, which advertisers aggressively seek out. See Eric Dash, "Internet News Sites Are Back in Vogue," *New York Times*, January 24, 2005, C1, C9.

55. Richard Petty and John Cacioppo, *Communication and Persuasion: Central and Peripheral Routes to Attitude Change* (New York: Springer, 1986), 5–24.

56. Randall Rothenberg, "Famed Disasters: Hindenburg, Chicago Fire and Banner Ads," *Advertising Age*, March 5, 2001, 19.

57. Marshall McLuhan, *The Gutenberg Galaxy* (New York: Signet, 1969), 298–330.

58. Helen Dewar and Dana Milbank, "Cheney Dismisses Critic with Obscenity," *Washington Post*, June 25, 2004, A4.

59. See, for example, Selena Roberts, "A Feeding Frenzy on the Web Shoves Sanity Right Out the Door, *New York Times*, July 27, 2003, sec. 8, 9.

60. Lincoln Dahlberg, "The Internet and Democratic Discourse," *Information, Communication and Society*, December 2001, 622–23.

61. Dahlberg, "The Internet and Democratic Discourse," 623–24.

62. Notable broadcast forums approximating reasonable deliberation stand out, including those led by Tim Russert (NBC's *Meet the Press*), Diane Rehm (NPR's *The Diane Rehm Show*), Tavis Smiley (PBS's *Tavis Smiley*), and Margo Adler (NPR's *Justice Talking*).

63. See, for example, Steven Vrooman, "The Art of Invective: Performing Identity in Cyberspace," *New Media and Society*, March 2003, 51–55; and Christine Fredrick, "Feminist Rhetoric in Cyberspace: The Ethos of Feminist Usenet Groups," *Information Society*, July–September 1999, http://web18.epnet.com/citation.asp?tb=1&_ug=sid+D.

64. "Topic: Kausfiles," *Slate*, June 22, 2004, http://fray.slate.msn.com/?id=3936&tp=kausfilesblog (accessed June 23, 2004).

65. For a discussion of the nature of argument, see Gary C. Woodward and Robert E. Denton Jr., *Persuasion and Influence in American Life*, 5th ed. (Long Grove, Ill.: Waveland, 2004), 86–106.

66. Chaim Pereman and L. Olbrechts-Tyteca, *The New Rhetoric: A Treatise on Argument*, trans. John Wilkinson and Purcell Weaver (Notre Dame, Ind.: University of Notre Dame Press, 1969), 31–35.

67. Vrooman, "The Art of Invective."

68. Vrooman, "The Art of Invective."

69. Katharine Seelye, "Congress Online: Much Sizzle, Little Steak," *New York Times*, June 24, 2003, A16.

70. Watts, *Six Degrees*, 157.

71. Unger, "Misplaced Metaphor."

72. Bruce Gronbeck, address to the Rhetoric Society of America, "Citizen Voices in Cyberpolitical Culture," May 2002.

73. See, for example, Duane T. Wegener, Richard Petty, Natalie Smoak, and Leandre Fabrigar, "Multiple Routes to Resisting Attitude Change," in *Resistence to Persuasion*, ed. Eric Knowles and Jay Linn (Mahwah, N.J.: Erlbaum, 2004), 13–38.

74. The original article was later removed from the site because of complaints about copyright infringement. For an overview of reviews of the book, see Jack Shafer, "The Clinton Book Blitz," *Slate*, June 30, 2004, http://slate.msn.com/id/2103167/#ContinueArticle (July 6, 2004).

75. Julie Lindquist, *A Place to Stand* (New York: Oxford University Press, 2002), 133 (italics added).

76. Goffman, *The Presentation of Self*, 51.

77. Goffman, *The Presentation of Self*, 253.

78. Review of *The Virtues of Aging*, Amazon.com, June 29, 2004, http://www.amazon.com/exec/obidos/tg/detail/-/0345425928/qid=1088530475/sr=1-5/ref=sr_1_5/102-8929642 (accessed July 20, 2004).

79. See http://www.tripadvisor.com/ShowUserReviews-g48245 (accessed July 21, 2004).

80. Netscape Network, June 22, 2004, http://home.netscape.com/ (accssed June 22, 2004).

81. Trippi, *The Revolution Will Not Be Televised*, 227.

Chapter Four

The Staging of the Contemporary Presidency

> All manners are a kind of plea. We judge according to the style of appeal being made, the conditions under which it is made, and the audience for which it is intended; in short, in terms of how it is *staged*.[1]
>
> —Hugh Dalziel Duncan

> The political idealist in me senses how challenging and instructive and uplifting and healing communication can be—especially communication offered by a president—and is thus doubly dismayed to find so little that could be called heroic, not to mention honest.[2]
>
> —Roderick Hart

Nowhere have theatrical assumptions about politics been in greater view than with regard to the presidency. Presidents are routinely described as the central agents of American civic life. In the polarized climate of national politics over the last decade, their actions stand as representations or perversions of the national will. Objects of reverential adulation by many, they are also cast as fools in films and the daily cycles of talk show satire. At their best, as White House adviser David Gergen has noted, presidents "engage the dreams and mobilize the energies of the country behind large, sustained drives." But revealingly, in his own study of decisive leadership, most of his best examples are *dissenters* rather than presidents, including Mohandas Gandhi, Golda Meir, Nelson Mandela, and Martin Luther King.[3]

In broad strokes, this chapter takes a look at contemporary presidential communication as both performance and narration. It also places the presidency in its privileged institutional place: as an office that can support initiatives of imaginative civic leadership or—less happily but more frequently—the familiar rituals of power politics. Walter Lippmann famously called for leaders of "creative will and insight."[4] But the political philosopher was also aware that inertia can limit needed change, leaving "enfeebled" governments verging on "paralysis."[5] In the modern presidency, we see both extremes, abetted by the final subject of the chapter: the uneasy relationship that exists between the presidency and the press.

VIEWING THE PRESIDENCY FROM THE DRAMATISTIC FRAME

The actions of any chief executive spawns memories of countless shadow chiefs reconstituted from the public record: FDR rallying the nation to war in 1939, LBJ declaring his own war on poverty, or Richard Nixon swimming against a tide of cover-ups to affirm that he was "not a crook." These stand-alone tableaus have entered the realm of common remembrance, functioning as accessible symbols of the use and abuse of authority, and matched in a parallel world of popular fantasies about power. The presidency of the Hollywood imagination ranges from the action hero in *Air Force One* (1997) to the practical ethicist that occupied *The West Wing*'s Oval Office. What reality and fiction share is an emphasis on the president as an active and decisive agent.

Presidential journalism naturally feeds this idea of dynamism in its use of the argot of performance. Current and former presidents may prefer to see their work in the instrumental terminology of bureaucratic management.[6] But most observers start from the premise that the president must demonstrate active leadership through an unremitting chain of symbolic acts. In Murray Edelman's words, news depends on "dramatization, simplification and personification."[7] We think in terms of the synoptic news stories that stand as representations of more complex phenomena, with their dependence on the mechanics and agents of melodramatic narrative. Verbs of active control give the president purpose, securing his (and, someday, her) place as the master of significant events. Presidents "decide," "affirm," "determine," "direct," and "order." Those who write admiringly of their work talk about "leadership," "influence," and "mastery." Time eventually amends these simple words of action, filling in with backstories that take into account larger structural and historical forces constraining even the strongest leaders. But in the short term, there is a sentimental preference for placing even the most inert leaders in narratives that make them decisive agents. Thus, for those in need of a heroic cause, Ronald Reagan "ended" the Cold War and cleverly engineered the demise of the Soviet Union by bankrupting its government. For students of the period, however, forces far more numerous and significant were at the center of Soviet disintegration.[8]

Journalistically, the dramatic frame is both convenient and opportunistic. Too busy or lazy to study the details of policy,[9] many journalists retreat to the safe conclusion that governing depends on "the triumph of imagery."[10] If the presidency is essentially a string of staged events, there is less need to do the homework required to understand the economic or social consequences of the policies they are intended to promote.[11]

There is no shortage of this kind of "red carpet" journalism providing daily updates of the political personalities appearing at presidential spectacles and responsible for enacting decisive strategies. In a representative forum like PBS's long-running *Washington Week in Review*, we typically get sketches of personalities falling in and out of orbit around the president. He is the agent that moves the plot forward; they have supporting roles in *his* play. A thirty-minute tour of the precincts inside the Beltway in November 2004, for example, reminded viewers that then Palestinian leader Yasser Arafat was "persona non grata" with the president, attorney general designate Alberto Gonzales was an "old friend," Secretary of State Colin Powell was a former ally leaving with "arrows in the back," and Senator Arlen Specter was in trouble with the president's conservative allies as the new chair of the Senate Judiciary Committee.[12] As much as we would like politics to be about ideas and ideals, our consciousness of civil affairs is more firmly anchored in seeing the White House as a kind of palace court consumed by shifting alliances and occasional treachery.

The melding of politics with the dramatic frame is so thorough and deep that we no longer seem to know which way the arrows run. Is it that politics is now but a species of theater or that theater has always been a form of politics? In more elemental terms, is the essence of campaigning and governing dramatistic, meaning that these broad objectives are not just *like* drama but essentially the heart of the dramatic imperative to construct and represent action?

An affirmative answer to the last question has important theoretical and philosophical implications. As master critic Kenneth Burke has argued, to take dramatism at face value is to view acts, motives, audiences, and scenes not as metaphorical conveniences but as primary terms with specific expectations. Drama is not simply a heuristic device for thinking about human conduct. It is the archetypal framework for understanding it.[13] To frame human behavior as *action*, we assume that there is an agent with choices to make and a consciousness of social settings that will affect those choices. As players in the dramas of everyday life, we adjust our actions to anticipate certain kinds of responses. As audiences to the actions of others, we reverse the process by decoding motives from behavior—the essence of the dramatic equation. One cannot easily know the exact course of, say, a grassfire in the dry eastern foothills of the Rockies. It will develop in accordance with conditions (wind, humidity, etc.) largely beyond anyone's complete knowledge. But a person can subjectively "know" the motives of Gerald Ford's 1973 pardon of Richard Nixon or George W. Bush's decision to center his presidency on the so-called war against terrorism. What we understand from witnessing the verbal and symbolic outcomes of human interaction are the internal causes of behavior, with inferences to their moral and biographical origins. And because this is drama and not science, it matters less that we may sometimes get things wrong (even while it matters a great deal to the agent). The measure of narrative is not objective knowledge but the intersubjective understandings of an audience.

Drama is thus the cognitive infrastructure for capturing the imagination. It is an abstractive and reductive process that, among other things, lets us see leaders as we *wish* they were. Drama also helps us retain enthusiasm for change that can be idealized through narratives of strong leadership. The nation's current challenge, as noted in the next section, is coping with media and political structures that seem better able to deliver to its fantasies than its principles.

THE FROZEN POLITICAL STRUCTURE

The makers of the Constitution foresaw and even welcomed divided government. But they probably did not intend a system where, in their words, "factions" would sometimes paralyze the fragile potential for political creativity. Virtually no one in American life looks to the White House or Congress for imaginative ways to respond to serious national problems. Historians occasionally give us glimpses of progressive and effective presidential leadership.[14] But incremental rather than original solutions are guaranteed by a range of forces: the tripartite constitutional split of powers, the continuous and virulent partisanship of Congress, the canceling effects of intensive lobbying by opposing corporate or single issue stakeholders, and a cautious nation that views most change as threatening.

There have been exceptions. One of the clearest examples of presidential innovation grew out of the merging of desperate economic times with the emergence of World War II. With the help of a supportive Congress, President Franklin Roosevelt promoted a legendary set of business and employment programs in the New Deal that sought to provide a social safety net and also prime the American economic machine that had faltered. Roosevelt enacted a vast web of initiatives embracing collections of innovations, ranging from public funding of artists in their own communities to much-needed reforms in banking and consumer protection. Social Security, various labor protection acts, and a host of public works projects made government an active agent in giving incentives to business and basic protections to individuals.[15]

Today Congress is stunningly independent and less likely to cede such power to a president. As we note in the next chapter, members of the same party are often comfortable going their own way. Even with ostensibly friendly pluralities in both houses, the second George Bush found it easier to articulate his domestic legislative agenda than enact it.

The rise in the independence of Congress has also been accompanied by polarized and often hostile public attitudes toward sitting presidents. This is not entirely new. Abraham Lincoln was famously vilified by the press and many Americans in his own day,[16] as was Warren Harding, Herbert Hoover, Johnson, Nixon, and others.[17] But compared with the recent past, the presidency has lost much of its mystique and, with it, the aura of authority that used to make it relatively easy to gain broad public sympathy for key decisions. While the office still confers enormous prestige on its staff and friends, it is far from a certainty that this prestige can be translated into action. Bill Clinton struggled and largely failed to rein in doubters who were ostensibly on his side regarding plans to end prohibitions against gays in the military and—more importantly—to enact his ambitious health care reform agenda.[18] Similarly, even after Bush won a second term in 2004, his approval ratings drifted steadily downward.[19] By contrast, Franklin Roosevelt, Dwight Eisenhower, and John Kennedy were still heroes in their time, partly because many associated the postwar success of the nation with their leadership.

A less distinct but significant cultural force has also been at work in the last four decades. Between 1930 and 1964, the legitimacy of presidential leadership was held together by greater emphasis on the *public office* than the *private* choices of its occupants. Faith in leaders was more certain because we did not "know" them in the same ways as we know their modern counterparts.[20] By the mid-1960s, deep and lasting political and national wounds began to expose the frailties of the executive. The public was famously soured by Johnson's relentless pursuit of a disastrous Vietnam policy and Nixon's involvement in a cover-up of the Watergate break-in. Each disaster—the first, policy driven; the second, political—unfolded at a time when cultural deconstructionists began to give preference to the personal over the institutional. The presidential hagiography that was routine in the past was partly replaced by unflattering insider accounts of administrations.[21] At the same time, revisionist biographies in this period cited the dysfunctions and marital infidelities of FDR, Kennedy, Johnson, and Eisenhower.[22] The nightmare of the Clinton-Lewinsky scandal in the 1990s may have been a new low in the diversion of the nation away from issues of importance. But the seeds for our national fascination were created with the rise of unrestrained press interest in the sideshows of political celebrity.[23]

Perhaps this is why the nation finds itself reenergized by faith-based politics. The application of religious absolutes and ideals to lifestyle choices and complex policy issues has always been an enduring American habit. Journalism that trades in the temptations of sex, drugs, and money fuels this tendency,[24] even while it moralizes and entertains us. Add in public displays of piety—vigils, prayer breakfasts, and the like—and the result is a special kind of ersatz religiosity that is *meant to be seen*. The battleground of school prayer is a case in point. In the simplest sense, anyone can pray anywhere and virtually at any time. If prayer is a conversation between oneself and God, it is beyond the notice or sanction of the state. But, of course, some public prayers function as back door attempts at social legitimation. Supplicants who insist that they must be noticed are usually trying to define a unified community under their definitions of the sacred and profane. When authorized by schools, football teams, and the like, public prayers function as a kind of theater of status endorsements, rewarding the compliant and reminding those beyond the pale that they are a minority.

EXPRESSIVE FUNCTIONS AND COMMON TROPES

One of the enduring functions of the presidency is to celebrate the free *individual* within *society*. But it is a balancing act that shifts over time as particular presidents emphasize the different values of each. Is the nation a culture that exists for the care and benefit of all—what we think of when we think of the "collective good"? Or is it charged only with maximizing the freedoms and potentialities of the individual? Robert Bellah and his colleagues address this and other tensions in their study *The Good Society.* As they see it, we are attached to the idea of individualism and its normative political correlate: a suspicion of any governmental efforts to act in "the public good." "We make greater demands on institutions for private satisfactions, while depleting the institutional infrastructure upon which any common good (or even the ability of the system to continue to produce individual goods) depends."[25]

It is a sign of our times that the ideological energies of most of our presidents since Reagan have been spent on the individualist side of the equation. In the absence of efforts to articulate specific common governmental objectives that can bind divergent interests together, presidents and their surrogates often retreat to evocations of external dangers ("terrorism") and internal strengths ("freedom" or "compassion")—terms that get a free pass because they sanction nearly any fantasy and offer no obligations to define standards or limits.[26] To propose a tax cut, the centerpiece of the Bush administration's domestic agenda in 2003, one need only claim that the cut was the rightful return of money "taken" from individuals by the government, as if government were an alien force existing in opposition to the needs or interests of the nation. Expectations for the maintenance or expansion of federal and state services (e.g., Medicaid, airport security, highways, and schools, to name a few) remain ingrained, but they are often interpreted as valuable only to the extent they are relevant to *personal* freedom.

There are exceptions, such as national crises that may momentarily set aside the rhetoric of individualism. In times of national trauma (i.e., 9/11, the loss of the two space shuttles, the devastation and slow governmental response to Hurricane Katrina), leaders are usually able to provide hopeful words that express a collective sense of loss. Mary Stuckey's apt description of the president as "interpreter-in-chief" suggests this function: "The president has become the nation's chief storyteller, its interpreter-in-chief. He tells us stories about ourselves, and in so doing he tells us what sort of people we are, how we are constituted as a community."[27] Kennedy, Reagan, and Clinton seemed especially adept at fulfilling this role. Reagan's apt speech on the day of the *Challenger* explosion in 1986 expressed sadness at the loss of the astronauts, while also reaffirming the value of the space program.[28] Presidents help convert crises into occasions that reaffirm an individual's sense of national identity.

Beyond this key interpretive role, chief executives must also defend administration policies. No other role is so deep or basic. These defenses usually take the form of broad and unchallengeable national commonplaces, with indications of how governmental action or withdrawal of action will fulfill them.[29] One can even feel empathy for the dour Nixon, who seemed compelled by his Quaker origins to repeatedly go to the public to explain legislative plans. Aide Leonard Garment recalls that he was often able to resist the advice of "hard-ass conservatives" in favor of some innovative ideas.[30] By today's standards, Nixon's initiatives on desegregation, Native American rights, and federal funding for the arts seem almost progressive.

Since the Reagan years, however, the norm has increasingly been in the other direction: lowering taxes and expectations about the delivery of governmental services; deregulating vital industries like broadcasting, banking, insurance, and airlines; and shifting a dwindling list of "safety net" programs to stretched private and state agencies. Presidents know they must still address our common dreams. But, with the recent exception of Bill Clinton, they have done so by largely downplaying the idea of *collective* prosperity. We are an "ownership society," George W. Bush noted many times.[31] Presumably, the assets of property will allow Americans to pretend to be atoms in their own universe, a fantasy that minimizes the indispensable role that government plays as the agent for fostering a civil society.

FINDING ACTS OF PRESIDENTIAL IMAGINATION

The act of communication assumes corollary acts of creation and imagination. At the simplest levels, the kind of invention undertaken by national leaders usually identifies and articulates norms and values already held and honored by audiences.[32] Leadership springs from reminding citizens of their common ideological roots. But any rounded view of leadership must also recognize a willingness to venture beyond the sometimes limited range of conventional belief. Asking that imagination be brought to the discussion of reflexive ways of thinking requires a meliorist orientation—a desire to find national correctives for national problems. This assumption was behind the conclusion of the bipartisan 9/11 Commission Report of 2004, which noted that one of the contributing factors that led to the terrorist attacks in New York and Washington was a "failure of imagination" within the intelligence communities.[33] The FBI and CIA might have taken preventive measures had they discovered patterns in questionable activities, including aviation school students with more interest in flying than landing commercial aircraft. As columnist Frank Rich has noted, we seem to live in times where we only think in terms of "small ideas, small plans, small schemes."[34]

Political imagination is nurtured in many ways. The Calvinist rectitude and love of oratory that led Woodrow Wilson to a professorship at Princeton seemed to stay with him through his years as a reformist governor and idealistic president. Wilson's rhetorical bent gave him the necessary equipment for imagining social and global transformations. For both Theodore Roosevelt and his cousin Franklin, there was a related sense of noblesse oblige: that those born into privilege have the obligation to govern in ways that protect the interests of the weak as well as the strong. All could have subscribed to Wilson's declaration of government as an agency for the collective good: "There is no idea so uplifting as the idea of the service of humanity. There is nothing that touches the springs of conscience like the cause of the oppressed, the cause of those who suffer, and we give not only our sympathy but our justice, our righteous action, our action for them as well as for ourselves."[35]

Our interest in communication also obliges us to acknowledge the generative possibilities of political language. Language is not just the slave of thought. It guides it as well. For example, Kenneth Burke has celebrated the power of language to upset usual ways of associating "what goes with what." As every reader knows, linking two dissimilar concepts to one common purpose can create a new perspective, a different way of seeing something familiar. Burke notes approvingly that when T. S. Eliot commented during a visit to the United States that he saw less "decadent athleticism" than during an earlier trip, the poet "offered a casual moral revaluation or perspective by putting the wrong words together."[36] In the dusty thinking of the time, athletics was rarely conceived as harboring any social malady.

It follows that presidents often do not know what they think until they see their ideas on paper. Working with staff on a speech is often indistinguishable from developing a policy.[37]

As dissenter, activist, playwright, and—finally—the unlikely president of a newly emerged Czech Republic, Václav Havel understood the generative power of language. Havel knew enough to sometimes avoid the hackneyed and watertight certainties of ritualized political discourse, allowing creative circumspection and even self-doubt. Superbly equipped to carry the ironies of the theater into public life, he has been perhaps the only modern leader to write political speeches as "voice-over" interior monologues. In one of his last addresses as a public official, for example, he admitted to "an experience of unbearable oppressiveness, a need constantly to explain myself to someone, to define myself, a longing for an unattainable order of things, a longing that increases as the terrain I walk though becomes more muddled and confusing."[38]

Few leaders would ever share such doubts with their constituents. As David Remnick notes, "Havel seemed not a President so much as Kafka reading from his diaries."[39] But there is something refreshing about a national figure with both the fluency and intellectual courage to recognize the uncertainties of leadership.

The Czech president's public career is a reminder that one can search for a long time to find creative and innovative presidential communication. Rod Hart has observed that "examining the *Public Papers of the Presidents* can be disheartening indeed. Such reading is not recommended to a reader already harboring significant doubts about the essential soundness of American governance."[40] He cites a modern penchant for a rising tide of inane comments on politically insignificant topics. Examples include a "rhetorically punch drunk" Richard Nixon rambling on to White House visitors about the virtues of long-distance bus travel or inadvertently highlighting his awkwardness by serenading a congressman with a piano rendition of "Happy Birthday." Hart notes that presidents spend "more and more of their hours saying less and less of substance."[41]

The well-documented nonfluencies of George W. Bush offer further evidence of a disabled presidential imagination. The inability of Bush to master basic syntax and word choice has been dismissed as a harmless, even endearing, personality tic. For many Americans suspicious of "too much" education and easy political glibness, such plain and mangled speech communicates its own populist message. But it remains disturbing to the rest of us who understand the capacity to speak well—to use language with precision and grace—as a measure of the quality of one's mind. Language use is not an adjunct to thought; it *is* the embodiment of thought. To say that "My education message will resignate among all parents" may be a simple malapropism, with the basic idea still intact. But to say "A tax cut is really one of the anecdotes to coming out of an economic illness" suggests deeper levels of confusion.[42]

Equally troubling has been Bush's failure to use countless opportunities to explain and properly argue the merits of controversial administrative decisions, including opting out of agreements to join the World Court and the Kyoto Protocol on global warming, or making the fateful decision to invade and occupy Iraq. That decision will forever define his presidency. But in forum after forum, the president failed to produce even the outlines of a prima facie case for so momentous a decision. Unlike predecessors such as his father and Bill Clinton, both of whom seized opportunities for laying out better cases to the American public in similar settings, Bush usually kept to a list of assertions-only "talking points."

A communications policy of a tight-lipped president may owe something to making official statements smaller targets for the often hostile news media.[43] But in joint press conferences with Bush's principal foreign ally, British prime minister Tony Blair, it was easy to see deeper contrasts in style separating a leader committed to the idea of public argument and the pale rhetorical opposite of issuing stand-alone assertions. In these meetings, Bush appeared to have neither the energy of Blair, who had honed his skills in the weekly give and take of parliamentary questions, nor the prime minister's talent for giving compelling reasons in support of a claim.

Consider their first joint press conference after an extended meeting at Camp David in 2001. Given the increasingly likely U.S. military invasion of Iraq, the most common news story of this meeting was Bush's bizarre response to a query about what he and the British prime minister had in common. To the accompaniment of nervous laughter, Bush informed the questioners that they both used the same brand of toothpaste.

Others got little more from the president on the critical issue of the effects of sanctions against Iraq.

> **Question**: Yes, sir. Could both of you explain how you keep the Iraqi sanctions from crumbling and how do you explain how the Iraqi sanctions could be reconstituted to keep them from—to help ease the strain on the Iraqi people?
>
> **The President**: We spent a lot of time talking about our mutual interests in Iraq and the Persian Gulf, and from our perspective, as you know, I made the famous

statement that our sanctions are like Swiss cheese. That means they're not very effective. And we're going to work together to figure out a way to make them more effective.

But I think the Prime Minister and I both recognize that it is going to be important for us to build a consensus in the region to make the sanctions more effective. Colin Powell left today, after lunch, to move around the Middle East, collect thoughts and to listen, with a policy of strengthening our mission to make it clear to Saddam Hussein that he shall not terrorize his neighbors, and not develop weapons of mass destruction.

Prime Minister Blair: Yes, I'd like to just add to that. I think that—I mean, of course, we look the whole time to see how we can make sanctions more effective. But don't be under any doubt at all of our absolute determination to make sure that the threat of Saddam Hussein is contained and that he is not able to develop these weapons of mass destruction that he wishes to do.

And as I constantly point out to people, I mean, this is a man with a record on these issues, both in respect to the murder of thousands of his own people, in respect to the war against Iran, in respect to the annexation of Kuwait. And we know perfectly well, given the chance he will develop these weapons of mass destruction; indeed, he's trying to do so and will get as much technology as he can to do so.

Now, of course, we've got to—we're all conscious of the fact that our quarrel is not with the Iraqi people who in many ways suffer under the yoke of Saddam Hussein. But—and therefore, it's important that we make sure that the sanctions hit him, Saddam, as effectively as they possibly can. But we need to contain that threat, and that's why the action that we took is right and justified.[44]

While neither answer is especially detailed or thoughtful, Blair made at least a token attempt to restate the case for sanctions, citing the record of violence Hussein used against his own people. In contrast, the president offered no expression of concern for the Iraqi people, no restatement of the threat posed by the Hussein regime, and no direct defense of sanctions as a tool of foreign policy. The heir to the rhetorical traditions of Jefferson and Lincoln, Wilson and Kennedy, seemed unwilling to grasp the political significance of a question that asked about the nominally innocent victims of economic sanctions.

Authentic acts of presidential imagination *can* be found, but in the day-to-day business of presidential governance, there is not much cream on the milk. Rarer still are presidential initiatives that take action to deal with endemic political and social problems that are widely discussed by think tanks and opinion magazine elites but are otherwise thought to be political poison. Any reasonable list could include the dubious practice of relying on military power as a prime instrument of foreign policy, a reluctance to pursue the causes of endemic American poverty, acceptance and even encouragement of unsustainable levels of consumption and public debt, tolerance of military indifference in counting civilian war casualties,[45] or tacit acceptance of what former Nixon aide Kevin Phillips describes as "the greatest gap between rich and poor" of any modern democracy.[46]

Occasions when presidents or politicians surprise us by creatively weighing in on issues central to the future of American society are relatively rare.[47] There is Dwight Eisenhower's 1961 farewell address, where he stepped outside the safety zone of his own persona to warn of the "unwarranted influence" of the growing "military-industrial complex." The phrase and its idea were prescient, living on to remind Americans of what he later described as a national compulsion for "unjustified military spending."[48] There was also Jimmy Carter's unsuccessful attempts in 1977 and 1979 to warn Americans they were wasting energy resources and to prepare them for the economic and political effects of scarcity. In the second address, he noted, "We can't go on consuming 40 percent more energy than we produce. When we import oil we are also importing inflation plus unemployment."[49]

Most Americans were not buying these unpleasant truths, and Carter was defeated before he could enact his program. But he deserves credit for shunning the impulse to pander to strong commercial forces addicted to cheap energy. In the longer term, one lesson taken from this rejection was that any talk of scarcity and sacrifice was political suicide, further solidifying a definition of the national interest that includes the use of American military power to leverage access to cheap foreign oil.

Bill Clinton used the imaginative resources of the presidency in a 1993 speech to African American ministers in Memphis. In that address, he spoke about intractable racial issues that have not usually been acknowledged by other recent leaders. His speech was an extended meditation on the disappointments that would come to Martin Luther King "if he showed up today."

> How would we explain to him all these kids getting killed and killing each other? How would we justify the things that we permit that no other country in the world would permit? How could we explain that we gave people the freedom to succeed and we created conditions in which millions abuse that freedom to destroy the things that make life worth living and life itself?[50]

What strikes a reader of Clinton's public statements is how often he helped Americans imagine lives that have fallen short of the American promise. Such rhetoric was not softheaded, as his critics sometimes complained, but—at its best—an enactment of the democratic ideal to protect the weak (i.e., youth raised in poverty, pensioners, the working poor) against the rampant economic Darwinism of the strong. As Clinton noted, "All spending is not the same. There is plainly a difference between spending money and investing it. We have got to change the character of federal spending toward investment in people."[51]

Presidential discourse must imagine the unpleasant and unwanted. It must address the social and political forces that have created victims as well as heroes. It acknowledges work yet to be done. To function only as the nation's official dreamer is to reduce the bully pulpit from what Theodore Roosevelt first envisioned to a place for merely comforting the self-satisfied.

COVERING THE PRESIDENT: THE PRESS IN REBELLION AND COMPLIANCE

When CBS's Robert Pierpoint began covering the White House in 1957, he recalls that the "regulars" in the pressroom numbered about fifteen.[52] Now 1,700 reporters hold press passes, with perhaps 100 who regularly track the president's words and activities for their news organizations.[53] These members are given one or two daily briefings from the administration's press secretary, and sometimes other federal officials. And they have an endless supply of press releases, photos, video, and audio copies of statements, as well as access to a staff that is available to comment on the thoughts of the administration.

The White House press performs a vital function. Although the nature of the beat makes them more reactive than proactive, they provide the essential frames for assessing an administration's activities. If the cliché is familiar, it is because it is true: the press functions as the nation's eyes and ears. At its best, it can hold in check an administration that has lost its ability to act with rationality or proportionality, as when FDR attempted to "pack" the Supreme Court in 1937[54] or when the Nixon administration ensnared itself in the web of Watergate deceptions. But the greater tendency is toward grudging but uncritical compliance.

If being close to a major source of news ought to be journalistic nirvana, the position of White House correspondent has increasingly been seen by insiders as its own kind of prison. Press secretaries have largely mastered the tactics of staying "on message" or declining comments on uncomfortable topics. Access to Oval Office visitors is often restricted. Press releases pass on good news and largely ignore the bad. And most problematic of all, presidents are less inclined to talk directly to the press, preferring instead to favor media venues that will produce softer questions. As Bill Wilt has noted, correspondents are "a captive audience, tied to the ground like Gulliver and

Figure 4.1. "Photo ops" are carefully constructed to suggest that presidents are patient and determined leaders. The White House usually offers one a day to the press, often with the understanding that the event will not include questions. Here, President Bush inspects the troops at Fort Stewart, Georgia, in February of 2001.

Source: White House Photo, *Public Papers of the Presidents, Vol. 1, 2000, George W. Bush* (Washington, D.C.: U.S. Government Printing Office, 2003), n.p.

subject to the whim of White House press briefers, communications specialists, and assorted underlings. Even more constricting: they're in the thrall of the president's schedule."[55]

This "news management" model of press relations comes with its increasingly familiar lexicon of public relations gimmicks, including photo ops, closed-event appearances, and stonewalling. As veteran reporter Tom Wicker has written, "Everything possible is done to centralize information favorable to the administration in the press office, and restrict the flow of any other information."[56]

The extent of what "everything" could mean came to light in early 2005, when it was discovered that a number of federal agencies were actually paying syndicated columnists to sell the administration's policies on issues ranging from marriage ideas to education programs.[57] At the same time, other agencies were passing on video news releases using fake "journalists" to excitedly relay their good news. Boldest of all was the accreditation of a White House "reporter" who had concealed his real name and had a habit of asking "softball" questions to the press secretary. Americans were asked to believe that the security-conscious White House had failed to notice that "Jeff Gannon" was actually a paid functionary of the GOP. Among his questions to Ari Fleischer was one about congressional Democrats that the administration must have loved: "How are you going to work with people who seem to have divorced themselves from reality?"[58]

Many serious journalists also feel like their obligations for fairness are easily co-opted by the White House. In the absence of other points of view that might serve the truth, they are captives to a single perspective.[59] And if a reporter shows ingratitude by asking tough or embarrassing questions, he or she may be isolated by other reporters who fear a further loss of access.[60]

Exceptions to the news management model emerge in crises when a president is under siege by a hostile Congress, a disenfranchised public, or—like the infamous Lewinsky affair—caught in a web of legal and moral issues. Political scientist Larry Sabato coined the phrase "feeding frenzy" to suggest what happens when a crisis draws sufficient blood to warrant intense press attention:

> It has become a spectacle without equal in modern American politics: the news media, print and broadcast, go after a wounded politician like sharks in a feeding frenzy. The wounds may have been self-inflected, and the politician may richly deserve his or her fate, but the journalists now take center stage in the process, creating the news as much as reporting it.[61]

Thomas Patterson has noted that a politician who stumbles "gives the press an opportunity to seize control" of their story.[62] Such was Nixon's fate in Watergate, Carter's with Americans held captive in Iran, and Reagan's during the Iran-Contra affair. And, of course, Clinton went to the edge of impeachment over the Lewinsky affair and his attempts to cover it up. The press covered each event as a crisis in presidential leadership, but there were vast differences in the dangers they posed to the nation. Watergate started as a low-level political crime but became a significant breach of law and the public trust. The Clinton scandal was less about malfeasance than lust. A zealous special prosecutor who was engaged in an unrelated dead end of a supposed money scandal (Whitewater) discovered the more lucrative target. It was not only the president who got excited about a moment of furtive sex in the Oval Office. In Clinton's weak denials to the press, prosecutor Kenneth Starr and Clinton's conservative critics suddenly found the perfect political platform.

Though the Lewinsky affair was not among them, some White House actions deserve but do not get intense and prolonged press coverage. The problem with the self-multiplying effect of "frenzy" reporting is that it feeds on an unhealthy appetite to satisfy commercial and public interests in tantalizing backstories. Scandals involving politicians or celebrities tend to sweep aside more sober assessments of what may be worthy of coverage, distorting the national news agenda in the process. The past is littered with scandal reporting that undeservedly ate up huge portions of public attention and kept other worthy news concealed. Through such periods, the public forum has been rendered mute on many of the nation's pressing problems. The nation was once awash in coverage of the love lives of Senator Gary Hart and Representative Gary Condit, and the court appearances of O. J. Simpson and style maven Martha Stewart. In the latter case, the July 2004 sentencing of Stewart to a short jail term got *more* network news coverage in one week than either the presidential political campaigns or the increasingly bloody war in Iraq.[63] To be sure, part of the difficulty lies with the public itself, which collectively succumbs to the timeless pleasures of watching the strong fumble. And part lies with a press that is only too willing to act as a procurer for audiences thirsty for the chance to peer into these sideshows.

Neither the news management or feeding frenzy models exist in pure form. Each serves as a check on the other. Even so, neither side sees the current arrangement predicated on either acquiescence or rebellion as a very healthy mix. After the excruciating loss of the White House to Reagan, in part because of the media obsession with the holding of American hostages in Iran,[64] Carter administration press secretary Jody Powell articulated what those in other administrations have also expressed:

> By the end of four years in the White House, I had reached the conclusion that this relationship between the press and the presidency is seriously flawed. It fails to provide the President with an adequate channel for communicating with, for moving, shaping, and directing the popular will. Perhaps more important, it also fails to provide the nation with the quantity and quality of reasonably accurate information its citizens need to make the decisions necessary for self-government.[65]

The stalemate that persists today is supported by the unchanging tensions created by the ritual cynicism of most of the press and the White House's attempts to counter it by organizing events that avoid the risks of unscripted encounters.

The choice favored by the second Bush administration was a refinement of press management techniques used by the Reagan and Clinton staffs: going around reporters to handpick journalists for one-on-one interviews or using forums guaranteed to contain only supportive audiences. Indeed, no president in modern times seemed more isolated than George W. Bush. By January

2004—after nearly four years in office—he had held only eleven formal press conferences, far fewer than Reagan's twenty-one for the same period and his father's seventy-one.[66] Ostensibly informal "meetings" with various publics—ranging from government leaders to ordinary soldiers serving in Iraq—conformed to secretly rehearsed scripts prewritten to give the illusion of spontaneity.[67] Even on the campaign trail in the same year, "rallies" were largely closed. Ordinary citizens who had been carefully issued tickets for an audience with the president were still asked to leave if they could be construed as not already a true believer.[68] Bush paradoxically declaimed his status as a tribune "of the people." But the nation could count itself lucky if he agreed to meet his opponent in a few hours of "debates" every four years. As Hart notes, "The older notion of dialectic—facing down one's accusers, joining the political fray on the enemy's territory—is now largely passé."[69]

There are no easy fixes for this problem. The Constitution is largely silent in asking for rhetorical accountability from a president.[70] And the federal system has evolved to the degree that a leader can be rhetorically isolated from Congress and other informed questioners. To be sure, there *is* an obvious presumption in favor of a *visible presidency*, with its communications apparatus supporting a host of message-of-the-day tableaux. But there is nothing that requires *dialogic* public discussion with anyone. The problem is not so much that presidents create their own events. They always have. Rather, it is that their appearance transforms other events into exercises in ritual obeisance. They participate on their own terms, usually declining to step away from the protective bubble of the office.

In this way, the presidency is distinctly inferior to its parliamentary equivalents. A weekly half hour or longer of Question Time for Britain's and Canada's prime ministers is typical, when their parliaments are in session. Although governed by their own rituals and posturing, these weekly public forums nonetheless offer a continuous opportunity for opposition representatives to hold to account the government in power. During a typical year, the British prime minister will have spent about twenty-four hours defending his or her government policies in the House of Commons.[71] And like all leaders in democratic states, he or she is also expected to routinely field questions from the press. By contrast, while U.S. presidents eagerly confirm common values to quiescent audiences, most will grudgingly spend as little as five hours a year in ad hoc interactive sessions with the White House press.[72]

The result is that American chief executives rarely have to listen to cogent and informed questions about their own initiatives.[73] Their denial of open access may sometimes result in being characters in someone else's story.[74] But they will compensate by successfully selling themselves as shapers of great events, especially given the American willingness to deploy the world's largest military against some of the planet's poorest nations (Libya, Somalia, Panama, Grenada, Afghanistan, Iraq, etc.).

The dialogic nature of policy debate, however, rarely provides the same opportunities to "perform" incisive leadership. With presidents such as Ronald Reagan and George W. Bush, the formerly cherished bully pulpit was literally just that: a safe forum used largely to target loyal followers with familiar pieties of faith from the American canon. Some of these values are durable and self-evident—for example, that the United States should help foster freedom around the world or help end starvation in failed states. But other values were reduced to code words such as "culture of life" or "family values" that rekindled long-festering "wedge" issues. True arguments asserting the merits of policy were often shunted to the margins of these administrations in part because they required a kind of statecraft that needed patience and inclusivity.[75] That patience was evident in the administrations of Ford and Carter. By contrast, a preference to "preach to the choir" leaves many more untouched or alienated—a problem that contributes to the divisive nature of modern presidencies.

CONCLUSION

So many of the lessons of the American chief executive touched on in this chapter were visited upon the capable but undisciplined Bill Clinton. It is hard to identify another modern American leader with a greater sense of curiosity about policy and its actual effects "on the ground." He was (and remains) a gifted communicator with the natural instincts to find inclusive appeals. As his two successful presidential campaigns demonstrated, he was a master at the outside game of "retail" politics but not the inside game of congressional politics. His administration was often disorganized and undisciplined, relegating innovative ideas to ivory tower policy forums and yearly Renaissance Weekend retreats. Even modest reforms gained ground slowly against the hardened defenses of an increasingly hostile Congress. Clinton sought the spotlight as the embodiment of progressive moral leadership, but he found himself mired in too many questions about his personal ethics. He distrusted the press, seeking—as most presidents do—to speak "directly" through the White House publicity machine to the American public. But he was drawn to almost any kind of forum. Clinton believed that no audience was beyond his ability to win over. Even before the gathering storm of impeachment, he captured the essential dilemma of modern presidents. "The job is much tougher than I realized," he observed. "I did not realize the importance of communications and the overriding importance of what is on the evening news. If I am not on, or there with a message, someone else is, with their message."[76]

NOTES

1. Hugh D. Duncan, *Communication and Social Order* (New York: Oxford University Press, 1962), 273.

2. Roderick Hart, *The Sound of Leadership: Presidential Communication in the Modern Age* (Chicago: University of Chicago Press, 1987), 192.

3. David Gergen, *Eyewitness to Power* (New York: Simon & Schuster, 2000), 12–13.

4. Quoted in Michael Schudson, *The Good Citizen* (Cambridge, Mass.: Harvard University Press, 1998), 211.

5. Walter Lippmann, *The Public Philosophy* (Boston: Little, Brown, 1955), 15.

6. Some reviewers of Bill Clinton's memoir, *My Life* (New York: Knopf, 2004), seemed disappointed that he was still the unrepentant "policy wonk," that so little space was spent on the Lewinsky affair, and that so much of the 900-plus-page book was a discussion of the ideas and initiatives that motivated his years in Little Rock and Washington.

7. Murray Edelman, *Constructing the Political Spectacle* (Chicago: University of Chicago Press, 1988), 90.

8. See, for example, David Remnick, *Lenin's Tomb: The Last Days of the Soviet Empire* (New York: Vintage Books, 1994). Remnick attaches a great deal of importance to the reforms of Mikhail Gorbachev, who hastened the exposure of economic and social flaws within the ailing Soviet state.

9. See, for example, James, Fellows, *Breaking the News* (New York: Pantheon, 1996), 116–24.

10. Sig Mickelson, *From Whistle Stop to Sound Bite: Four Decades of Politics and Television* (Westport, Conn.: Praeger, 1989), 151.

11. For a case study where this is a factor, see Kathleen Hall Jamieson and Joseph N. Cappella, "The Role of the Press in the Health Care Reform Debate of 1993–1994," in *The Politics of News, the News of Politics*, ed. Doris Graber, Denis McQuail, and Pippa Norris (Washington, D.C.: CQ Press, 1998), 110–31.

12. *Washington Week in Review*, November 12, 2004, http://www.pbs.org/weta/washingtonweek/transcripts/transcript041112.html (accessed May 23, 2006).

13. Kenneth Burke, *Dramatism and Development* (Barre, Mass.: Clark University Press, 1972), 12.

14. See, for example, Alan Dawley, *Changing the World: American Progressives in War and Revolution* (Princeton, N.J.: Princeton University Press, 2003), 341–58.

15. Dawley, *Changing the World*, 342–46.

16. Robert Harper, *Lincoln and the Press* (New York: McGraw-Hill, 1951), 303–10.

17. With regard to the Johnson years, see Kathleen Turner, *Lyndon Johnson's Dual War* (Chicago: University of Chicago Press, 1986), 134–211. The stormy struggles between Nixon and the press are described in Joe Spear's *Presidents and the Press* (Cambridge, Mass.: MIT Press, 1984), 45–235.

18. See Clinton, *My Life*, 481–86.

19. "President Bush Opens Second Term with Job Performance Rating at 48%; 47% Say the US Headed in the Right Direction, New Zogby Poll Reveals," Zogby International, November 15, 2004, http://www.zogby.com/news/ReadNews.dbm?ID=933 (accessed May 23, 2006).

20. See, for example, Joshua Meyrowitz, *No Sense of Place* (New York: Oxford University Press, 1985), 268–304.

21. Ronald Reagan was partly the exception. Far closer to the norm are the "warts and all" accounts of former presidential staffers, such as Johnson aide George Reedy's *Twilight of the Presidency* (New York: Signet, 1971) or Clinton aide George Stephanopoulos's *All Too Human: A Political Education* (Boston: Little, Brown, 1999).

22. See, for example, Carlo D'Este, *Eisenhower: A Soldier's Life* (New York: Holt, 2002); Micheal O'Brian, *John F. Kennedy: A Biography* (New York: St. Martin's, 2005); and Doris Kearns Goodwin, *No Ordinary Time: Franklin and Eleanor Roosevelt: The Home Front in World War II* (New York: Touchstone, 1995).

23. See, for example, Larry Sabato, Mark Stencel, and Robert Lichter, *Peepshow: Media and Politics in an Age of Scandal* (Lanham, Md.: Rowman & Littlefield, 2000).

24. John Zaller, "Monica Lewinsky and the Mainsprings of American Politics," in *Mediated Politics: Communication in the Future of Democracy* ed. W. Lance Bennett and Robert M. Entman (New York: Cambridge University Press, 2001), 253.

25. Robert Bellah, Richard Madsen, William M. Sullivan, Ann Swidler, and Steven M. Tipton, *The Good Society* (New York: Knopf, 1991), 133.

26. By one count, "freedom" and "war" were the most common references in a typical day of speeches at the 2004 Republican National Convention. See "The Statements," *New York Times*, September 2, 2004, 4.

27. Mary Stuckey, *The President as Interpreter in Chief* (Chatham, N.J.: Chatham House, 1991), 1.

28. "President Reagan's Speech on the Challenger Disaster," January 28, 1986, *The Reagan Information Page* http://presidentreagan.info/speeches/challenger.cfm (accessed May 23, 2006).

29. In Richard Nixon's 1971 State of the Union message, for example, a range of policy principles were laid for legislative initiatives, among them "to restore and enhance our natural environment," "improving America's health care and making it available to more people," and "full prosperity in peacetime." "Richard Nixon, "A New American Revolution," January 22, 1971, in *Presidential Rhetoric (1961–1980)*, 2nd ed., ed. Theodore Windt (Dubuque, Iowa: Hunt, 1980), 150–53.

30. Leonard Garment, *Crazy Rhythm* (New York: Times Books, 1997), 205–12.

31. James Surowiecki, "The Risk Society," *New Yorker*, November 15, 2004, http://www.newyorker.com/printable/?talk/041115ta_talk_surowiecki (accessed November, 23, 2004).

32. See, for example, Joshua Gunn, "Refiguring Fantasy: Imagination and Its Decline in U.S. Rhetorical Studies," *Quarterly Journal of Speech*, February 2003, 41–47.

33. Peter Grier and Faye Bowers, "Failure of 'Imagination' Led to 9/11," *Christian Science Monitor*, July 23, 2004, http://www.csmonitor.com/2004/0723/p01s03-uspo.htm (accessed May 23, 2006).

34. Rich quoted in Paul Simon, *Our Culture of Pandering* (Carbondale: Southern Illinois University Press, 2003), 176.

35. Wilson quoted in James Andrews, "President Woodrow Wilson's First Inaugural Address, 1913," in *The Inaugural Addresses of Twentieth-Century Presidents*, ed. Halford Ryan (Westport, Conn.: Praeger, 1993), 20.

36. Kenneth Burke, *Permanence and Change* (New York: Bobbs-Merrill, 1965), 90–91.

37. For an example of policy shaped *through* the process of writing speech drafts, see Robert E. Denton Jr. and Gary C. Woodward, *Political Communication in America*, 2nd ed. (Westport, Conn.: Praeger, 1990), 245–49.

38. David Remnick, "Letter from Prague," February, 17, 2003, *New Yorker*, http://www.newyorker.com/printable/?fact/030217fa_fact1 (accessed September 28, 2004).

39. Remnick, "Letter from Prague"

40. Hart, *The Sound of Leadership*, 198.

41. Hart, *The Sound of Leadership*, 199.

42. George W. Bush quoted in Geoffrey Nunberg, *Going Nuclear: Language Politics, and Culture in Confrontational Times* (New York: Public Affairs Press, 2004), 60.

43. Ken Auletta, "Fortress Bush," *New Yorker*, January 19, 2004, 53–55.

44. "Remarks by the President and Prime Minister Blair in Joint Press Conference," February 23, 2001, http://www.whitehouse.gov/news/releases/2001/02/20010226-1.html (accessed May 23, 2006).

45. Sabrina Tavernise, "U.S. Quietly Issues Estimate of Iraqi Civilian Casualties, *New York Times*, October, 30, 2005, A10. Prior to October 2005, the networks generally followed the lead of the Pentagon and largely ignored tallies of Iraqi casualties. One exception: a small October 29, 2004, segment mentioning a British study (citing one hundred thousand deaths) on CNN. Vanderbilt University Television News Archive, *CNN Evening News*, October 29, 2004, http://tvnews.vanderbilt.edu/TV-NewsSearch/fulldisplay.pl?SID=20041207612243652&UID=&CID=18781&auth=&code=TVN&RC=769677&Row=2 (accessed December 7, 2004).

46. Kevin Phillips, *Wealth and Democracy* (New York: Broadway Books, 2002), 4.

47. For examples from congressional politics, see Simon, *Our Culture of Pandering*, 52–58.

48. Dwight D. Eisenhower, *Waging Peace: 1956–1961* (Garden City, N.Y.: Doubleday, 1965), 614–15.

49. Jimmy Carter, "Televised Address to the Nation, July 15, 1979," in Windt, *Presidential Rhetoric (1961–1980)*, 265.

50. "Excerpts from Clinton's Speech to Black Ministers," *New York Times*, November 14, 1993, A24.

51. Clinton quoted in Richard Parker, *John Kenneth Galbraith: His Life, His Politics, His Economics* (New York: Farrar, Straus & Giroux, 2005), 630.

52. Robert Pierpoint, *At the White House* (New York: Putnam, 1981), 32.

53. Martha Joynt Kumar, "The Office of Press Secretary," in *The White House World: Transitions, Organization and Office Operations* (College Station: Texas A&M University Press, 2003), 241.

54. See Samuel Rosenman and Dorothy Rosenman, *Presidential Style* (New York: Harper & Row, 1976), 352–54.

55. Bill Wilt, "How Technology Could Free the White House Press Corps," *Columbia Journalism Review* (May/June 2004), http://www.cjr.org/issues/2004/3/voices-wilt.asp (accessed May 24, 2006).

56. Tom Wicker, *On Press* (New York: Viking, 1978), 77.

57. Mark Jurkowitz, "Communication or Manipulation? Press and President Clash over Approach," *Boston Globe*, March 7, 2005.

58. Jurkowitz, "Communication or Manipulation?"

59. There is a vast library of case studies and analyses of press acceptance of presidential and governmental perspectives. Representative studies include Allan Rachlin, *News as Hegemonic Reality* (New York: Praeger, 1988); Kathleen Hall Jamieson and Paul Waldman, *The Press Effect* (New York: Oxford University Press, 2003), 1–23; and Mark Hertsgaard, *On Bended Knee: The Press and the Reagan Presidency* (New York: Schocken Books, 1989).

60. See, for example, James Wolcott, "Round Up the Cattle," *Vanity Fair*, June 2003.

61. Larry Sabato, *Feeding Frenzy: How Attack Journalism Has Transformed American Politics* (New York: Free Press, 1991), 1.

62. Thomas E. Patterson, *Out of Order* (New York: Knopf, 1993), 155.

63. *Tyndall Weekly*, July 12–16, 2004.

64. ABC started a nightly show about the hostage story called *America Held Hostage*. It eventually became *Nightline.*

65. Jody Powell, *The Other Side of the Story* (New York: Morrow, 1984), 35.

66. Auletta, "Fortress Bush," 60.

67. David Green, "Take One: President Bush via Satellite," *All Things Considered*, National Public Radio, October 13, 2005.

68. Darrell Rowland, Alan Johson, and Mark Niquette, "Presidential Campaign: Screening Can Ensure Adoring Audiences," *Columbus Dispatch*, August 16, 2004.

69. Hart, *The Sound of Leadership*, 132–34.

70. The clear exception is a small one: the constitutional requirement for the president *"from time to time give to Congress information of the State of the Union and recommend to their Consideration such measures as he shall judge necessary and expedient"* (Article II, sec. 3).

71. House of Commons Information Office, "Parliamentary Questions," June 2003, 6, http://www.parliament.uk/documents/upload/p01.pdf (accessed May 24, 2006).

72. Auletta, "Fortress Bush."

73. Former Johnson administration press secretary George Reedy made this compelling conclusion in 1970, based in part on his experiences. See Reedy, *Twilight of the Presidency*, 3–17, 48–60.

74. Gary Woodward, *The Idea of Identification* (Albany: State University of New York Press, 2003), 142.

75. For example, encouraging "freedom around the world" is an easy value to assert. The challenge is a sensible policy to support it.

76. Clinton quoted in Bob Woodward, *The Agenda: Inside the Clinton White House* (New York: Simon & Schuster, 1994), 313.

Chapter Five

Congress and the Courtroom

On the second day of Judge John Roberts's confirmation hearings, CNN's Jeff Greenfield felt moved to ask a question. The guest was Sen. Charles Grassley of Iowa, and Greenfield inquired why his fellows on the Judiciary Committee felt the need to use their limited time for bloviation instead of actually asking the judge questions. Senator Grassley replied with one word: "television."[1]

—Anna Quindlen

The true American theatre is the courtroom.[2]

—Lloyd Chiasson Jr.

Congressional observers could not remember anything quite like it. It was unusual even given the volatile tectonics of political conflict. In March 2005, congressional leaders took the extraordinary action of calling House members back into session from their spring recess to pass a law permitting the parents of a brain-dead Florida woman, Terri Schiavo, to reinsert a feeding tube that doctors—with court approval—had removed. Schiavo had been in a "persistent vegetative state" for more than a decade, and her husband had decided to carry out what he explained were her wishes to not continue extraordinary efforts to maintain basic body functions. An autopsy would later confirm the obvious: because most of her brain had withered away, she had virtually no cognitive processes. But even though the federal courts repeatedly sided with the husband's decision, congressional leaders passed a bill that allowed her parents to appeal again to the courts to have the feeding tube reconnected. Shortly before the midnight vote, House leaders marched together through the Capitol, letting cameras capture their legislative rescue mission. And the

White House made a point of noting that the president was immediately awakened to sign the bill.

What struck so many as odd about these events, aside from the decision to call back the entire Congress to pass a single item, was the miscalculation that it represented. The passing of the Schiavo law was unusual not just because it applied to only one family but also because it was defiantly *public*: apparently—according to a leaked Republican memo—because it is "an important moral issue and the pro-life base will be excited."[3] Millions of Americans every year are allowed to quietly pass away when it is clear that they will not regain even minimal brain function. But a decision was made in this instance to make Schiavo's life a public spectacle. The result was that many reporters recounted these events as if they were reviewing a repertory group who had taken on more than they could master:

> Occasionally politics turns into national theater, and when it does, the politicians love playing a lead role. So when the case of Terri Schiavo came along—a brain-damaged woman, grieving parents, a husband painted as a villain and a Greek chorus of protesters—many in Congress leaped into the stage lights. Lawmakers interrupted their Easter recess for a mad dash back to Washington and a midnight vote on a measure to allow the federal courts to intervene in Ms. Schiavo's case. President Bush flew back from his Texas ranch to sign the legislation in the wee morning hours. The public was riveted. But by week's end, when the poll results rolled in, it turned out that the high drama in Washington was not playing well in Peoria.[4]

The president and Republican leaders in the House and Senate took a great deal of heat for intervening in one of the most painful and private moments a family can have and making a show of defiance of federal court rulings. Most Americans thought they had gone too far.[5] In this case, at least, the machinery for managing the impressions of a weary nation was artless and obvious.

The focus of this chapter is on the publicity apparatus of two key political institutions: the national legislature and those who are subject to the decisions of the courts. Although they are very different, any consideration of how both affect political and social attitudes must now include the performance possibilities of their advocates. In some senses, Congress has always been a grand repertory theater. Americans know that there are as many natural performers on Capitol Hill as ever walked the studio lots of Hollywood. By contrast, the use of public relations strategies in high-profile court proceedings is newer and still outside the norm. But intense media coverage of white-collar crime and "megatrials" now entice prosecutors and defense attorneys to appeal not only to juries and judges—but frequently to the American public as well. Both arenas have press and public galleries that cannot be ignored.

WASHINGTON'S *OTHER* CENTER FOR THE PERFORMING ARTS

A first-time visitor to Capitol Hill is perhaps most impressed with the old symbols of the national legislature and the continuity of its rituals. The rules of Congress seem positively old-fashioned. Comments about the rhetoric of other members of the House or Senate are still worded in gentle euphemisms, such as "the honorable member from Kentucky" or "the senior senator from Nebraska." And senators continue many of the old customs, such as carving their names into the drawers of their desks next to those of earlier occupants such as Daniel Webster and Henry Cabot Lodge. But if the formal parliamentary rules for debate have changed little in the two hundred years since the government moved from Philadelphia to Washington, the instinct for legislating *through* publicity has never been stronger. Television and the press are everywhere: in the galleries above the floors of the House and Senate, in its committee rooms and basement television studios, and perched precariously on the grassy "swamp" near the southeast corner of the Capitol grounds.

Publicity-seeking members are now identified for their dogged "media entrepreneurship."[6] And virtually all new senators and representatives discover that public relations skills are essential to statecraft.[7] The constant urgency to reach the press, the need to work with professional lobbyists with valuable connections and constituencies, and the impulse to explain oneself to constituents back home are now all part of the mix. From the lawmakers' standpoint, all are critical to gaining the kind of power and longevity that will allow them to stand apart from the other 539 members of the House and Senate.

The primary task of Congress is obviously lawmaking. Bills are introduced in the Senate or the House. After bills are assigned to committees, those with some support within the majority party are usually scheduled for committee hearings. When a bill is "marked up" or changed, it may be voted out of committee and eventually considered by the entire body. Hurdles for legislation typically pop up several times, starting with procedural votes that measure a bill's support. A final vote is taken later, after a series of amendments have been offered and usually rejected, and after supporters and opponents have organized their forces. Before a president can sign or veto it, different versions of a bill must be reconciled in a conference that involves representatives from both Houses.

This is the simplest systemic outline of congressional action, but it misses the drama of related congressional roles that include investigation, oversight, and confirmation. Under an expansive view of the enumerated powers granted by the Constitution, both bodies are free to observe and gather information on virtually any topic or issue that is potentially the subject of lawmaking or federal action. In addition, the Senate carries the additional power of confirming the president's top appointees, including federal judges, ambassadors, and agency heads. Exercising just this function in 2005, the Senate was the subject of extensive television and news coverage focused on the confirmation of two Supreme Court nominees, a controversial United Nations ambassador, and a handful of cabinet appointments.[8]

All of these processes—approving high-ranking federal appointees, conducting hearings, and legislating—are largely unchanged functions. And they are primarily activities of communication and consensus building that require motivating like-minded activists outside Washington, defending views that have come under attack, holding together coalitions of supporters, and maintaining positive relationships with opponents who may be future allies. Congress is preeminently a place for public bargaining, posturing, and explaining. If the rude old joke is right that "politics is Hollywood for the ugly," Congress is surely the route to enduring political stardom.

Stable Processes and New Pressures

Though the fundamental processes of legislating are largely unchanged, significant transformations have occurred in the ways members communicate influence and power. The Congress that our grandparents understood from news reports was a very hierarchical institution. With notable exceptions, members knew their place and more readily accepted party and presidential loyalty as fundamental axioms. The political professionals around them—the long-serving party leaders in both chambers and the Speaker of the House—were given powers that were nearly absolute. The roll call of the famous senators that John F. Kennedy described in *Profiles in Courage*—John Quincy Adams, Daniel Webster, Robert Taft, and others—suggests a continuity of unquestioned moral authority that is difficult to match in the modern Senate.[9]

Several decades ago, a freshman Democrat serving his first term in the House would have risked more of his political future ignoring the wishes of Speaker Sam Rayburn than a modern counterpart who rebels against the wishes of contemporary legislative leaders. MSNBC's Chris Matthews, who served as an aide to former House Speaker Tip O'Neil, recalls that Rayburn had a "quiet capacity to deal with congressman after congressman, again and again," turning "the mob scene of the House floor into a disciplined army carrying laws and policies that had seemed unachievable."[10]

Leaders today seem less able to build coalitions and command broad respect than Rayburn. But what have changed most are the pressures that shape congressional behavior. The parties in Congress have lost some of their clout. The general fragmentation that has occurred in much of American life relating to ethnic, gender, and social issues—the trinity of political passions—have created alliances and commitments that often supersede party identification. Newer members are reluctant to serve a long apprenticeship behind senior members. Patience is no longer considered a virtue. Moreover, after the rise and fall of House leaders Jim Wright, Newt Gingrich, Tom Delay, and others, members have little patience for the kind of power politics that gave legislative kingmakers their legendary control.

The largest change, however, is that political power is projected differently in Congress than has been the case in its long history. Party leaders and key committee chairpersons still exercise enormous control over the congressional agenda. But they are no longer the public face of Congress. Competing with them are larger numbers of autonomous members with their own agendas and constituencies.[11]

It is still suicide to bolt *both* parties.[12] But it is easier now to survive in legislative life as an independent agent, using a wide collection of public relations skills (see textbox 5.1) to offset the now-diminished dangers of rebelling against the president or congressional leader. Membership on several of the 250 committees and subcommittees is the most important way to stand out.

Textbox 5.1. The Basics: Planning a Statement for the Press or a Press Conference

Essential considerations in planning a single event for reporters include the following:

- Have an initiative or new information to announce. Most journalists need more than your opinions as a reason to show up. If you want television coverage, try to have something to *show* as well as say. (If the news value of the event is limited, stop here and consider a separate route: Give the news to a respected journalist as a short-term exclusive.)
- Fax advisories of the event to the news media. Ask for coverage from editors and producers. Don't overlook relevant trade and social action publications.
- Be ready in case the press does do not show up. (Beyond a narrow range of events and high-profile figures, television is especially a tough sell.) Cover the event yourself and issue press releases and video news releases to the press.
- Put releases and videos on the web, and distribute them to your web list of news outlets and stakeholders.
- Pick a light news day, such as Monday.
- Choose a location appropriate to the topic and convenient for the press.
- Consider the news cycle in scheduling your event. Mornings are preferable to allow time for print journalists and evening news shows to file.
- Outside Congress, build alliances with others, including recognized experts, celebrity advocates, and like-minded organizations. Share resources and—where appropriate—the spotlight

The Theater of Fact Finding

Congress remains the preeminent national forum for consideration of the nation's hopes, fears, and fantasies. To note that most of the talk that takes place within its walls does *not* result in legislation is to miss its central role as a national lyceum. The Schiavo case provided such a platform. But consider the less lethal topic of baseball.

Congress has a long history of interest in the business of sports. Because the Supreme Court exempted baseball from antitrust laws in 1922, legislators have always played a role in oversight of the game, ranging from the expansion of franchises in the 1950s to charges of rampant drug use in the new century. Several bills were introduced in the House and Senate to settle the long baseball strike that abruptly ended the 1994 season.[13] Supporters of the legislation argued that the sport had a special place in American life. Senate and House bills known as the Baseball Strike Settlement Act followed on the heels of a well-publicized but failed effort by President Clinton to negotiate a compromise over the issue of salary caps. Both the Speaker of the House and the majority leader in the Senate indicated a reluctance to get involved in the dispute. Even so, the Senate Judiciary's Subcommittee on Anti-trust, Business Rights, and Competition held well-publicized hearings in which owners and players testified.

In 2005, another round of widely anticipated hearings were held to focus attention on the use of steroids by key players. Stars such as Jose Canseco, Sammy Sosa, and Mark McGwire testified, even though the specific legislative purpose of the hearings was never very clear. Representative Tom Davis offered the view that it was "about people seeing baseball players as role models for their kids."[14] Others saw the drama of sports stars responding to congressional questions as a warning to the team owners to police themselves. And more than a few viewed the proceedings in terms of a familiar dramatistic lexicon: "political grandstanding," a "media circus," and a "theater of congressional Klieg lights."[15]

Like most bills in Congress, all of the proposed legislation relating to ending strikes or enacting new drug laws died a quiet death without votes in either house. That is normal. But it is also true that the bills served as vehicles for congressional discussion of an issue—in this case, one with widespread public interest and significant financial stakes for the businesses involved.

Hearings such as these are a fixed reference point for navigating the nation's political life. Traditional functions of hearings, according to Roger Davidson and Walter Oleszek, include the desire to "explore the need for legislation," "build a public record in support of legislation," "publicize the role of committee chairmen," and "provide a forum for citizen's grievances and frustrations."[16] Among other *rhetorical* uses, hearings serve the function of allowing members to display concern or support in behalf of their constituents and to perform the role of advocacy about problems that have no hope for legislative redress. An illustration of the first was in widely reported Senate hearings where a number of members grilled oil company executives on their rising profits during a period of huge increases in gas and fuel prices.[17] Part of the point of the hearings was to publicly question their motives. Hearings in September 2005 to dramatize the negative effects of the American occupation of Iraq illustrate the second function. Because the majority leadership opposed the purpose of the hearings, antiwar Democrats found that the only space available was in a cramped room in the basement of the Capitol—a fact that added even more drama to their cause.[18]

Hearings represent the primary work of legislating. National and trade press journalists are used to covering them. C-SPAN devotes hours to live and tape-delayed coverage of committee meetings.[19] And news consumers are primed to pay attention to the melodrama that results when institutions and personalities clash. Such fact finding can even have unexpected effects, as members discovered in 1987 when the president of the old Soviet Union began to tailor comments in Moscow to testimony heard in Washington before the Joint Economic Committee. Apparently statements of Reagan administration officials before the committee estimating Mikhail Gorbachev's chances of pulling off planned economic reforms had caught the Soviet leader's attention. To the surprise of committee members, references to the generally pessimistic assessments of the administration suddenly started showing up in Gorbachev's speeches.[20] Somehow the leader of what was still the Soviet Union had decided that these hearings deserved serious counterarguments that would affirm his domestic reforms and peaceful intentions. It would not be the first time that others around the world eavesdropped on a national conversation carried out in front of a congressional panel.

The functions of fact finding and oversight of agencies can be broadly defined. Members may study proposed legislation or hold hearings in advance of concrete proposals. Committees may also investigate the work of federal agencies such as the Federal Emergency Management Agency (FEMA), the CIA, or the Office of Homeland Security—all the objects of recent attention because of the national jitters fashioned from man-made and natural disasters. During virtually every week that Congress is in session, a range of hearings is held to record expert or stakeholder testimony or to request information from federal officials about their agencies' performance (see textbox 5.2).

No subject is too large or small, too specialized or too general. Over the last few decades, Americans have read about or viewed excerpts of hearings covering the broadest possible diversity of American life, including the effects of "obscene" music lyrics, gas efficiency of automobiles, terrorist

Textbox 5.2. One Day of Committee Hearings in the Senate: Thursday, October 6, 2005

9:30 A.M. Armed Services
To hold hearings to examine the nominations of Michael W. Wynne, of Florida, to be Secretary of the Air Force, and Donald C. Winter, of Virginia, to be Secretary of the Navy.

9:30 A.M. Environment and Public Works
To hold hearings to examine actions of the Environmental Protection Agency, the Army Corps of Engineers, and the Federal Highway Administration relating to Hurricane Katrina.

10 A.M. Banking, Housing, and Urban Affairs
To hold hearings to examine U.S. investment policy.

10 A.M. Energy and Natural Resources
To hold hearings to examine Hurricanes Katrina and Rita's effects on energy infrastructure in the Gulf Coast region.

10 A.M. Finance
To hold hearings to examine the future of the Gulf Coast by using tax policy to help rebuild businesses and communities and support families.

10 A.M. Homeland Security and Governmental Affairs
To hold hearings to examine Federal Emergency Management Agency's (FEMA) status report on recovery efforts in the Gulf states.

2:30 P.M. Homeland Security and Governmental Affairs
To hold hearings to examine how the federal government leases needed space.

2:30 P.M. Judiciary
To hold hearings to examine pending judicial nominations.

2:30 P.M. Homeland Security and Governmental Affairs
Oversight of Government Management, the Federal Workforce, and the District of Columbia Subcommittee. To hold hearings to examine improving Department of Defense logistics.

2:30 P.M. Finance
International Trade Subcommittee. To hold hearings to examine the U.S.-Bahrain Free Trade Agreement.

2:30 P.M. Select Committee on Intelligence
To receive a closed briefing regarding certain intelligence matters.

3:00 P.M. Energy and Natural Resources, Water and Power Subcommittee
To hold hearings to examine S.1025, to amend the act for various water and environmental projects.

Source: Edited summary from http://www.capitolhearings.org, October 4, 2005.

threats, veterans' health benefits, "payola" in the music industry, college loan programs, concentrated ownership of the media, the use of snowmobiles in national parks, care of the elderly in national emergencies, drug company profits, the problems and potentials of stem cell research, military base closings, conversion to digital television, and many other issues.

If the manifest function of the legislature is to pass laws, its nearly equal latent function in the age of the mass media is to use committee hearings to publicize the concerns of its most powerful members. Rules continue to give chairs wide latitude in deciding when to organize informational sessions. But the results have sometimes served neither truth nor the rights of participants, as Americans repeatedly witnessed in the landmark Army-McCarthy hearings in 1954. That widely covered witch hunt for phantom communists in government and the military turned a senator's name into a noun of reprobation.[21] "McCarthyism" remains as a label for the special kind of demagoguery that weds the worst impulses of political life with the most irrational fears of the public. Eventually, it took one dramatist, CBS journalist Edward R. Murrow, to help undo the damage of McCarthy's corrosive morality plays. And still more dramatists have emerged over the years to create their own cautionary tableaux of the Wisconsin senator's purification crusade.[22]

More useful public discussion *has* been served in scores of hearings over the long history of the modern Congress, notably in the Senate's inquiry into Vietnam policy in 1966,[23] the landmark Watergate inquiry of 1973, and the Iran-Contra investigations of 1987.[24] Some members from humble backgrounds have risen to the need to be effective chairpersons in critical periods. Few thought that Democratic "machine politician" Peter Rodino, who led the House impeachment hearings of President Nixon, would turn out to be so fair and wise. More recently, Republican Senate Judiciary Committee chair Arlen Specter has been widely judged a thoughtful, thorough leader of the high-stakes process of confirming judicial nominees.[25]

Americans also benefited from the independent, bipartisan 9/11 Commission established by Congress in 2002. Because they exist partly outside the constraints of the usual political pressures, commissions represent an especially useful way to explore policy questions on behalf of Congress or the president.[26] Members are typically former representatives, governors, or business leaders. Their nonelected status and experience often allow them to bring a broader range of options to the discovery process.[27] Working on behalf of Congress, the intensely covered 9/11 Commission heard from members of the Clinton and Bush administrations, New York City emergency personnel, and victims' families. Hearings effectively organized by the chairperson, college president and retired Republican governor Thomas Kean, often surfaced in nightly news broadcasts.

The final report released in July 2004 offered a comprehensive critique of the nation's intelligence services prior to the terrorist attacks.[28] Members lost their staff and subpoena power at that time. But especially the chair has attempted to keep the commission's recommendations in play, firmly chiding the Bush administration for dragging its feet in implementing key recommendations.[29]

Confirmation Hearings

The Senate's prerogative to confirm key presidential appointments is one of its most cherished and observed functions. Under most circumstances, members yield to the executive on his "right" to pick members of his own cabinet. Lower-level appointees such as ambassadors and cabinet appointees often sail through the confirmation process with little attention. But high-level federal appointees can pose a challenge for presidents and members.[30] In some cases, the appointee is simply a vehicle for a larger divisive issue, as when the Clinton administration nominated Henry Foster to be surgeon general. The confirmation began an intense struggle for public opinion waged between the White House and key Republican leaders, who opposed the nomination because Foster had performed abortions in his duties as a gynecologist. Foster's nomination became the center of the ongoing battle in the United States over the legitimacy of existing protections for women seeking to end a pregnancy.

In other cases, a president may make what seems to many others like a serious miscalculation by mismatching a candidate and the position for which he or she is nominated. The nomination of the State Department's George Bolton to be ambassador to the United Nations raised this concern. Most of the country's representatives have been selected because of their inclusive inclinations and patience. But Bolton had a very different reputation as a brusque street fighter and a bully to members of his own staff. Moreover, he seemed to have a perspective seriously out of sync with the fundamental values of the UN. At one point, he expressed the surprising view that the UN "does not exist" in any meaningful way,[31] a grotesque overstatement given the world body's long record of humanitarian achievements.[32] To many in the nation and the Senate, both facts made him an unlikely choice for a sensitive diplomatic post. Support among Republicans on the Foreign Relations Committee was mostly lukewarm. And Democrats thought Bolton was ill suited for the job—less a potential ambassador than an enforcer who would use the post to bludgeon the sluggish international body to change. When extended hearings of the committee failed to produce a positive vote, George W. Bush was left with the task of making an awkward "recess appointment." It would allow Bolton to serve without the consent of the Senate until the end of its next session. Before it was over, the confirmation broke the semblance of co-operation that had prevailed in White House–Congress relations. Everyone from the committee's Senator Joe Biden to the *Daily Show*'s Jon Stewart weighed in on a process that easily penetrated the national consciousness.

Confirmation hearings for judges and key cabinet officials are often a kind of echo chamber of debate reverberating through the national psyche. There is inherent drama in a process that focuses on the competence of one figure and a parade of supporting players who testify in support or opposition. The final act is written when the committee votes. The outcome is an instant indicator of *who* among a range of competing interests has been at least implicitly embraced or ignored.

DRAMATIZATION IN MEGATRIALS AND LITIGATION

The institution of the courts offers another set of forums for dramatizing causes and issues. But there is a crucial difference. The agents of drama in the courtroom are not usually local, state, or federal judges but almost always the legal teams who intend to use publicity to further the prospects of their clients. After briefly considering crime and punishment as a narrative model, we turn to uses of publicity in both criminal and civil cases.

Changing Villains into Victims

Graphic descriptions of criminal acts often dominate the headlines and the prime-time television schedule. Trials condense in one place and one cast of characters many of the social tensions that permeate our culture. Perhaps it has always been so. Shakespeare's plays regularly gave their often impoverished audiences vivid glimpses of justice served on the powerful and mighty. Even as *King Lear* and *Macbeth* vainly attempted to remake human law in their own image, Shakespeare was quick to reassure his audiences by Act III that the higher laws of God and nature would still hold them accountable.

Popular media in the form of television news, crime novels, and courtroom dramas give us newer ways to witness the completion of this predictable cycle, but they still offer the same frail but final accounts of justice confirmed or denied. If legal truth is rarely as simple as others would make it seem, and if the requirements of justice are not easy to define,[33] we are still drawn to the idea of a perfect reckoning visited upon those who have done their part to make an imperfect world.

In a broad sense, journalism has always had an uneasy but profitable alliance with its audiences when it comes to portraying murder, rape, and other forms of brutality.[34] As perhaps a warning to ourselves, it publicizes acts that have violated definitions of civility. But our focus here is less on "routine" crimes against persons and property, and more on cases involving wealthy or celebrated defendants caught in the web of criminal or civil trials. For these kinds of cases, there is a newer trend of strategic communication that owes something to the publicity arts practiced in Congress. In the last decade, cases in this heavily scrutinized realm have involved persons such as Calvin Klein, the parents of JonBenét Ramsay, William Kennedy Smith, Michael Jackson, Marion Barry, Martha Stewart, Kobe Bryant, Mike Tyson, and organizations like the accounting firm Arthur Andersen. Andersen reportedly spent more than $1.5 million in a vain attempt to salvage its reputation during the Enron scandal.[35]

Sensationalistic news coverage of "megatrials" is arguably on the upswing, but they are not entirely new. Richard Stack reminds us that Thomas Jefferson saw the Declaration of Independence itself as a play for world opinion against the judgments of colonial courts and governments.[36] And the twentieth century is filled with cases that became national obsessions, including the trials of Nicola Sacco and Bartolomeo Vanzetti, Julius and Ethel Rosenberg, Bruno Hauptmann, Sam Shepard, the "Chicago Eight," and John Hinckley.[37] Hauptmann's 1935 trial was perhaps the most flamboyant. He was charged with the kidnapping of Charles and Anne Morrow Lindbergh's son. The reporting and publicity seeking that transformed the sleepy farming town of Flemington, New Jersey, into a national media circus is still a measure of media and scapegoating excess.[38]

In recent years, television has increased our "direct" access to trials, not only giving these representations of the legal process new immediacy and visibility but setting the stage for greater use of the media by prosecution and defense teams. Aided by the judiciary's increasing willingness to allow cameras in the courtroom[39] and by the enormous amounts of time available to cable television programmers, live trial coverage can now approximate what had been available only to spectators on the scene. Janice Schuetz calls this "telelitigation," noting that the media spectacle of a trial forces all involved to play to the "court" of public opinion.[40] Add in defendants with deep pockets, or their surrogates who see the trial as an identity group struggle, and the prospect of a trial puts in play the sinews of public opinion.

Exhibit A for all of these forces is still perhaps the 1995 criminal trial of O. J. Simpson for the double murder of Nicole Brown-Simpson and Ronald Goldman. No court proceeding had ever received so much live television coverage and accompanying media speculation. The case saturated the American consciousness for nearly a year. The day the not-guilty verdict was announced, Americans watched in numbers massive enough to affect patterns of national phone, airline, and utility use.[41]

Simpson's defense team responded to charges by building a case for two audiences: the jurors in the courtroom and the public at large. A "memoir" was quickly produced to tell the defendant's side of the story.[42] The "dream" defense team of Johnnie Cochran, Alan Dershowitz, and others appeared frequently on television to soften the widespread public opinion that Simpson was guilty.[43] For their part, the prosecution leaked their own information about Simpson's earlier abuse of his wife, a factor that significantly reframed public perceptions.[44]

Consulting to help stage-manage the courtroom labyrinth for high-profile clients is now common. In the charged atmosphere of the Clarence Thomas confirmation hearings in the Senate, Thomas was advised by political lobbyists Kenneth Duberstein and Tom Korologos. Anita Hill, who alleged that Thomas had made inappropriate advances, was advised by Louise Hilsen, a vice president of Devillier Communications.[45] More recently, Martha Stewart's legal team included Citigate Sard Verbinnen, a firm that specializes in crisis communication.[46] The firm's team created a website defending her against charges of conspiracy and obstruction of justice relating to the sale of stock. They also provided services used by many other high-profile litigants: press releases, carefully managed press conferences, interviews, and other attempts to neutralize the natural tendency in the press to focus on the formal charges. Although Stewart eventually served prison time for obstructing justice in a fraud investigation, one could make the case that they paved the way for her quick postsentence recovery as a valued "brand."

Not all cases with a public relations strategy feature celebrities. The defense team working for the alleged "American Taliban," John Walker Lindh, waged their own campaign to moderate the charges against him and public attitudes shaped by the terrorism hysteria in the aftermath of 9/11.[47] But most cases come from the need to control the news agenda when a lucrative public reputation is at risk.

Consider the rise of television's Dr. Phil McGraw. He is now known for his homey psychological counseling on network television and elsewhere, but he started his career as a litigation consultant. Among his clients at Courtroom Sciences Incorporated was Exxon (now ExxonMobil) after the ecological and public relations disaster of the oil spill from the *Exxon Valdez*. Soon after, he was "discovered" by Oprah Winfrey during litigation against her by the cattle industry. After interviewing a guest who described mad cow disease, the talk show host and potent opinion leader ventured to note that she would not be eating hamburgers anytime soon. That statement—and a sudden dip in the wholesale price of beef—was enough for an industry trade association to pursue charges against her for slander. McGraw was hired to help "soften" her image and keep Americans from reaching the view that she was prone to irresponsible comments that can affect others' livelihoods.[48]

Litigation counselors usually share McGraw's confidence that even the most dire public charges can be redefined with the right presentational skills. His belief in the malleability of public opinion shows in his various incarnations as a counseling psychologist, trial consultant, truth-telling talk slow therapist, and diet and lifestyle author. And it confirms what we know about the constant need to reframe and relabel events that have spun away from the control of their players. McGraw has refashioned himself just as he attempted to shape a new and warmer Oprah, helping shift her role from accuser to victim. The obvious lesson is that no legal jeopardy is so hopeless or dark that it cannot be recast in a softer, friendlier color.

In designing a strategy for salvaging a career threatened by legal action against a client, consultant Todd Felts offers a number of suggestions. Among his imperatives: Keep control of the media message. Rein in talkative clients. Pick a respected and consistent spokesperson for the client. And counsel clients on how to prepare for interviews or other public statements.[49] While some firms offer advice he sees as "humbug," Felts is adamant that "sound communications planning and strategy at the very beginning of a prosecution" will "positively influence the outcome of the case and allow defendants to pick up the pieces of their lives afterward."[50]

Litigation as Theater

In the last quarter century, the United States has seen a dramatic rise in the number of lawsuits brought against manufacturers, doctors, government agencies and the providers of many kinds of services. Typically, these are not criminal cases but proceedings involving tort law, which covers the liabilities of corporations, institutions, or individuals over their alleged negligence. Damages awarded in such suits typically require the payment of fines or compensation and usually an agreement to end certain kinds of practices.

There is almost no end to the range of suits that are filed in federal and state courts, ranging from class action suits against carmakers alleging faulty design, to efforts to seek damages from school officials over the broken bones of high school athletes.[51] The sheer number of these cases seems to challenge the original intentions of laws covering—among other things—product liability and medical malpractice. Building on the widely held view that some in the legal profession would sue their own parents for passing on inadequate genes, Republicans in Congress and the White House now regularly agitate for restrictions against lawsuits, especially those against product and service providers.[52] In 2005, for example, Congress passed legislation to indemnify the gun industry against most lawsuits initiated by victims of gun-related crimes.[53] Arguably, gun manufacturers got better protection from Congress than the American public did.

One reason for GOP opposition to litigation is that it can be used by public interest groups to reform and shame industries not easily brought to heel through legislation. In an era of deregulation, tobacco companies, gun manufacturers, and the makers of high-fat foods can be held to *public* account through high-visibility legal action. As Michael McCann points out, "Media-oriented stagecraft and legal advocacy . . . constitute complementary tactics of modern policy advocates."[54]

Even against American hostility against to the explosion in the number of practicing attorneys and various forms of "junk litigation," defenders of the lawsuit as a weapon for accountability argue that it allows an important kind of redress. "Litigation works," according to Michael Jacobson of the Center for Science in the Public Interest.[55] An early battle waged by the Environmental Defense Fund (EDF) against the use of the pesticide DDT, for example, resulted in both the manifest objective of controlling the chemical's use and increasing the EDF's status and ability to influence the public agenda. As Joel Handler notes, "From the very start, EDF used the litigation to dramatize the dangers of environmental degradation and to launch a massive, and successful, fund-raising drive."[56]

Longtime consumer activists such as Ralph Nader, Joan Claybrook, Richard Daynard, and John Banzhaf III clearly have understood the value of highly visible lawsuits as ways to agitate for increased corporate accountability. Nader first became a national force with his highly visible attempts to gain accountability from General Motors on what he considered a car that was lethal to its owners.[57] Banzhaf's group, Action on Smoking and Health, went even further. Banzhaf understood that lawsuits against the tobacco industry brought by victims of smoking would be noticed. But he also knew that various state attorney generals familiar with the public health costs of caring for smokers would feed the cause of reform in ways legislation could never achieve. "He is a man who loves to generate publicity for his legal campaigns," notes Michael McCann and William Haltom, "and he is exceptionally successful at both."[58] Litigation and negative publicity against the tobacco companies in 1998 resulted in settlements with the states that will pay $246 billion over twenty-five years.

Earlier agitators for product safety often came from the fields of medicine, academe, and the political parties. But these traditional sources of change have been partially eclipsed by not-for-profit groups and their activist legal staffs. Among the better known have been the Environmental Defense Fund, U.S. Public Interest Research Group (USPIRG), the Center for Auto Safety,

Common Cause, the Center for Science in the Public Interest, and Public Citizen. By using lawsuits to mandate court enforcement of the increasingly complex web of state and federal laws protecting individual and community rights, they have pushed the judiciary into territory that it has been reluctant to claim. Judges and juries frequently must now decide how public institutions will be administered and how broad policies—everything from Title IX access to school sports to sex discrimination on the job—will actually be implemented. This gradual but important shift has not been lost on members of the news media, who now cover the courts not just as deliverers of verdicts defining responsibility or guilt but as de facto legislators defining the specific responsibilities of agencies and organizations.

Suits brought against manufacturers, polluters, and government agencies have intrinsic news value. With some exceptions, they are typically not the kinds of actions that corporations or governmental agencies want to debate in the court of public opinion, even though they may well win. A long and drawn-out civil suit accusing a corporation of neglecting its public responsibilities is inevitably going to harm its image, possibly triggering further litigation or punitive legislative action.[59] In 2003, for example, Wal-Mart undertook a massive public relations campaign to restore its battered image after a series of lawsuits brought by a variety of different interests: municipalities trying to block the building of megastores, labor organizers claiming strong-arm efforts to resist organizing workers, and employees claiming discrimination. A spokesman conceded that their engagement of the public relations firm Fleishman-Hillard was in part a response to the federal suit brought on behalf of women who claimed to be passed over for promotions.[60]

The food giant McDonald's also learned the cost of a public fight when vegetarians and Hindus sued by noting that the company enhanced its french fry cooking oils with beef flavoring. The company eventually reached a $10 million settlement—small potatoes in financial terms. The bigger win was its acknowledgment that consumers were not informed that a product reasonably represented as one thing was actually something quite different. The case set off a flurry of suits against McDonald's and many other companies for not clearly disclosing the presence of harmful "food" ingredients, such as trans fats, in descriptions of their products. Even though federal judge Robert Sweet eventually dismissed another case against McDonald's brought by several families of obese children, he noted that a reformulated lawsuit against one of their products might have merit:

> Chicken McNuggets, rather than being merely chicken fried in a pan, are a Frankenstein creation of various elements not utilized by the home cook. . . . Chicken McNuggets, while seemingly a healthier option than McDonald's hamburgers because they have "chicken" in their names, actually contain twice the

> fat per ounce as a hamburger. It is a question of fact as to whether a reasonable consumer would know—without recourse to the McDonald's website—that a Chicken McNugget contained so many ingredients other than chicken and provided twice the fat of a hamburger.[61]

With such statements issued from the bench, the company must have wondered what would have happened had it actually lost.

In the immediate future, we can probably expect more high-profile cases against food companies, retail chains regarding the sources of their products, drug manufacturers, and employers who have allegedly used discriminatory personnel practices. Successful litigation against American tobacco companies will remain the model. For their part, corporations will continue to settle in advance of court proceedings.[62] And others will sign onto the Republican Party's ongoing battle against trial lawyers and its call for even more legislation restricting "frivolous" liability lawsuits.

CONCLUSION

Congress and the courts are institutions dominated by insiders capable of negotiating their labyrinthine rules and structures. The idea that their agents would be compelled to find ways to dramatize their work to the public seems vaguely misplaced. Members of Congress need to master "the inside game" of cooperating with other members to carry legislation. Courtrooms are similarly sentimentalized as bastions of fact finding insulated from the thrall of public opinion. Why does either place such importance on reaching the public outside?

Perhaps *the* classic answer has been given by Robert Hariman, who borrows from the work of Plato. Legal and deliberative processes "perform" our laws. They bring statutes and codes to life by showing their consequences on the living and the dead. And "the performance of the laws is essential for their becoming realized in lawful living." Those who make and enforce the civil and legal system are therefore the natural "rivals" of dramatists. Both are in the business of "reproducing" through performance the critical elements of a society.[63]

The newer answer speaks to the relative decline of civic life against the rise of the corporate state. Money and power are now inseparable in campaigns, institutions of civic life, and our definitions of success. The old powers and prerogatives of Congress and the courts are still in place. But in the slippery environment of instant and incessant news, the instabilities of public opinion more clearly affect the fortunes of commercial and industrial stakeholders. It is obvious that corporate millions were tied to the fates of Martha Stewart and

Oprah Winfrey, as well as the firms of Arthur Andersen, Wal-Mart, and the Exxon Corporation. The pressures of other vital constituencies are at work in House or Senate hearings on farm supports, transportation subsidies, or insurance reform. Just as water finds its way even through the densest of rock, commercial interests that depend on public acceptance have found their way into the very core of governmental and legal advocacy. More than ever, the nation depends on professional advocates—for hire by interested individuals or groups, or in the employ of Congress—who then use their skills to capture distracted news consumers.

As noted earlier, news comes in short segments to largely disengaged citizen-consumers. Events are offered as a kind of transaction. We will attend to them, but only to the extent that they have value as entertainment or information. Congressional committee members know that even high-visibility hearings will yield only a limited number of sound bites. Questions must be brief, and answers must be sharp. Within the crowd that makes up any session of Congress, there is awareness and regret that only melodrama will rise to the surface of what is otherwise a thick column of buried news.

Beyond protecting financial interests, high-profile litigation offers other challenges. Court proceedings are now actually the third act of a narrative loaded with pretrial conflict. Earlier acts unfold in the phases of discovery and indictment. Each puts a defendant's character in question, requiring the services of script doctors who must do face-saving rewrites on the fly. They know that they must counter charges that have reversed the burden of proof in the court of public opinion. They are challenged to write scripts of innocence or extenuation before juries can render a harsher judgment.

These consultants succeed in part because their stories now appeal to our postmodern preference for alternative endings and outsider narratives. We frequently decry the public relations "game" and its superficial manipulations. But we have also learned its rules and honored its effective practitioners. Did lawyer Johnnie Cochran help free a double murderer? Many thought so. But others admired his ability to stage a morality play about institutionalized racism that turned O. J. Simpson into a victim.

NOTES

1. Anna Quindlen, "By the Tube, for the Tube, *Newsweek*, October 3, 2005, EBSCO Academic Search Premier, October 4, 2005.

2. Lloyd Chiasson Jr., ed., *The Press on Trial* (Westport, Conn.: Greenwood, 1997), x.

3. Maura Reynolds, "After Schiavo, GOP's Push on End-of-Life Issues Fades," *Los Angeles Times*, April 7, 2005.

4. Sheryl Stolberg, "The Dangers of Political Theater," *New York Times*, March 27, 2005, sec. 4, 3.

5. Susan Page, "Poll: Public Disliked Schiavo Intervention," *USA Today*, April 6, 2005, 1A.

6. See Karen Dedrowski, *Media Entrepreneurs and the Media Enterprise in the U.S. Congress* (Cresskill, N.J.: Hampton, 1996), 3–8.

7. Hedrick Smith, *The Power Game: How Washington Works* (New York: Random House, 1988), 128–29.

8. Just the issue of federal judge nominations was the most-covered story of the networks for the weeks of May 16 and October 31, 2005. *Tyndall Weekly*, May 2 and November 5, 2005.

9. John Kennedy, *Profiles in Courage*, Memorial Edition (New York: Perennial Library, 1964).

10. Christopher Matthews, *Hardball: How Politics Is Played* (New York: Summit, 1988), 50.

11. These varied agendas are often seen in the House of Representative's morning sessions of "one-minute speeches."

12. Few have tried. One who did is Senator Jim Jeffords of Vermont. He is now an independent rather than a Republican.

13. David Hosansky, "President Swings and Misses at Baseball Strike," *Congressional Quarterly Weekly Report*, February 11, 1995, 447–49.

14. Mark Sappenfield and Gail Chaddock, "U.S. Congress as Baseball's Cleanup Hitter," *Christian Science Monitor*, March 17, 2005.

15. Sappenfield and Chaddock, "U.S. Congress as Baseball's Cleanup Hitter."

16. Roger Davidson and Walter Oleszek, *Congress and Its Members*, 7th ed. (Washington, D.C.: Congressional Quarterly Press, 2000), 217.

17. Jad Mouawad, "An Oil Price Duel on Capital Hill," *New York Times*, November 6, 2005, C1.

18. See Edward Epstein, "Anti-War House Members Press for a Withdrawal Plan," *San Francisco Chronicle*, September 16, 2005, A3.

19. C-SPAN was initiated to carry the proceedings of the House. Coverage of the Senate was added later. On its first two networks that primary commitment remains. What was perhaps not foreseen was how much extra time would be available when the House and Senate are not in session. The networks use much of this time to broadcast hearings and public affairs meetings. All combine to make C-SPAN an enormously important national resource. For a dated but useful history, see Stephen Frantzich and John Sullivan, *The C-SPAN Revolution* (Norman: University of Oklahoma Press, 1996).

20. Clyde Farnsworth, "Gorbachev Lends an Ear to Proxmire's Hearings," *New York Times*, November 9, 1987, B8.

21. See, for example, Robert J. Donovan and Ray Scherer, *Unsilent Revolution: Television News and American Life* (New York: Cambridge University Press, 1992), 23–34.

22. See, for example, George Clooney's 2005 film, *Good Night and Good Luck*. Arthur Miller's allegorical 1953 play, *The Crucible*, remains the strongest indictment of groupthink hysteria produced in public witch-hunts.

23. See Fred Friendly, *Due to Circumstances beyond Our Control* (New York: Vintage Books, 1968), 212–65. Interestingly, Bill Clinton cites his own work as a young staffer at the Senate Foreign Relations Committee as the reason for his opposition to the war. See William J. Clinton, *My Life* (New York: Knopf, 2004), 161.

24. Smith, *The Power Game*, 616–37.

25. Life for a *new* member of the House is very different, and not likely to be filled with high-profile committee assignments or dramatic encounters. For a sense of the challenges to surface above the din of competing voices, see David Price: *The Congressional Experience: A View from the Hill* (Boulder, Colo.: Westview, 1992), 31–56.

26. For a slightly less optimistic estimate of the effects of commissions, see David Rosenbaum, "Commissions Are Fine, but Rarely What Changes the Light Bulb," *New York Times*, October 30, 2005, E14.

27. See, for example, Steve Schwalbe, "Independent Commissions: Their History, Utilization and Effectiveness," n.d., http://www.naspaa.org/initiatives/paa/pdf/Steve_Schwalbe.pdf#search='Congressional%20commissions (accessed May 24, 2006).

28. For a downloadable copy of the report, see "9/11 Commission Report," *Washington Post*, July 22, 2002, http://www.washingtonpost.com/wp-srv/nation/911report/911reportbychapter.html (accessed May 24, 2006).

29. Philip Shenon, "9/11 Group Says White House Has Not Provided Files," *New York Times*, August 7, 2005, A18.

30. The classic cases, of course, involve Supreme Court nominees. Perhaps the 1991 hearings of the Senate Judiciary Committee to confirm George H. W. Bush's nomination of Clarence Thomas was the low point in modern confirmation battles. Near the end of the hearings, Professor Anita Hill came forward with allegations that Thomas had tried to engage her in the crudest forms of sexual discussion, widening gender sensitivities already at the source of a number of political disputes. For a contemporary account, see J. Biskupic, "Thomas Drama Engulfs Nation," *Congressional Quarterly Weekly Report*, October 12, 1991, 2948.

31. Steven Weisman, "Nominee to U.N. Defends Record at Senate Panel," *New York Times*, April 12, 2004, A1.

32. Working with many states, the UN's agencies have made genuine progress eradicating poverty and fighting infectious diseases. As Ved Nanda notes, "The World Health Organization is credited with ridding the world of smallpox, leading the battle against SARS and polio, and now creating worldwide awareness of the threat of the avian flu. Similarly, UNICEF is in the forefront of the effort to improve children's well-being." See Ved Nanda, "The U.N. as It Turns 60," *Denver Post*, October 23, 2005.

33. See, for example, Chaim Perelman, *The Idea of Justice and the Problems of Argument*, trans. John Petrie (London: Humanities, 1963).

34. For a series of classic cases, see Chiasson, *The Press on Trial*.

35. Constance Hays and Leslie Eaton, "Martha Stewart, Near Trial, Arranges Her Image," *New York Times*, January 30, 2004.

36. Richard A. Stack, "The Genie Is Out of the Bottle: Publicity vs. the Press Ban in the Information-Age Courtroom," in *Litigation Public Relations: Courting Public Opinion*, ed. Susanne A. Roschwalb and Richard Stack (Littleton, Colo.: Rothman, 1995), 225.

37. Studies of these cases are collected in Janice Schuetz and Kathryn Snedaker, eds., *Communication and Litigation: Case Studies of Famous Trials* (Carbondale: Southern Illinois University Press, 1988).

38. See Carol Wilkie, "The Scapegoating of Bruno Richard Hauptmann: The Rhetorical Process of Prejudicial Publicity," *Central States Speech Journal*, Summer 1981, 101–10.

39. For a comprehensive discussion of the introduction of cameras in trial proceedings, see Marjorie Cohn and David Dow, *Cameras in the Courtroom: Television and the Pursuit of Justice* (Lanham, Md.: Roman & Littlefield, 2002).

40. Janice Schuetz, "Introduction: Telelitigation and Its Challenges to Trial Discourse," in *The O. J. Simpson Trials: Rhetoric, Media and the Law*, ed. Janice Schuetz and Lin Lilley (Carbondale: Southern Illinois University Press, 1999), 1–18.

41. N. R. Kleinfield, "A Day (10 Minutes of It) the Country Stood Still," *New York Times*, October 4, 1995, A1, A12.

42. Kleinfield, "A Day," 13–15.

43. Simpson was later tried in federal civil court in 1997 and held responsible for the deaths of two people.

44. Lin Lilley, "The Trial of the Century in Retrospect," in *The O. J. Simpson Trials*, ed. Schuetz and Lilley, 162–63.

45. Susanne Roschwalb, "The Role of Public Communication in the Judicial Proceedings of Anita Hill and Clarence Thomas," in *Litigation Public Relations*, ed. Roschwalb and Stack, 177.

46. Hays and Eaton, "Martha Stewart."

47. William Glaberson, "Defending, and Recasting, an Unloved Client," *New York Times*, December 19, 2001, A1.

48. Alessandra Stanley, "Blunt Advice and No Pity Get Ratings for Dr. Phil," *New York Times*, September 24, 2002, E1.

49. Todd Felts, "Some Things Are Worse Than Going to Jail," *Of Counsel*, January 2005.

50. Felts, "Some Things."

51. Jethro Lieberman, *The Litigious Society* (New York: Basic, 1981), 4–5.

52. See, for example, John F. Harris and Jim VandeHei, "Senate Nears Revision of Class Actions," *Washington Post*, February 10, 2005, A4.

53. Richard Simon, "Bill to Shield Gun Makers is Approved," *Los Angeles Times*, October 21, 2005.

54. Quoted in Michael McCann and William Haltom, "Framing the Food Fights: How Mass Media Construct and Constrict Public Interest Litigation," unpublished paper, n.d., http://www.law.berkeley.edu/institutes/csls/McCann%20paper.pdf#search='public%20interest%20litigation (accessed May 24, 2006).

55. Michael Jacobson, "A Time to Sue," *Nutrition Action Healthletter*, March 2003, 2.

56. Joel Handler, *Social Movements and the Legal System: A Theory of Law Reform and Social Change* (New York: Academic Press, 1978), 216.

57. Ralph Nader, *Unsafe at Any Speed* (New York: Grossman, 1972).

58. McCann and Haltom, "Framing the Food Fights."

59. Of course, some corporations or trade groups are extremely willing to fight lawsuits, and they have financial resources that are usually much greater than their opponents'. For an extended case study, see Jonathan Harr, *A Civil Action* (New York: Vintage, 1996). Even the cattle industry's ill-fated suit against Oprah Winfrey could be interpreted as a warning to others to expect an expensive legal fight for defaming a large industry.

60. Constance Hays, "Wal-Mart, Aware Its Image Suffers, Studies Repairs," *New York Times*, August 14, 2003, C1.

61. Quoted in McCann and Haltom, "Framing the Food Fights."

62. See, for example, Andrew Skolnick, "Spate of Lawsuits," *Journal of the American Medical Association*, July 19, 1995, 1080–81; and Christopher Stern, "ABC Would Rather Not Fight," *Broadcasting and Cable*, August 28, 1995, 18.

63. Robert Hariman, "Performing the Laws: Popular Trials and Social Knowledge," in *Popular Trials*, ed. Robert Hariman (Tuscaloosa: University of Alabama Press, 1990), 17.

Chapter Six

Nationalism, Foreign News, and War Reporting

> News you can use may help you with your diet or your next car purchase, but it offers little of utility for the major issues that Americans face when making up their minds about who will occupy the White House or lead the Congress or what challenges the United States can expect in its relations with the rest of the world.[1]
>
> —Donald Shanor

> Only one of five Americans hold a passport and the only stories that make their news are floods, famine, and wars, because it makes them feel good to be an American.[2]
>
> —T. R. Reid

Perhaps there is no greater challenge for media and citizen alike than the decision to fully enter into a world beyond their own. We are creatures of habit and convenience. Without the curiosity and inclination to believe that we have lessons to learn from others, we are not easily induced to explore other cultures. Just as narcissism usually cripples an individual's full potential, ethnocentrism can lead a nation to sad and unpleasant surprises. Americans have long sought to thrive *outside* the class and political constraints of the old world, projecting power beyond their borders only on their terms. But if it ever really existed, the luxury of this kind of isolation died long ago in the ashes of two cataclysmic world wars.

This chapter explores the serious deficit in foreign news reporting that exists in the most widely used media in the United States. Our task is to account for some of the causes and consequences of low levels of journalistic and public interest in the rest of the world. The deficit is dramatic and profound, especially if we exclude news focused on American military action or natural disasters. Of course, we cannot and should not ignore these categories. But when a nation's understanding of its place in the world is seen almost exclusively through the lens of political conflict and catastrophic events, the effects may be more isolating than broadening.

Studies in the last two decades have shown repeatedly that foreign news as a percentage of all print and broadcast journalism usually hovers in the single digits. In one study in the 1990s, CNN *Headline News*, CBS, and other American outlets ran in *last* place on time spent on foreign news stories compared with their counterparts in Sweden and the United Kingdom, among others.[3] And even for 2001—a year that contained wall-to-wall terrorism coverage in the final quarter—domestic datelines on the major American networks dominated foreign datelines by a ratio of 5 to 1.[4] Notwithstanding the global implications of a war on terrorism and an ostensible coalition of nations to fight it, most reporting came from Washington or other domestic news bureaus.

Our specific focus here is on recurring patterns of foreign news reporting in popular news outlets such as regional newspapers and the broadcast television networks. A second section describes the American tendency to look inward, tracing its exceptionalist and nationalist origins. The final extended section applies these concepts to past and current patterns of war reporting, with special reference to the "war on terrorism."

FOREIGN NEWS WITH AN AMERICAN SLANT

Depending on the source and news agenda—and excluding war news for the moment—foreign news generally represents between 2 and 30 percent of the content of general news sources. The low end is represented by many regional newspapers in the United States and some television outlets such as Fox and MSNBC, which usually emphasize domestic news coverage.[5] While subject to variations depending on how foreign news is defined and the length of the period surveyed, American media also spend less time on international news items than their counterparts in other Western nations. Former *Baltimore Sun* reporter John Schidlovsky notes that it "is perhaps the single most negative development" of his lifetime."[6]

To be sure, there are a number of notable exceptions: the "big four" of American print journalism, including the *New York Times, Wall Street Journal, Los Angeles Times*, and *Washington Post*; the broadcast coverage of CNN International and National Public Radio; the growing presence of the BBC on public television and radio; the exceptional reporting of the *Christian Science Monitor*; and news services such as the Associated Press, Agence France

Presse, and Reuters. In addition, some regional papers are blessed with inventive foreign reporting.[7] And especially after the 2003 invasion of Iraq, more Americans have sought out alternative perspectives from a wealth of overseas Internet sources. In January 2003, nearly half of the web users of Britain's *Guardian* newspaper came from North America.[8]

Even so, among the traditional American broadcast networks and many smaller newspapers, the political world still hardly exists beyond the stories and frames of reference originating from American strategic interests.

It is easy to identify the fundamental forces that produce narrow and self-serving forms of international news. Nearly all of the American media depend on ratings, circulation numbers, and advertisers. In this familiar equation, foreign news must find a significant number of receptive readers and viewers. News organizations tend to respond to this imperative in two ways. One is represented by the *New York Times*' Joseph Lelyveld, who concedes that "stories that really matter in the world may or may not be stories that move ratings or sell papers." But they deserve coverage because we cannot escape the realities of living in an interconnected world. "If you build trust, your readers will understand that these stories matter to their lives."[9] The more common response is to write off the possibility that Americans are curious about events outside their borders, unless reports can build on exceptionalist commonplaces of American uniqueness. From this perspective, events elsewhere have significance only if they fit into recognizable frames of reference—for example, as natural disasters—or if the story involves American economic or military interests.

Consider the output of all of the three broadcast networks for 2004. As tallied in the annual *Tyndall Report*, *none* of the top twenty stories for the year originated outside the Middle East. The only foreign locations were Israel and Iraq: the first, a primary client state and the largest recipient of American foreign aid; the second, a military and public relations project that was costing the United States $1 billion a week in 2004. For the entire year, nearly 40 percent of all the stories dealt either with the Iraq war and the hunt for terrorists or with the presidential campaigns of George W. Bush and John Kerry.[10] And virtually all foreign stories, including Iraq and Israel, originated within three American agencies: the White House, Department of Defense, and State Department. Among the networks' most heavily used field reporters, the only one outside the United States was in Baghdad.[11]

Similarly, the Pew Research Center's running tally of news stories followed "very closely" by Americans indicates a decided preference for domestic stories, except wars and terrorism involving the United States (see table 6.1).

Table 6.1. Public Attentiveness to News Stories, Other Than War and Terrorism: 1986–2004

This list reflects the top of the list of news stories followed "very closely" by the Pew Research Center's rolling sample of Americans. It exempts stories on war and terrorism involving American interests, which comprised eighteen of the top thirty. On each occasion, respondents were asked if they were following the story "very closely," "fairly closely," "not too closely," or "not at all closely." Stories include the month and year in which the question was asked, since attention to the same story changes over time. Note that all the top stories are domestic. None focus on international news such as famines or civil strife on other continents, national elections, the opening of the Berlin wall, world conferences on economic, environmental or human rights issues, and so forth.

% Followed Very Closely	*Subject*
80	Challenger disaster (July 1986)
73	San Francisco earthquake (Nov. 1989)
70	Rodney King case/verdict and riots (May 1992)
69	Crash of TWA flight 800 (July 1996)*
69	Little girl in well, Texas (Oct. 1987)
68	High school shooting in Littleton, Colo., (Apr. 1999)
66	Hurricane Andrew (Sept. 1992)
65	Floods in the Midwest (Aug. 1993)
65	Sniper shootings near Washington, D.C. (Oct. 2002)
63	Earthquake in Southern California (Jan. 1994)
61	High gasoline prices (May 2001)
60	Hurricane Hugo/destruction (Oct. 1989)

Source: Adapted from "Public Attentiveness to News Stories: 1986–2004," Pew Research Center for the People and the Press, http://people-press.org/nii/ (accessed May 25, 2006).

*This crash was initially thought to be the result of terrorism but was later determined to be caused by a mechanical failure.

A Small Keyhole

The United States is a huge nation that looks outward only through a very small keyhole.

Consider some significant but disturbing benchmarks:

• *In the last ten years, most American broadcast networks have closed most of their foreign news bureaus.* CBS once had fourteen major bureaus supporting reporters and producers who had a chance to learn about the regions they were covering. Now they have almost none. Gone are outposts in Cairo, Rome, Johannesburg, Nairobi, Beirut, and Cyprus.[12] The same is true of the other networks, which depend on receiving video feeds from external sources, which are then frequently narrated by a "reporter" in New York. "I don't believe that buying footage and looking at it second-hand is a substitute for going there yourself," observes veteran CBS reporter Betsy Aaron. She notes that in narrating someone else's footage:

> I am not seeing the story. I'm relying on someone else to gather that story for me. I have no idea what the person's agenda was—as there always is an agenda. And we're putting that on the air with the CBS label or the NBC label or the ABC label and we're doing it in a cavalier fashion that we never would have done twenty years ago, ten years ago or five years ago.[13]

NBC and ABC have even abandoned full-time news bureaus in the vital city of Moscow, requiring "fly-ins" by sometimes clueless New York correspondents to cover fast-breaking stories. One wonders whether viewers of an October 2002 segment of *Good Morning America* were aware that Bill Blakemore had only been on the ground just a few hours when he went on the air with a live report from a Moscow theater attacked by Chechen guerrillas.[14] Reporters are usually not very insightful when they have spent no more time at a location than the average tourist.

• *9/11 exposed a dangerous media myopia that left Americans and national leaders in the dark about changes in world attitudes.* "We did not examine the country's anti-terrorism efforts adequately, our intelligence capabilities, our immigration policies, or the reasons for anti-Americanism," noted the former president of the American Society of Newspaper Editors. "While we can debate whether this failure played a role in our national lack of preparedness, there is no question that we failed our readers."[15]

Even residents in the cosmopolitan precincts of New York City are hardly prepared to be citizens of the world if their news diet is limited to the hugely popular *New York Daily News*, Fox News, or MSNBC. The *Daily News* duplicates the pattern of many papers to focus almost exclusively on domestic stories. And beyond reporting on American military and security topics, none of the three have much interest in world opinion or in regional solutions to shared concerns such as the environment or human rights. Especially for the two cable news outlets, the solutions to the most vexing world problems are likely to come from "talk jockeys" in the studio rather than reporters in the field. Typical is Fox's studio-bound Fred Barnes, for whom many of the world's problems can simply be solved by "the strong exercise of American power."[16]

• *In geographic terms, news organizations have simply written off entire continents.* For decades there has been little coverage of noncatastrophic developments in Latin America, the vast nations of Asia, the Pacific Rim, and Africa. These regions represent well over half of the world's total population, but they receive only a tiny fraction of our attention.[17] Given the fact that *less* than 20 percent of young American adults can locate Iraq, Saudi Arabia, or Afghanistan on a world map,[18] the news blackout of these huge regions is even more disturbing.

Interestingly, during the initial invasion of Kuwait by Iraq in 1990—arguably the defining moment of the presidency of George Bush senior—there was only *one* American correspondent stationed within the emirate: the *Washington Post*'s Caryle Murphy.[19] Moreover, of the many American reporters who had to be quickly flown into Saudi Arabia to cover the military buildup in Persian Gulf, few were prepared for the task, neither speaking Arabic nor understanding the sensitivities of Islamic culture.[20]

• *What foreign coverage there is tends to assume a narrow American perspective.* One of the difficulties researchers have had in assessing the extent to which any nation's news media focuses on international affairs is locating the point that divides foreign from domestic news. A report about American tourists detained in a Latin American country is arguably less about the country than about the plight of U.S. citizens traveling abroad. Most such stories are, in a word, ethnocentric. Events have meaning or significance only to the extent they seem to affect one's own group or culture. In their own study, Roger Wallis and Stanley Baran make the useful distinction between "stories reported in wholly international terms" versus "stories reported in terms of home nation involvement." They found that American outlets were more likely to include a foreign news story if it was seen as affecting some dimension of domestic life. "British and Swedish news media, while offering almost twice as much foreign news as some of their U.S. counterparts, showed only half as much ethnocentricity."[21]

"Owing to cutbacks in our news department, here is Rod Ingram to guess at what happened today in a number of places around the globe."

American farmers have learned about the virtues of selling "Chernobyl wheat" to replace the radiation-contaminated grains once grown around the Ukrainian city of Kiev. And autoworkers in Honda's Tennessee factory have a natural interest in trade barriers and quotas that could affect the sale of finished automobiles. But Americans remain reluctant internationalists, preferring a view that sees the nation as largely separate from the regional interdependence that is now increasingly taken for granted in other Western nations.

• *Most foreign news reporting is framed in the contexts of conflict or mayhem.* Wars, civil strife, natural disasters, and terrorist attacks represent the dominant share of American foreign reporting. For the first week of January 2005, for example, network news coverage was completely focused on two stories: the effects of a devastating tsunami wave in Asia and violence against Americans and Iraqis by Iraqi insurgents. Combined, they represented 90 percent of the network's time.[22] At one level, who could quarrel with coverage of a natural disaster that killed more than 160,000 Asians and produced a world outpouring of aid? And why wouldn't American networks want to cover the bloody effects of its long military occupation of Iraq? The obvious answer is that both were important stories. The problem is when the willingness to cover foreign news is *only* triggered by human and natural disasters. The disturbing corollary—suggested in T. R. Reid's observation that opens this chapter—is that the world beyond America's borders is a violent and chaotic place. As determined by foreign editors and television producers, most news functions to reassure Americans that others' experiences have little to offer.

For example, consider two stories from Russia that recently ran on CNN International but not on its sister network in North America. One segment described the growing boom in shopping malls throughout Russia. A second report documented the widespread adoption of Western-style childbirth practices, including active participation from fathers-to-be.[23] By themselves, these were small stories. But the subtext of normalcy within them—when consistently *subtracted* from the American news diet—has the effect of keeping Russia a troubled and alien nation. This absence of the kinds of *stories we would tell about ourselves* fuels the presumption that the only role the United States has to play in the world is to police the human and natural disasters that pass for foreign news or to provide aid that might help those who suffer from them. Not surprisingly, a study of by the Center of Media and Public Affairs found that the American media response to the rest of the world is most likely to include suggestions for the use of military force, not diplomacy, and—of course—not just listening for what others may be able to teach us. Such coverage, they conclude, continues "the media's longstanding practice of presenting the United States as the principal actor on the world stage."[24]

Foreign News from Washington: Covering the "Golden Triangle"

There is some irony to the fact that many stories about the affairs of other countries carry a Washington dateline. But that reality reflects two basic organizational features of foreign news reporting. The first is the prevailing view among the nation's editors that important events in other countries should be framed in terms of government-to-government contacts. We frequently make our interpretations of life in another country in terms of the quality of official relations that its capital maintains with our own. Patterns of international diplomacy—whether cordial or hostile—tend to extend into public perceptions about even the nongovernmental characteristics that we attribute to people in other countries. For example, our sometimes uneasy official relations with Japan over trade issues, and with France over differences in security and foreign policy matters, have undoubtedly shaped the collective impressions we have of their cultures. The stormy past that once characterized diplomatic relations with Japan—from Pearl Harbor to American perceptions of Japan's alleged economic protectionism—still lay down the tracks that guide attitudes about Japanese national life.[25]

The second feature that often dictates a Washington dateline is the wealth of information that federal agencies accumulate and propagate. Reporters with prestigious assignments in the "golden triangle" of the White House, State Department, and Pentagon can depend on a range of daily briefings from armies of press staffers. And that is only the beginning. All of these venues are organized to help reporters construct stories on a wide range of subjects, feeding them a vast array of intelligence data on trade and military issues, as well as information on political and social conditions. In the vast press operations of these three centers is an endless flow of press releases, interviews, research reports, and documents. Reporters are also encouraged to travel with top officials and sometimes pay the price by losing their journalistic independence.

At their best, the public relations arms of the foreign policy establishment do provide useful information. In most cases, a reporter may view his or her private sources and general knowledge about a region as miniscule compared with the resources of the foreign and military establishments. But at their worst, governmental press offices contribute to a false sense of uniformity in reporting. Not only are Washington-based correspondents indebted to the agencies they are supposed to be writing about for much of their information, but the fact they are all listening to the same officials contributes to a kind of "groupthink." Before he retired, ABC's Ted Koppel suggested part of the problem in the opening of one of his *Nightline* broadcasts:

> We are a discouragingly timid lot. By we, I mean most television anchors and reporters and most of our colleagues of the establishment press. . . . We tremble

> between daydreams of scooping all of our competitors and the nightmare of standing alone with our scoop too long. . . . People whose job it is to manipulate the media know this about us. They know that . . . many of us are truly only comfortable when we travel in a herd.[26]

Critics often point out the failures of reporting that depends too much on official sources.[27] Former CBS diplomatic correspondent Marvin Kalb recalls a time in Moscow in the 1950s and 1960s when he "generally cooperated with [the] U.S. embassy" and readily accepted "the ambassador's interpretation of Kremlin policy."[28] Kalb believed that he had ample reason to develop some of his stories with the help of the American embassy staff. Until the late 1980s, much of the Soviet Union was officially off-limits to reporters. But in less exotic locales, reporters who rely on American sources may do so for other reasons. Either their editors may only want to offer their readers "the American perspective" on a region, or the reporter may be looking for a shortcut to filing a quota of stories, using views from American foreign service personnel in place of the more bothersome task of taking an independent look at a nation's national affairs.

THE EXCEPTIONALIST CONCEIT

The idea that the United States is the natural agent for world leadership is not new. Indeed, its effects are so old and durable that it rarely gets the scrutiny it deserves.

To be sure, every nation-state narrates and nurtures its own fantasies of uniqueness. A society's history, achievements, and shared values are essential parts of its national identity. But the breadth and extent of American nationalism carries this process at least one step further. It defines not only a collective identity but also a familiar set of universal values that assert "legitimate" terms of engagement for all states.[29] As a nation we may not acknowledge it, but these values can function as *covering rationales* that exempt ourselves from the multilateral approaches that govern other global partners. Through them, we universalize American interests as the natural interests of others, and we often do so by interpreting opposition to American *strategic goals* as an affront to universal democratic values.

The rhetoric and assumptions of American exceptionalism fuel this process. This rhetoric constructs our place in the world by arguing that the unique circumstances of our history can instruct other nations. It emphasizes the rights and obligations we have to other Americans rather than those beyond our borders.[30] And its preferred vocabulary is couched in terms of natural rights, democratic values, and destiny.[31] All of this is offered as a prime export, where we measure our foreign policy successes by the degrees to which we gain compliance from others.

Specific forms of this rhetoric have accompanied crises as divergent as the attacks on military vessels in the Gulf of Tonkin in 1967 ("The United States has the right to be anywhere") or on the Pentagon and World Trade Center in 2001 ("The attack on us was an attack on all civilized nations"). Each event becomes an occasion for endlessly recycled narratives of American virtue vehemently argued by successive presidents and amplified by compliant news outlets.[32]

All of this nationalistic piety functions rhetorically as the legitimizing agent for a foreign policy dominated by unilateralism but "covered" in rationales of moral and historic inevitability. Hence, former deputy secretary of state Strobe Talbott has noted, without any apparent sense of irony, that "American foreign policy is consciously intended to advance *universal* values."[33] Journalists William Kristol and Robert Kagan similarly conclude that the United States "infuses its foreign policy with an unusually high degree of morality."[34] Apparently, Americans are the lucky custodians of most of the world's civic virtues.

It is these kinds of benign attributions that oil the mechanisms of national self-denial. We naturally want to think the best of our own motives, largely avoiding the dominating role of national self-interest in the actions of the United States.

The Unilateralist Impulse after 9/11

By American decree, terrorism policy remains the new organizing principle for judging the soundness of state-to-state relations. Listen to a president, his surrogates in the defense establishment, and most members of Congress, and one sees the presumption that other states must accommodate this agenda. We relish the certainty that our wounded nation will seek its revenge against alien forces around the globe and that it will do so unilaterally, notwithstanding the fig leaf of "coalitions." This stance is reflected in Joseph Nye's view that the United States has mastered only one of three dimensions of international relations. He notes that the American government is uncontested in its ability to project *military power*. But in terms of both *economic supremacy* and support for various *nongovernmental groups*—two vital realms for global cooperation—the United States is now often seen more as a drag on innovation than a leader.[35] Attitudes toward the United States among traditional allies in the United Nations, human rights groups, and other important extragovernmental organizations often verge on contempt (see table 6.2).

Table 6.2. Percentage in Various Nations Who Agree That U.S. Foreign Policy Considers Others

Country	*Percentage*
United States	67
Jordan	17
France	18
Turkey	14
Canada	19
Poland	13
Netherlands	20
Spain	19
Russia	21
Great Britain	32
Lebanon	35
Germany	38
Pakistan	39
China	53
Indonesia	59
India	63

Source: Adapted from the Pew Research Center, Pew Global Attitudes Project, "Opinions of U.S. Policies," June 24, 2005, http://pewglobal.org/reports/display.php?PageID=803 (accessed May 25, 2006).

The American presumption for accommodation *from* other states often goes unnoticed here but not elsewhere. A Paris-based journalist for the *International Herald Tribune* has noted that European foreign ministers now tend to regard "their most serious foreign-relations problem as that of dealing with the United States."[36] American foreign policy is seen as a major obstacle to the achievement of their own objectives. And it is easy to see why. In the recent past, the United States has operated with the assumption that it is not legally or morally bound to support the cooperative legal and environmental efforts of other friendly nations. The list of initiatives and treaties that the United States has recently rejected is extensive. The second Bush administration refused to sign onto a Comprehensive Test Ban Treaty, the Rome Treaty for the International Criminal Court, the Land Mines Convention, the Convention on the Rights of the Child, and the landmark Kyoto agreement on global warming.[37] In its first term, it backed away from several tentative starts at a Middle East peace initiative. It was slow to allow international peacekeepers to secure vast regions in Afghanistan. Moreover, it sought to exempt scores of prisoners captured in Afghanistan and Iraq from traditional American and Geneva Convention protections.[38] In addition, in a number of high-visibility speeches, the Bush administration snubbed supposed allies against terrorism, including Russia, Canada, and "old Europe,"[39] the latter phrase serving as an especially clumsy taunt of most of America's traditional

European allies. We expect that other nations will consult with us before they act. But many in those nations understand that whether the United States does the same depends on a narrow calculus of potential gains.

Samuel P. Huntington has noted that, from the perspective of many other nations, the United States is perhaps the world's only "rogue superpower." Not only do we "grade countries according to their adherence to American standards on human rights, drugs, terrorism, nuclear proliferation, missile proliferation, and now religious freedom," but we also "bludgeon other countries to adopt economic policies and social policies that will benefit American economic interests."[40] The flags and ribbons that blossom after every crisis, the "get tough" rhetoric, and benevolent interpretations of our motives all play a role. Such rhetoric makes it much more difficult to visit alternative conclusions about the needs and legitimate claims of other states.

Evidence of these blind spots is found in nearly every paragraph of George Bush's pivotal 2002 State of the Union address and the subsequent assertions on the imperative of invading Iraq in 2003. In that speech, he noted that recent events are a reminder that "we've been called to a unique role in human events." He also observed that "some governments will be timid in the face of terror. And make no mistake about it: If they do not act, America will."[41]

Statements like these offered a domestic performance advantage. They communicated firmness and resolve. But no one would want to live next door to a neighbor who likes to issue ultimatums. As the *Sydney Morning Herald* editorialized with regard to the command for other states to either fall in line or get out of the way:

> [There is] no hint here that he understands that he is talking of sovereign nations, some of whose governments are not so much timid as bankrupt and powerless. No acknowledgement, either, that "terrorist" is a term used not only to describe misguided fanatics intend on destroying Western civilization, but also by oppressive regimes to demonize their internal enemies, who are often drawn from suffering ethnic or religious minorities.[42]

"What is most curious about these speeches," notes Francis FitzGerald, "is the combination of triumphalism and an almost unmitigated pessimism about the rest of the world."[43] In the days leading up to the second Iraq war, cooperation with our allies and the United Nations on the consensus issue of containment of the Hussein regime held little appeal. By the time the United States began to search for an exit strategy after the ill-fated Iraq occupation, the normal effects of diplomacy had been turned upside down. With a few exceptions, American policy had managed to make enemies of friends and cashed in the reserves of international goodwill built up over decades.

Media and Nationalism as Fuel for Conflict

As we noted in the first part of this chapter, our foreign news coverage mirrors a nationalistic orientation to American policy. Moreover, as many in the press have since conceded, much of the coverage of the pivotal decision of the younger Bush to invade and occupy Iraq was uncritical.[44] It was not just that the press had conspired to suppress dissident opinions at home or around the world about American policy. Instead, many journalists seemed to accept the premise that it was the United States' destiny and fate to act.

Attributions of "rights" and destinies are fed by such nationalism. The impulse to find a separate identity in a society's common values and histories is strong, contributing to two world wars and, more recently, countless tribal feuds in Serbia, Bosnia, Somalia, the Middle East, and Africa. Even as alleged "citizens of the world," populations in most states at least partly define their societies by what they are *not*. The issue has even resurfaced within the increasingly powerful European Community, where nationalists fret about the degree to which identification with specific national traits must be sacrificed to achieve economic security.[45] Even so, many Europeans regret that American nationalism has not devolved into more harmless forms of patriotism.[46] A *majority* also believe that American foreign policy contributed to the September 11 attacks.[47]

Hubris born of an inflated sense of national destiny is paradoxically lethal *and* sentimental, especially if a state has the military capacity to act. And the United States clearly has that capacity. It spends nearly as much ($466 billion) as the combined defense budgets of *all* the rest of the world ($500 billion).[48] The sheer mastery of modern weapons technology becomes its own show, which perhaps accounts for why many Americans can find at least three cable television channels now devoted solely to American military affairs.[49] Moreover, the collective memory of Americans who have paid the ultimate price in military action requires its own theater of formalized funerals, memorials, and eulogistic narratives. Each new conflict comes with its own reified antecedents: past wars and sacrifices to be honored in new trials that affirm the nation's unique separateness. As veteran American war correspondent Chris Hedges notes, conflict can easily become the state's means for demonstrating greatness:

> Daily wartime episodes are central to the nationalist vision. The carefully choreographed performances come to define and make up the body politic. The lines between real entertainment and political entertainment blur and finally vanish. The world, as we see it in wartime, becomes high drama. It is romanticized. A moral purpose is infused into the trivial and the commonplace. And we, who yesterday felt maligned, alienated, and ignored, are part of a nation of self-appointed agents of the divine will. We await our chance to walk on stage.[50]

Disillusion sets in, according the Hedges, only when the "mythic" war of noble leaders and battle-scarred heroes begins to give way to the "sensory" war of pointless death and destruction. The issue, of course, is *if* and *when* a nation's news media will finally deliver the awful truth.

WAR REPORTING: FINDING TRUTH IN THE NATIONAL INTEREST

In his landmark study of war journalism from the Civil War to Vietnam, Phillip Knightley provides a vivid picture of journalists who sought to bring the terror of battle to readers and viewers. Every age has identified with some of these colorful figures: photographer Mathew Brady with the Union Armies at Bull Run and Gettysburg, Ernest Hemingway seeking out stories from the battle lines in the Spanish Civil War, Ernie Pyle with infantry units in World War II, and CBS's Jack Laurence covering an ambush and firefight in Vietnam.[51] During the 2003 invasion of Iraq, reporters such as CBS's Scott Pelley and NBC's Fred Francis served as the nation's witnesses to battle. Such front-line correspondents have always provided the most vivid images of war. In unexpected ways, they put a human face on the most inhuman of all activities. By describing the ugly and often senseless consequences of war, they provide a valuable check on the lofty political rhetoric that often justifies it.

In peacetime, journalists have been aided by a Pentagon that is often more open and receptive to press coverage than even the State Department. But "hot" wars can severely strain the relationship. No governmental action so tests the vaunted ideals of a democracy and a free press than the decision to commit Americans to combat overseas. The dominant staging issue here is often represented in a difficult dilemma: to what extent can the raw and often unpleasant facts of modern industrial warfare be presented to audiences and advertisers who have a clear preference for narratives of national honor?

Military News Management: Then and Now

Since World War I, few journalists have bothered to argue with what has become a standard list of restrictions regarding military actions. These prohibitions have included detailed information on the location of troops or weapons; discussions of planned tactics; the location of missing troops, planes, or ships still subject to possible rescue; and news about operational weaknesses that could be used by the enemy. But with the partial exception of the Vietnam War, commanders and reporters have seldom agreed on how to report less strategic types of information.

Edward R. Murrow's experiences with Britain's Ministry of Information in 1940 are illustrative. The popular journalist sought permission to do several live broadcasts to his CBS radio audiences in the United States during the massive German air attacks on London. Permission was initially declined. It is difficult to figure out what kind of news might have compromised British secrecy; the devastation of the nighttime raids on central London's docks and homes would have been obvious to German air crews. More likely, the ministry was bothered by the prospect of the world witnessing the nightly pounding of the capital city at the hands of the Luftwaffe's incendiary bombs. Murrow kept asking and agreed to record his reports in a number of practice runs that would prove to the ministry that he would not expose military secrets.[52] The ministry finally relented, slow to realize that his accounts of the stoic resolve of the city's residents would help achieve Winston Churchill's objective of motivating Americans to enter the war.

Murrow and other reporters were often less successful in getting stories cleared through American military censors. Drew Middleton recalls that "total censorship prevailed. Everything written, photographed, or broadcast was scrutinized by censors. Anything that did not meet the high command's considerations of security was deleted."[53] In the Pacific Theater, for example, Americans were not initially told of the heavy damage to the U.S. Navy inflicted by Japan at Pearl Harbor. Even at the end of the war, information about the desperate kamikaze attacks of the Japanese Air Force against American ships was largely kept out of the American press by military censors.[54]

Despite strict censorship rules in World War II, the press generally gave the military and its planners high marks. Several factors explain why. One reason is that the adversary model that is so common today was less clearly a part of the journalistic ethos. Members of the press suffered less from the antipolitical bias that is now a fixture in contemporary American life. In addition, most reporters were personally committed to the broad political objectives of the Allies, and they were routinely allowed to join specific units, talk to their members, and fly on bombing and supply missions. Key commanders from Dwight Eisenhower to George C. Marshall were willing to provide thorough briefings "off the record" on the effects of particular campaigns. As in World War I, correspondents soon learned to engage in self-censorship to avoid the delays that rewriting stories sometimes entailed.[55]

The stalemated and deadly "police action" in Korea signaled a gradual shift away from this pattern of broad access but strong official censorship, a pattern that would be complete by the time the Vietnam War had escalated into a major conflict. Partially because Vietnam was an undeclared war, journalists had a freer rein in determining for themselves what they would file to their editors and producers.

Vietnam has been called the "uncensored war," a label that is technically accurate but also misleading. In the last half of the 1960s, correspondents in Vietnam found that they had wide access to individual units in the field. Many became effective chroniclers of the peculiar hell that results when the "enemy" becomes indistinguishable from the inhabitants of jungle villages. Along with others, UPI's Neil Sheehan, the Associated Press's John Wheeler, and NBC's Greg Harris captured in words and images much of the incredible horror of the conflict, usually shipping their reports back to their offices without prior military screening. The continuous intensity of this reporting on the networks' evening newscasts left Americans with few illusions about the high costs and muddled objectives of the conflict.

But the absence of military censorship of outgoing dispatches conceals what Middleton describes as the common practice of "censorship at the source."[56] Especially in the case of Vietnam, an enormous credibility gap developed that increasingly pitted journalists—and, soon, a sizable portion of the American public—against their sources, including the president and military commanders in Saigon. The gap was created by the enormous discrepancies between what reporters were seeing in the countryside and what briefers were more optimistically describing in Saigon and Washington. The daily afternoon sessions between correspondents and representatives of the Joint U.S. Public Affairs Office became a notorious symbol of purposeful equivocation. What was dubbed "the five-o'clock follies" provided abundant evidence that the bureaucracy was intentionally attempting to manage news about the overall scope of the conflict, often by claiming that information was not available or by inflating estimates of the number of enemy soldiers killed in combat.

In deploying resources in Vietnam for long-term coverage, news organizations were able to overcome one of their major liabilities: the fact that *the press is naturally a reactive institution*. As the Nieman Foundation's Bill Kovach has observed, the press typically responds only after other organizations have already put their plans in motion.[57] At least in the short term, the press is easily led. It has a strong tendency to cover an event initially from the perspective of those who have orchestrated it. But because the Vietnam conflict grew incrementally over a decade, many in the press had the time to establish an independent presence in the region.

It was, ironically, a small operation on the island of Grenada in 1983 that would signal the weakness of the media to cover short-term military actions, a weakness that would surface again in the Afghan war at the end of 2001.

Grenada: A Time for Press–Military Negotiation

The Grenada invasion was a quick military strike—what then White House chief of staff James Baker accurately described as a commando raid—

centered on the airport of that small Caribbean island. The primary objective was the rescue of American students thought to be held by a government friendly to Cuba. The invasion occurred without the press and was virtually over before any were able to fly to the island. Although news organizations voiced strong objections, most had no choice but to grudgingly relay after-the-fact accounts of the invasion provided by the Pentagon and the White House.[58] Even the Pentagon's public affairs spokesperson at the time, Pete Williams, later conceded that it was a "journalistic disaster."[59]

The political consequences of the Grenada invasion may have been as important as its strategic value. It pushed the military into meetings with news executives and reporters about how to arrange coverage of the smaller combat operations that were now predicted in a world no longer dominated by East–West tensions. The primary result of these meetings was the so-called Sidle Commission Report, named after retired army general Winant Sidle, who oversaw the deliberations. Sidle worked with retired military officers and journalists to establish a set of recommendations governing press–military planning in future operations. The most essential proposals included the following:

- That public affairs planning for military operations be conducted concurrently with operational planning. . . .
- When it becomes apparent during military operational planning that news media pooling provides the only feasible means of furnishing the media with early access to an operation, planning should provide for the largest possible press pool . . . and minimize the length of time the pool would be necessary. . . .
- That a basic tenet governing media access to military operations should be voluntary compliance by the media with security guidelines or ground rules established and issued by the military. These rules should be as few as possible. . . .
- Public affairs planning for military operations should include sufficient equipment and qualified military personnel whose function is to assist correspondents in covering the operation adequately.[60]

The same general guidelines remained in effect for the American invasion of Panama in December 1990 and the Persian Gulf War the following year.

Military News Management I: The Persian Gulf War

"With an arrogance foreign to the democratic system," CBS's venerable Walter Cronkite told readers of *Newsweek* magazine, "the U.S. military in Saudi Arabia is trampling on the American people's right to know."[61] What he objected to was a series of restrictions given to the approximately one thousand accredited reporters and technicians who covered the 1991 war to retake Kuwait from Iraqi occupation. Of this number, no more than 126 were ever assigned to a pool for coverage of the half million Americans in the area during the five-week air war. During the three days of ground combat that began on February 24, approximately 250 journalists were allowed to join combat pools.[62]

Built on the Sidle Commission model, the military's rules in the Middle East put heavy and burdensome restrictions on members of the press. To be sure, they were less onerous than the strict Iraqi government censorship imposed on reporters still in Baghdad, but not by much. Even before the massive air offensive began, Pentagon rules issued to the Washington bureaus of news organizations required that all reports not disclose sensitive military information, that access to combat units would be limited to preselected pools of reporters, and that reports from members within a pool would have to be submitted to "security review."

The small number of reporters who ignored the Pentagon's guidelines in the weeks that followed discovered that they sometimes gained protection from commanders who were sympathetic to their desire to break free of Pentagon restrictions. At other times, however, these so-called unilaterals were rounded up by military MPs and detained in rear-staging areas.[63] The most unlucky of the unilaterials was CBS's Bob Simon and his crew, who were captured by Iraqi troops and held until the end of the war.

The two-page list of restrictions that would be placed on the press included the obvious and traditional limits on coverage. Reporters were reminded to restrict the use of lights at night. They were told that they would have to carry their own gear, and they were cautioned against giving out information regarding the names of casualties, the movements of troops, and specific information on individuals or aircraft behind enemy lines. The more troublesome limitations involved the requirement to travel in military-escorted *pools* and the indication that some materials might be reviewed by military censors.

The idea of using a representative group of journalists in a specific setting was not new. In some cases, the sheer number of accredited reporters in a given location can make it impossible for press offices to arrange access for all who seek it. The White House, presidential campaigns, NASA, and other agencies have often put limits on coverage by selecting a limited number of reporters to relay impressions to others. Those who are selected relinquish the right to claim an "exclusive" on the events they witness. Much like wire service reporters, their job is to provide a factual running narrative of what took place. In the early days of the air war, fewer than ten pools were initially established, with sizes ranging from seven to eighteen members. The largest pools were assigned to the Army and Marines. Smaller groups were established to cover the Air Force, Navy, the military hospitals, and any unexpected events. Even so, large gaps remained. According to the *New York Times*'s

R. W. Apple, out of a total of eight Army or Marine divisions numbering more than one hundred thousand men and women on the ground near Kuwait, only thirty spots existed for the press.[64] Most of the approximately one thousand journalists who wanted to cover the war in the Persian Gulf were left at the Dhahran International Hotel or the Riyadh Hyatt, able only to receive pool reports and the daily military briefings issued by the Joint Command.[65]

The use of pools as a way to manage press coverage was especially evident in efforts by the Pentagon to keep pilots and members of the press apart. Members of a pool hoping to fly with the crews of the massive B-52 bombers that contributed to the seventy-two thousand sorties during the war were instead given ground interviews with air force commanders or a single preselected pilot. At one point, they ended up interviewing drivers in a motor pool, where the commander suggested stories about their "unsung" role. Apparently only one reporter—ABC's Forest Sawyer—actually flew on a bombing mission, even though aircraft had ample space.[66]

Military News Management II: Afghanistan and Iraq

Two months after the attacks on the World Trade Center and Pentagon in 2001, the United States began air and ground offensives against the Taliban government of Afghanistan. The refusal of the extreme theocratic government to turn over Osama bin Laden sealed their fate. Throughout most of October and November, B-52s and scores of fighters launched repeated raids on mountain bunkers and Al Qaeda hideouts, accompanied by efforts on the ground by commando and U.S. Marine units to drive Taliban leaders from Kabul and Kandahar. The air assaults were intense but largely unseen by the American public. Perhaps five thousand Afghan civilians were killed in the air attacks of "Operation Enduring Freedom," and another twenty thousand died from the chaos that the attacks created on the ground.[67]

Afghanistan duplicated the Grenada experience of denial of press access. Most reporters conceded that the relatively brief military efforts on the ground in Afghanistan's remote cities would preclude extensive on-the-scene reporting. But many were annoyed that even reporting about the air attacks was *after* the fact and usually from military briefers cowed into near silence by Secretary of Defense Donald Rumsfeld. Journalists were kept out of land and sea bases from which the strikes were launched, and they were usually denied the chance to interview pilots and others.[68]

The war to overturn the Taliban regime certainly had worthwhile political goals and consequences, but at the expense of a news blackout on its human costs. There was little question that the failed state of Afghanistan under the Taliban was a danger to its citizens—especially women—and other nations.

The subsequent decision of the second Bush administration to link the "war on terrorism" to the overthrow of Iraq was much more problematic, even while it produced opportunities for more accessible press coverage.

The 2003 invasion and occupation of Iraq was, as noted earlier, a foreign policy fiasco. The original motive for removing the government and occupying the nation was to take control of what was presented as an extensive cache of "weapons of mass destruction." But, of course, none were found—a confirmation of what United Nations' inspectors had been telling the American government. At the height of the conflict in 2004, weekly American casualties where edging into the upper teens, and the occupation force of 160,000 troops (many called to active duty from the National Guard) struggled against horrible odds to maintain civil order. Throughout most of 2004 and 2005, news reports tallied the daily toll of death wreaked by bloody ambushes of American and Iraqi forces by Sunni guerillas. To many observers, media representations of the conflict looked like Vietnam all over again. Official optimism in Washington competed with nightly accounts of deadly skirmishes with "enemies" indistinguishable from the citizens who had ostensibly been "liberated." Military information about the occupation was controlled from the Pentagon, the elaborate CentCom stage set in neighboring Qatar, and journalists "embedded" with military units. The latter was a relatively new twist, at least since World War II. The idea at the start of the war was to place willing journalists inside specific units during the initial invasion. At the height of the campaign to capture Iraq's key cities, as many as seven hundred reporters were embedded with units.[69] Traveling with specific units meant that journalists were dependent on them for safe passage and support.

One representative report featured CBS's Scott Pelley with the Second Battalion of the Fifth Marine Regiment in Ramadi. The story that aired on *60 Minutes* in January 2005 documented the dangerous process of patrolling a deadly street known by the troops as "Route Michigan." Patrols were regularly hit by residents in the city wielding everything from bricks to mortars. In Pelley's narrative, viewers saw the group hit by a rocket-propelled grenade "seemingly from nowhere" and then blood spilling onto the sidewalk from a wounded soldier. The camera followed as his comrades pulled him into the safety of a sheltered corner. Then Pelley and his crew followed another patrol down the same street in a later attempt to defend the office of a local American-backed politician. This part of the story narrated by Pelley focused on Captain Pat Rapicault: "He's an unusual Marine. Born in France, he came to the United States as a student. His accent is part France, part Mississippi. His men tease him about it and some of them call him Frenchie."[70] Pelley followed him on more urban street patrols, briefly cutting away to footage of a young Iraqi insurgent wiring explosives placed under a road. The insurgent's goal was to detonate the homemade bomb when American patrols passed by. But most of the camera time was given to Rapicault, who was seen clinging to the shadowed edge of a building, his eyes and rifle trained on a deserted alley around the corner. A voice-over script filled in the grim statistics:

> Rapicault, 34, and married, may have been born to be a Marine officer. He was first in his class in Ranger school. When we met him he'd already lost six men. And there was something we noticed about him. As he talked with us he never took his eyes off the potential threats to his Marines down the road. He told us the enemy was always watching, so you could never look away. . . . Rapicault "leads from the front," as the Marines like to say, and he's focused on getting the rest of his men home. Most often, Rapicault's men never see the enemy—they don't truly know who he is or what he's fighting for. They have never seen the enemy like this—that watches for an approaching American patrol and prepares to set off a roadside bomb.[71]

As the story concluded, Pelley told of another attack that had taken three more members of the 160-person company, among them the same Captain Rapicault viewers had just come know.

Not all reports from embedded reporters were this dramatic. But most carried the same essential features: close-up profiles of troops with familiar American accents moving through dusty and hostile Iraqi streets. It was the kind of up-close urban warfare Pentagon planners had hoped to avoid when the invasion of Iraq began. Yet this level of access also provided essential evidence of the enormous gap between the lofty rhetoric of liberation coming from Washington and the harder realities of military occupation.

As in all other conflicts, the military in Iraq imposed limits on reporting any information that—in their view—would compromise the safety of the troops or security of actions.[72] But embedded reporters were clearly less affected by formal restrictions than by the bonds they built with their subject-protectors. These connections carried their own problems. Most of those who traveled with troops recognized the awkward arrangement that made reporters fully dependent on their ostensible news source. Marvin Kalb notes, "'Embedding' is part of the massive, White House–run strategy to sell a single message about the American mission in this war—that the United States is liberating Iraq from a bloody dictator."[73] It almost requires "patriotic reporting," a conclusion that some journalists openly admitted and more detailed content analysis confirms.[74] As ABC's John Donvan observes, "These people have been so nice to us. . . . I could see how it'd be hard to write critically if they made a mistake. I don't think I could do it. They're my protectors."[75]

What this reporting lacked was a larger and longer perspective.[76] With no Pentagon assistance and a general reluctance by most American media to keep their own tally, it fell to groups of academics, enterprising journalists, and researchers to track the cumulative cost of the war in terms of civilian casualties. The conclusion of one such study released in July 2005 made for unpleasant reading. Using firsthand news accounts of specific instances, the writers concluded that nearly 25,000 civilians had died in Iraq, including 2,500 women and children, mostly from American fire. Another 42,500 were listed as wounded.[77]

Whatever the lasting consequences of the occupation of Iraq, it is clear that military news management practices that began after Vietnam are still in place. A likely future of confrontations involving rapid and intense skirmishes puts the press at an enormous disadvantage. In short wars, journalists have less time to establish an independent presence in a region. And with fewer reporters for major news organizations stationed overseas, editors have fewer resources to resist the sometimes heavy-handed terms that govern access to military operations.

CONCLUSION

As we have seen, foreign news lies at one of the busy thoroughfares of American life. The long-standing American wish to exist on a continent separated from the discontent of other nations has been steadily eroded by a combination of factors. Since World War II, the United States has acted on a strong desire to project American power beyond its borders. We have entered into wars—both "hot" and "cold"—for altruistic and selfish reasons. And we have found new Soviets to replace the old; real and imagined terrorists now remind us who we are not, offering a simple way to understand America's place in a more multilateral world. The result is that we have become a more militaristic society. In summarizing the ideas of Andrew Bacevich, a graduate of West Point and a Vietnam veteran, Tony Judt notes that the nation "is becoming not just a militarized state but a military society: a country where armed power is the measure of national greatness, and war, or planning for war, is the exemplary (and only) common project."[78]

Overall, the response of media and governmental forces to the globalization of politics and information has been enormously varied, but it includes several conclusions reached in this chapter:

- a tendency by media organizations to focus more on domestic rather than international affairs, or foreign reporting that emphasizes an American angle to events;
- a reduction of "in-house" foreign news gathering by the broadcast networks, in favor of greater use of international video news services;

- a reliance on government sources to set the context for foreign reporting; and
- deep ambivalence by the military and news organizations about the role of the press in wartime.

To be sure, the task facing correspondents who deal with foreign affairs is enormous. They must deal with editors and producers who are reluctant to commit resources to the coverage of foreign news, especially if it is *not* given a frame of reference in concurrent American events. And they must attempt to interest an American public that—in the mass—lacks knowledge about even the most elemental issues affecting other societies.

NOTES

1. Donald Shanor, *News from Abroad* (New York: Columbia University Press, 2003), 74.
2. T. R. Reid, *The United States of Europe: The New Superpower and the End of American Supremacy* (New York: Penguin, 2004), 18.
3. See Gary C. Woodward, *Perspectives on American Political Media* (Boston: Allyn & Bacon, 1997), 153–55. See also James F. Hoge Jr. "Foreign News: Who Gives a Damn?" *Columbia Journalism Review* (November–December 1997): 48–52.
4. *Tyndall Report*, "Top Stories of 2001."
5. Lucinda Fleeson, "Bureau of Missing Bureaus," *American Journalism Review*, October–November 2003, http://www.ajr.org/article_printable.asp?id=3409 (accessed May 25, 2006).
6. Quoted in Fleeson, "Bureau of Missing Bureaus"
7. Michael Parks, "The Future of Foreign Coverage," World Press Institute, n.d., http://www.worldpessinstitute.org/parks.htm (accessed January 7, 2005).
8. Leander Kahney, "Media Watchdogs Caught Napping," *Wired.com*, March 17, 2003, http://www.wired.com/news/print/0,1294,58056,00.html (accessed January 3, 2005).
9. Quoted in Shanor, *News from Abroad*, 38.
10. *Tyndall Report*, "Top Stories of 2004."
11. *Tyndall Report*, "Top Stories of 2004."
12. Scotti Williston, "Global News and the Vanishing American Foreign Correspondent," *Transnational Broadcasting Studies*, Spring–Summer 2001, http://www.tbsjournal.com/Archives/Spring01/Williston... (accessed January 3, 2005).
13. Quoted in Tal Sanit, "The New Unreality: When TV Reporters Don't Report," *Columbia Journalism Review*, May–June 1992, 18.
14. Fleeson, "Bureau of Missing Bureaus."
15. Edward Seaton quoted in Parks, "The Future of Foreign Coverage."
16. Quoted in "Global News: TV News Coverage of Global Issues," Center for Media and Public Affairs, *Media Monitor*, November–December 2002, 4.

17. Roger Wallis and Stanley Baran, *The Known World of Broadcast News* (New York: Routledge, 1990), 256.

18. "Global Goofs: U.S. Youth Cannot Find Iraq," Associated Press, November 22, 2002, CNN.com, http://archives.cnn.com/2002/EDUCATION/11/20/geography.quiz/ (accessed May 25, 2006).

19. Jude Wanniski, *1991 Media Guide* (Morristown, N.J.: Polyconomics, 1991), 55.

20. Chris Hedges, "The Unilaterals," *Columbia Journalism Review*, May–June 1991, 27–29.

21. Wallis and Baran, *The Known World of Broadcast News*, 179.

22. *Tyndall Weekly*, January 8, 2005.

23. Fleeson, "Bureau of Missing Bureaus."

24. "Global News," 4.

25. This is a continuing theme in T. R. Reid's impressionistic account of a Western family (his) living in Japan. See his *Confucius Lives Next Door: What Living in the East Teaches Us about Living in the West* (New York: Random House, 1999), 152–204.

26. Quoted in Martin A. Lee and Norman Solomon, *Unreliable Sources: A Guide to Detecting Bias in News Media* (New York: Stuart, 1991), 337.

27. Nik Gowing, "Journalists and War: The Troubling New Tensions Post 9/11," in *War and the Media*, ed. Daya Thussu and Des Freedman (Thousand Oaks, Calif.: Sage, 2003), 231–40.

28. Marvin Kalb, preface to *The Media and Foreign Policy*, ed. Simon Serfaty (New York: Macmillan, 1990), xvi.

29. Consider the variations just on the single term *freedom* that George W. Bush used in his January 29, 2002, State of the Union address: "freedom's fight," "hope for freedom," "price of freedom," "freedom's power," "freedom's victory," and "We choose freedom and the dignity of every life." *New York Times*, January 30, 2002, A22.

30. See, for example, Martha Nussbaum, *For Love of Country: Debating the Limits of Patriotism* (Boston: Beacon, 1996), 4–5.

31. For a useful discussion of the idea of exceptionalism, see Seymour Martin Lipset, *American Exceptionalism* (New York: Norton, 1996), 31–52.

32. Mainstream news organizations reflect public opinion by safely challenging political leaders on the veracity of small claims of fact, but they rarely challenge the assumptions behind the projection of American economic and military power. See, for example, Todd Gitlin, "Showtime Iraq," *American Prospect*, November 4, 2002, 34–35.

33. Quoted in Samuel Huntington, "The Lonely Superpower," *Foreign Affairs*, March–April 1999, emphasis added.

34. Quoted in William Pfaff, "The Question of Hegemony," *Foreign Affairs*, January–February 2001.

35. Tony Judt, "Its Own Worst Enemy," *New York Review of Books*, August 15, 2002, http://www.nybooks.com/articles/article-preview?article_id=15632 (accessed May 25, 2006).

36. Pfaff, "The Question of Hegemony."

37. Peter J. Spiro, "American Exceptionalism and Its False Prophets," *Foreign Affairs*, November 2000.

38. In its decision to treat prisoners of the "war on terrorism" as "unlawful combatants," the second Bush administration undermined American values and international faith in its traditional role as a protector of human rights. Most news stories have described the restricted rights of prisoners at Guantánamo Bay Cuba (see Neil Lewis, "U.S. Judge Halts War-Crime Trial at Guantanamo," *New York Times*, November 9, 2004, A1) or sadistic prisoner abuse at Abu Ghraib prison in Iraq (for summarizing essays and reports on this scandal, see Mark Danner, *Torture and Truth: America, Abu Ghraib and the War on Terror* [New York: New York Review Books, 2004]).

39. Frances FitzGerald, "George Bush & the World," *New York Review of Books*, September 26, 2002, http://www.nybooks.com/articles/article-preview?article_id=15698 (accessed May 25, 2006).

40. Huntington, "The Lonely Superpower."

41. Bush, State of the Union address.

42. Quoted in June Thomas, "Hate of the Union," *Slate*, January 31, 2002, http://slate.msn.com/id/2061450 (accessed May 25, 2006).

43. FitzGerald, "George Bush & the World."

44. Michael Massing, *Now They Tell Us: The American Press in Iraq* (New York: New York Review of Books, 2004).

45. See, for example, Christopher Caldwell, "The Anti Europeanist," *New York Times Magazine*, January 9, 2005, 26–31.

46. "Americans and Europeans Differ Widely on Foreign Policy Issues," Pew Research Center, April 17, 2002, http://people-press.org/reports/display.php3?ReportID=153 (accessed May 25, 2006).

47. Chicago Council on Foreign Relations and the German Marshall Fund of the United States, "Europeans See the World as Americans Do, but Critical of U.S. Foreign Policy," September 4, 2002, http://www.worldviews.org/key_findings/transatlantic_report.htm (accessed May 25, 2006).

48. "World Wide Military Expenditures," 2004 estimates, Global Security.org, http://www.globalsecurity.org/military/world/spending.htm (accessed May 25, 2006).

49. They are the Military Channel owned by Discovery Communications, the Military History Channel owned by A&E, and the Pentagon Channel run by the Department of Defense. See Mark Glassman, "Military Channels Are Competing on Cable TV," *New York Times*, January 24, 2005, C8.

50. Chris Hedges, *War Is a Force That Gives Us Meaning* (New York: Public Affairs Press, 2002), 54.

51. Phillip Knightly, *The First Casualty* (New York: Harcourt, Brace Jovanovich, 1975).

52. A. M. Sperber, *Murrow: His Life and Times* (New York: Freundlich, 1986), 161–74.

53. Drew Middleton, "Barring Reporters from the Battlefield," *New York Times Magazine*, February 5, 1984, 37.

54. Knightley, *The First Casualty*, 273–74, 297.

55. Richard Steele, "News of the 'Good War': World War II News Management," *Journalism Quarterly*, Winter 1985, 707–83.

56. Middleton, "Barring Reporters." 61.

57. Bill Kovach, "Speech to the Cambridge Forum," National Public Radio, July 26, 1991.

58. Mark Hertsgaard, *On Bended Knee: The Press and the Reagan Presidency* (New York: Schocken Books, 1989), 205–37.

59. Pete Williams, "Statement before the Committee on Governmental Affairs, Washington, United States Senate, February 20, 1991."

60. Winant Sidle, "Report by CJCS Media-Military Relations Panel," appendix in Peter Braestrup, *Battle Lines: Report of the Twentieth Century Fund Task Force on the Military and the Media* (New York: Priority, 1985), 161–78.

61. Walter Cronkite, "What Is There to Hide?" *Newsweek*, February 25, 1991, 43.

62. David Lamb, "Pentagon Hardball," *Washington Journalism Review*, April 1991, 33–36.

63. Hedges, "The Unilaterals," 27–29.

64. R. W. Apple, "Correspondents Protest Pool System," *New York Times*, February 12, 1991, A14.

65. Lamb, "Pentagon Hardball," 33; Michael Massing, "Another Front," *Columbia Journalism Review*, June 1991, 23–24.

66. Jason DeParle, "Keeping the News in Step: Are the Pentagon's Gulf War Rules Here to Stay?" *New York Times*, May 6, 1991, 23–24.

67. Daya Kishan Thussu, "Live TV and Bloodless Deaths: War, Infotainment and 24/7 News," in *War and the Media*, ed. Thussu and Freedman, 126.

68. Neil Hickey, "Access Denied: The Pentagon's Reporting Rules Are the Toughest Ever," *Columbia Journalism Review*, May–June 2003, http://archives.cjr.org/year/02/1hickey (accessed January 14, 2005).

69. Steve Ritea, "Media Troop Withdrawal," *American Journalism Review*, December/January 2004, http://www.ajr.org/Article/asp?=3477 (accessed January 1, 2005).

70. "Under Fire, Alongside the Fallen," transcript of January 16, 2005, segment on *60 Minutes*, CBSNews.com, http://www.cbsnews.com/stories/2005/01/16/60minutes/printable667271.shtml (accessed May 25, 2006).

71. "Under Fire."

72. Section 6.a of the Pentagon's military ground rules reflects the general tone of the "security review" process: "Security at the source will be the rule. U.S. military personnel shall protect classified information from unauthorized or inadvertent disclosure. Media provided access to sensitive information, information which is not classified but which may be of operational value to an adversary or when combined with other unclassified information may reveal classified information, will be informed in advance by the unit commander or his/her designated representative of the restrictions on the use of disclosure of such information. When in doubt, media will consult with the unit commander or his/her designated representative." Greg Mitchell, "Pentagon Ground Rules May Limit Reporting," *Editor and Publisher*, February 24,

2003, http://www.editorandpublisher.com/eandp/search/article_display.jsp?vnu_content_id=1822054 (accessed January 10, 2005).

73. Marvin Kalb, "Journalists Torn between Purism and Patriotism," *Editor and Publisher*, March 24, 2003, http://www.editorandpublisher.com/eandp/news/article_display.jsp?vnu_content_id=1848137 (accessed June 7, 2006).

74. Michael Pfau, Michel Haigh, Mitchell Gettle, Michael Donnelly, Gregory Scott, Dana Warr, and Elaine Wittenberg, "Embedding Journalists in Military Combat Units: Impact on Newspaper Story Frames and Tone," *Journalism and Mass Communication Quarterly*, Spring 2004, 80–84.

75. Quoted in Howard Kurtz, "The Ups and Downs of Unembedded Reporters," *Washington Post*, April 3, 2003, http://www.washingtonpost.com/wp-dyn/articles/A16094-2003Apr2.html (accessed January 10, 2005).

76. Pfau et. al., "Embedding Journalists in Military Combat Units," 80–82.

77. Hassan Fattah, "Civilian Toll in Iraq Is Placed at Nearly 25,000," *New York Times*, July 20, 2005, A8.

78. Tony Judt, "The New World Order," *New York Review of Books*, July 14, 2005, http://www.nybooks.com/articles/18113 (accessed May 25, 2006).

Chapter Seven

Art, Entertainment, and Politics

> If you can write a nation's stories, you needn't worry about who makes its laws.[1]
>
> —George Gerbner

> One needs to ask . . . not how one can eradicate entertainment from politics, but how one can entertain the citizen instead, how the current entertainment culture can be articulated with the requirements of political citizenship, and what kind of civic virtues can be evoked and maintained through popular culture.[2]
>
> —Liesbet van Zoonen

Politics is part of the ocean of popular culture to which we are all tied. Some of us regularly swim in its waters or visit its restless edge. Others of us claim to show no interest in it. But all of us are at least affected by its environment and the periodic storms created by its sheer vastness. To a large extent, we live *through* politically infused portraitures of daily American life that can be as commonplace as an episode of *The Simpsons* or as evocative as a satire of the president.

Art and politics have never been completely comfortable companions. But the *forms* of fiction and news spring from the same representational resources. Most share the same conventions of narrative and characterization. Most acknowledge audience expectations to be met or challenged. And in various ways, most address the forces that unite and sometimes divide us. In truth, political and imagistic dramas about society are not easily separated. Beethoven is reported to have torn up the dedication page of his Third Symphony after hearing that Napoleon Bonaparte had declared himself emperor of the French. Apparently the grand work known as the "Eroica" would not be tainted by association with the "new tyrant."[3] Reversing the roles, the great Mexican painter Diego Rivera came under the wrath of the industrial titan John D. Rockefeller, who had commissioned frescos to decorate the public entrances of the New York office complex bearing his name. Rockefeller was willing to condone Rivera's sympathetic murals of toiling workers, but not when one of them included Vladimir Lenin, the founder of the Soviet state.[4] He had that particular panel destroyed.

Art and politics intersect at one of the busiest thoroughfares of American culture. The commercial arts of novels, films, and television help establish the frames of reference against which issues are discussed or judged. As underscored in this chapter, the traffic of ideas carried within a society's art defines its priorities and asserts its collective identity. It is little wonder that this intersection is subject to repeated and angry clashes.

When a recent secretary of education felt it necessary to warn PBS that its animated series *Postcards from Buster* was out of line, many could regret the specific reason but not the assumption. The offending scene of an episode included two moms who happened to be lesbians observing the process of gathering maple sugar. The child-friendly animated rabbit never uttered the feared "L" word. And to virtually all but the secretary and a few culture police, this was just a scene of children and parents in the Vermont woods. But Margaret Spellings made it clear that such moments in a program originally intended to celebrate diversity could jeopardize PBS support. "Many parents would not want their young children exposed to the lifestyles portrayed in the episode," she noted.[5] But are gay parents really so different? We doubt that the young audience witnessed anything more than the reassuring sight of two nurturing parents. Yet, if Spellings was a mile wide of the mark in her comments, she was theoretically correct to assume that political meaning is potentially embedded in all forms of expression.

Even the most harmless forms of mass-produced culture carry their own messages of cultural praise and blame. Characters are heroes or fools. They make good choices or bad ones. Some live enviable careers that feed on fantasies of success. Others survive nightmares that extend and dramatize the nightly horrors of the evening news. When we observe their lives—mostly by gazing into our television screens—they clearly represent some of the most vivid sources of our national consciousness.

Our goal in this chapter is to consider art as a kind of political discourse. We start by identifying core assumptions about narrative and collective representation. The section that follows breaks down three progressively subtle levels for assessing meaning in narrative content, with a special emphasis on film.[6] We look at the "culture wars" that have placed art and the media at the center of some of our most heated political battles. The chapter concludes by examining the uniquely American tendency to see many products of commercial entertainment as instruments in the alleged "subversion" of American values.

THE CREDIBILITY OF NARRATIVE: CORE ASSUMPTIONS

The rhetoric of art lies in its power to compress and heighten experience. Those large segments that are representational (as opposed to purely abstract) communicate a wealth of judgments about human and institutional relationships that make up the fabric of life. *To a large extent, we judge art by assessing how efficiently it functions as commentary on these relationships*. As Hugh Duncan has noted, drama and portraiture offer their own forms of journalism,[7] inviting assessments of motives and choices that others have made.

Several conclusions underpin this view. First, there are times when fiction is more accommodating to truth than the decontextualized news narratives that dominate contemporary journalism. News stories are especially bound by a limited range of acceptable outcomes, often chipping away bits of inconvenient reality that cannot fit into a tight narrative arc.[8] Truth can sometimes be better served by an imaginative artist who is nimble enough to capture the essences of motives, persons, or eras. We enter the older and more constrained worlds of E. M. Forster and Virginia Woolf not just to step into a different era but to discover what their characters still tell us about ourselves. Similarly, we can perhaps get closer to the absurdities and tragedies of the first Iraq war by viewing David O. Russell's film *Three Kings* (1999) than from reading the pool reports that were issued out of Dhahran. And there is arguably as much of the essence of Richard Nixon or Bill Clinton in the film portrayals of Oliver Stone's *Nixon* (1995) and Joe Klein's *Primary Colors* (1998) than in their subjects' own labored memoirs. "Fiction" and its kindred form of biography allow writers to more easily essentialize the pivot points of a life.

Second, art is less stipulative in its meaning than more instrumental types of communication. Because it invites interpretation and comment, it sometimes refracts the light of wish fulfillment and experience into its primary forms. Perhaps—but only perhaps—will Beethoven's Third or Ninth Symphonies communicate political attitudes to modern audiences. Different listeners will hear different motivations reflected in scores and texts. Those who know the recording of conductor Leonard Bernstein's famous Berlin concert celebrating the end of a divided Germany may associate the famous *Ode to Joy* conclusion of the Ninth Symphony just as Bernstein intended it and as

Beethoven intended the Third: as celebrations of human freedom. But in music, as in other cultural forms, audiences construct rather than simply discover meaning.

This refraction into levels of meaning also gives art a calculated depth, a third function that plays out in meanings revealed at both latent or subtextual levels. The very evident realities of a film or any entertainment can be easily extended into symbolically rich layers of meaning that comment on other times, people, and places. *The Wizard of Oz* (1939), for example, allegedly began as a cautionary tale by L. Frank Baum about the inaction of President William McKinley. We no longer pick up that latent message, but we still like to see its innocents gently unmask the pretensions of power. In similar ways, music uses evocative chord and rhythm structures to deliver compelling word images. Anthems such as Joni Mitchell's "Big Yellow Taxi" or Hugh Masekela's "Bring Him Back Home (Nelson Mandela)" have been their own agents for change.

Every epoch contributes its own forms that speak to audiences in the soft language of allegory. John Sayles's films such as *Lone Star* (1996), *Sunshine State* (2002), and *Casa de los Babys* (2003) are rewarding as explorations of cultural blind spots without the histrionics of melodrama. His work especially stands in contrast to most filmmakers' for his willingness to peer into divisions of class and culture usually hidden behind a scrim of forced optimism. Steven Spielberg's very different films—including *E.T.: The Extra-Terrestrial* (1982), *Empire of the Sun* (1987), and *A.I.: Artificial Intelligence* (2001)—offer more conventional plot-driven dramas. But seen through the moral purity of their children, these stories suggest something altogether darker about the lost innocence of adulthood.

Because art is understood to be expressive and additive—we want its richness to evoke dreams and ideals—we sometimes understand its significance by noting what it *omits*. This fourth assumption is both an observation about the selective nature of all narration and portraiture as well as a methodological reminder of how we should "read" the stories a nation tells about itself. Representations of collective identity are sometimes best understood by noting what is *not* present. Seasoned observers on the content of prime-time television have often discovered that what is *excluded* from programming is just as revealing as what is affirmed. Omission functions as its own commentary.

Several years ago, for example, Beth Austin took on the makers of classic "emotional blockbuster" films such the now-iconic *When Harry Met Sally* (1989) for being too socially insular. Austin argued that many older films managed to tell interesting stories about people absorbed in relationships who at the same time had well-developed senses of public responsibility. In *On the Waterfront* (1964), *High Noon* (1952), and *To Kill a Mockingbird* (1962), the central characters were not only governed by their personal desires and needs but by duties to the communities they were apart of. "A little looking out for the next fella," she writes, "is precisely what filmmakers are leaving out of their family pictures—a dangerous signal to be transmitting to our kids."[9] Others have long noted the absence of *serious* portrayals of differences of class in American films,[10] as well as the neglect of fully developed portrayals of older Americans, mature women, and others on the supposed margins of marketplace culture.[11]

Finally, a core assumption that exists especially in the audiences for the popular arts is that, on the whole, they should be celebratory or inspirational. Without doubt, one function of art in the context of the political world is that it should sustain the myths the nation wants to validate and endorse.[12] In the words of the writer and art critic Robert Hughes, American art institutions operate under the mistaken belief that they are "good for us." We expect that their work will be "therapeutic."[13] In this tradition, Rivera's Rockefeller Center murals communicated the dignity of people engaged in ordinary work. Even with the sly addition of a Soviet leader, the murals were generally meant to confer honor on their patron and pride to their viewers.

But what do we make of Robert Mapplethorpe's controversial "X Portfolio"? In the 1980s and 1990s, his photography severely tested traditional views about the nature and uses of creativity. It is an understatement to say that his images flaunted social conventions. Mapplethorpe's photographs are graphic and sometimes confrontational. Before he died of AIDS, he surely knew that the homoeroticism of his images would incite the very kind of the gay bashing he opposed. When the pictures were displayed in a Cincinnati museum, the director was hauled into court for "pandering obscenity." After the exhibit was scheduled for a show at Washington's Corcoran Gallery (*Robert Maplethorpe: The Perfect Moment*), objections multiplied like cherry blossoms.[14] The prestigious gallery had entered the political realm by giving a flamboyant perspective the imprimatur of a national forum.

Hughes and most others in the art establishment are quick to rebuke the idea that what hangs on a gallery wall needs to be beautiful.[15] But the fact that this expectation remains widespread helps explain why dissonant messages can generate controversy and discord—the same effects so often associated with political discourse.

LEVELS OF POLITICAL MEANING

There is no simple line separating art from politics and entertainment from political persuasion. And, to be sure, countless films and cultural ephemera satiate audiences with diversions of total irrelevance. But it is useful to look at three levels of political meaning that can exist in the products of the artistic and entertainment industries. First, content may preference a political position, as in Michael Moore's searing documentary critique of George Bush, *Fahrenheit 9/11* (2004). Second, it may reconstruct an event from the political past with a certain emphasis or perspective, such as in the classic Watergate film, *All the President's Men* (1976). Third and most subtle, content may indirectly endorse or devalue certain groups for whom political influence is essential: women, homosexuals, corporations, and others. That was the clear intention in Robert Greenwald's 2005 feature documentary, *Wal-Mart: The High Cost of Low Price*. In this realm, narratives cannot help but confer legitimacy to some, while denying it to others.

Content as Political Advocacy

Narrative and art are often a visible part of the mix of public discussion. Political cartoons, popular satire, films, plays, novels, and music are resonances of events already in the public's consciousness. They may openly advocate a specific attitude, as in Tim Robbins's play about press complicity in the second Iraq war, *Embedded* (2003).[16] Far more commonly, narratives suggest directly or indirectly that discourse in the public sphere is ruled by hypocrisy or stupidity. Any list is arbitrary but suggestive: Gary Trudeau's president watching in "Doonesbury"; monologues on the *Tonight Show* or Comedy Central's *The Daily Show*[17]; the Internet's *The Onion*; John Sayles's film parable about a politician who is the captive of his handlers (*Silver City*, 2004); or antiwar films that started as novels, including *M*A*S*H* (1970), *Dr. Strangelove* (1964), and *Catch-22* (1970).

Art is frequently used to identify the political villains of a society. In 1937, for example, Germany's Nazi Party held official exhibitions of allegedly "degenerate painting," including the works of Paul Gauguin and Vincent van Gogh. Their work was thought to be a danger to the public and a threat to the glory of the Third Reich.[18] Orson Welles famously took on another threat in the form of Charles Foster Kane (*Citizen Kane*, 1941), his proxy for the imperious William Randolph Hearst.[19] Most professions that exert considerable power over a culture have faced their own artistic Jeremiahs: corporate leaders in *Barbarians at the Gate* (1993) and *The Insider* (1999), opportunistic preachers in *Bob Roberts* (1992), and ruthless legal operators in *The Firm* (1993) and *Runaway Jury* (2003).

More common is the justifiable instinct among members of every creative community to channel their own convictions into their work. Gay activist Randy Shilts, for example, was encouraged to speed up the writing and release of his book defending homosexuals in the military in order to take advantage of the public debate that emerged in the early months of the Clinton administration. *Conduct Unbecoming* eventually became an important reference point on that issue.[20] On the same theme, Tony Kushner's play *Angels in America*, later converted into a 2003 HBO series, interlaces the horrors of AIDS with evocations of a complacent Reagan-era America.

For sheer innovation, the great Russian symphonist Dmitri Shostakovich deserves special credit. His stormy Fifth Symphony speaks to its listeners in an ironic subtextual code. Under pressure from the political and music bureaucracies that dominated Soviet arts in the 1930s, the composer apparently used this symphony as a response to criticism that his music was too dour and "modern." Much of the work develops a deliberately forced optimism that brilliantly mocks the music that the Soviet establishment wished that he would write. The result is a romantic symphony in meltdown, with marches that are grotesquely heroic and "pretty" themes that sound vaguely dissonant. Perhaps only Shostakovich could have converted the negative forces of persecution into something so vibrant.[21]

Content as the Reconstruction of the Political Past

Another kind of political content flows from the work of artists and writers intent on re-creating a past event with political significance. Painters, illustrators, and even stained glass artisans working in the great medieval cathedrals of Europe were perhaps the first narrators of events deemed important to a community. Then as now, official benefactors with clear propagandistic goals frequently determined their subjects. A beautiful frieze in the Capitol rotunda in Washington, for example, presents idyllic scenes of early American history. The unbroken ring just under the dome's tall windows holds Constantino Brumidi's continuing narrative of Indians who are noble and agreeable, and settlers and conquerors who are mostly peaceful[22] (see figure 7.1). Like the massive paintings of John Trumbull also below the dome (including his iconic painting of the signing of the Declaration of Independence), this art simplifies and purifies a much more complex political past.

By contrast, modern film depictions of political history usually carry themes of corruption or malfeasance. *All the President's Men* (1976) was an effective reminder of the value of adversary journalism in the face of the official paranoia that characterized Richard Nixon's last year in office. Costa Gravas's film about a political assassination in Greece, *Z* (1969), unravels the threads of compromise and moral culpability deflected in every government's justifications of its actions. The same director followed up with *Missing* in 1982, a chilling fable about an American idealist who disappears under

Figure 7.1. "William Penn and the Indians," a section of Brumidi's Frieze in the Rotunda of the United States Capitol.
Source: Architect of the Capitol, "Art of the Capitol Complex," http://www.aoc.gov/cc/art/rotunda/frieze/william.cfm (accessed June 7, 2006).

mysterious circumstances. Told from the perspective of the missing man's relatives who travel to South America to find him, the film captures what headlines usually miss: temporizing functionaries within the American community who seem too comfortable with corrupt right-wing regimes. Along with *The Quiet American* (2002), *Syriana* (2005), and similar films, these stories function as alternate narratives about how life on the ground differs from lofty dictates issued from the world's capitals. The best political films are cautionary tales against judging governments only by their official stories.

Because of the timidity of the major television networks, direct portrayals of momentous political struggles are rare.[23] The case of CBS's film *The Reagans* is illustrative. Slated to originally air on the network in 2003, the four-hour, $16 million film was pulled from the schedule by CBS chairman Leslie Moonves, who said it "did not present a balanced portrayal" of its subjects.[24] Balance is a curious standard to impose on any fully rounded narrative, even about actual events. But the larger problem seems to have been complaints from keepers of the flame. By all accounts, the actor James Brolin captured Reagan's style and was—according to one critic—respectful of the character.[25] But conservatives complained and threatened boycotts, noting the criticism implied by the portrayal of the president as indifferent to the growing AIDS crisis in the United States. Like the old Soviet apparatchiks who entombed Lenin in the Kremlin wall, they sought to impose their own fantasies about the president, limiting the risks of narrative disfigurement. CBS succumbed, eventually moving the film into less visible precincts of the Showtime Channel.

Both direct advocacy and historical recreation are the easiest kinds of political content to observe. But a third category is of special importance when looking at the products of popular culture.

Content Portraying the Just and Unjust Distribution of Power

From Karl Marx to contemporary writers such as Robert Bellah,[26] politics makes sense largely in terms of the quality of the relationships that exist between members or groups within society. Marx, for example, was preoccupied with the abuse of power in uneven and exploitative hierarchical relationships.[27] Such power may be financial, involving an organization's or individual's ability to influence the actions of others. It may also be legal, as when judges, legislators, and the police are vested with authority to defend governmental edicts. In either case, prestige or legitimacy flows *to* some groups and *away* from others. Films or novels that portray individuals as prospering or withering communicate a great deal about the social distribution of power. Themes of class have been treated in film classics adapted from evocative novels such as John Steinbeck's *The Grapes of Wrath* (1940), E. M. Forster's *Howards End* (1992), and Patricia Highsmith's *The Talented Mr. Ripley* (1999). Those that have lifted the veil of race in America have also had their own successes. Any list is arbitrary, but it might include insightful films such as *To Kill a Mockingbird* (1962), *Do the Right Thing* (1989), *Mississippi Masala* (1991), and *Smoke Signals* (1998) (see table 7.1). Indeed, in the recent past, Hollywood has arguably done a better job of focusing on race and its hidden injuries than most presidents.

With regard to relations between the sexes, women in film and fiction frequently seem to change to win the approval of successful men. Narrative almost always carries the promise of the transformation of a pivotal character. But should that transformation necessarily be accommodation?

Consider the cultural-political meanings embedded in countless Cinderella or Pygmalion fantasies.[28] In Garry Marshall's popular 1990 film, *Pretty Woman*, Julia Roberts's prostitute is transformed by her contact with Richard Gere's accomplished businessman. It is a variation found in hundreds of versions of a winning Hollywood formula, including *Sabrina* (1954, remade in 1995), *Bridget Jones's Diary* (2001), and *The Wedding Date* (2005). Each performs the sly cinematic trick of emotionally loading the deck in favor of a dependent female character. The audience is drawn in to identify with the attractive women cast in the pivotal title roles. But their fates are usually in the hands of more distracted or controlling males. In relational terms, it is the women who must do most of the learning and growing. It is also largely the men who are given the power to validate their worth.

Table 7.1. Explorations of Social and Political Issues in 2004 Films: A Sampling

Film	*Setting*	*Number of Theaters**	*Issue*
Vera Drake	1950s England	95	A kindly neighborhood woman helps others end their unwanted pregnancies, running afoul of the law
Fahrenheit 9/11	Documentary using news footage and interviews	2,004	Michael Moore's stinging polemic against the war and foreign policies of President George W. Bush gained notoriety before the 2004 elections
Hotel Rwanda	Rwanda, 1994	824	An account of the mass genocide against Africa's Tutsi tribe in the absence of significant attempts by world powers to stop it
Million Dollar Baby	Woman boxer in contemporary America	3,035	A three-way character study that gives dignity to the idea of assisted suicide
The Sea Inside	Contemporary Spain	53	The story of quadriplegic who seeks assisted suicide and wins support from others
The Passion of the Christ	Graphic portrayal of the sadism of crucifixion	3,408	Reportedly reedited to soften the idea of Jewish culpability in the death of Christ
Control Room	Documentary about cable news service Al Jazeera during the Iraq war	74	Suggests different realities as seen by a non-Western news source allegedly targeted by the American military

Source: Screen data taken from Internet Movie Database, http://us.imdb.com.
*Number of theaters showing film during best week of run, United States.

As Exhibit A, there is Bridget Jones's terminally unstable life. In this satire of modern obsessions, audiences are meant to want the endearing character created by Renée Zellweger to succeed: to find herself and to find the man that will give her life meaning. In voice-over diary entries that make up much of the first installment, she vows to get her life "on track" while still dreaming about men that will cause her grief: "Equally important: will find nice sensible boyfriend and stop forming romantic attachments to any of the following: alcoholics, workaholics, sexaholics, commitment-phobics, peeping toms, megalomaniacs, emotional fuckwits, or perverts. Will especially stop fantasizing about a particular person who embodies all these things."[29] Many stories in this genre play like male fantasy films of the 1950s and 1960s, when women were similarly portrayed as objects to be captured by strong protecting men (as in the continuing James Bond franchise). Colin Firth's Mark Darcy offers a cautious stability that seems the right antidote to Bridget Jones's chaotic life. He is by no stretch a better person. But we are meant to cheer for the salvation of women at the hands of such "centered" and successful men. Hollywood actresses who made their careers playing tough-minded women in the 1940s (i.e., Katharine Hepburn, Barbara Stanwyck, Carole Lombard, etc.) would have cringed at the empty vessels that their modern counterparts have been asked to create. The conferring of power or powerlessness in many forms of art can be a significant form of indirect political advocacy.

CULTURE WARS: THE POTENCY OF NARRATIVE

Much of our public discourse is centered on issues that make up battle lines in the nation's ongoing "culture wars." A major cause of these "wars" is the recognition that the organs of popular culture and the mass media have the power to define what kind of society we are or want to be. In this view, consciousness *is* reality, and the media hold most of the cards in offering perspectives we are likely to internalize. To simplify, conservatives who sit on what James Davison Hunter calls the "orthodox" side of this conflict are largely energized by the belief that media outlets should project positive, prosocial, "mainstream" values emphasizing personal responsibility and respect for traditional Judeo-Christian beliefs.[30] The counterweight is a modernist impulse to embrace secularism and experimentation in the arts and media, as well as a general tolerance for social diversity.

These two views represent nothing less than different worldviews: different assumptions about what constitutes moral authority and "progress" in a complex society. In the orthodox view, one's character is capable of being assessed and judged, because it either conforms to or fails to meet the essences of what it means to live a virtuous life. By contrast, secular "progressives" in these battles are likely to accept variations of conduct as merely human extensions of the natural pluralism that one expects to find in a complex world.[31] We see these different perspectives played out in response to Supreme Court rulings on school prayer, abortion, and gay rights, among many other issues (see table 7.2). And they are fed from an old impulse to define those at the margins of mainstream values as less worthy of having their stories dramatized. According to Todd Gitlin:

> Citizens of the United States have been given to purification crusades from the moment there was a United States to purify. . . . In the Alien and Sedition Acts of 1798, the nativist upsurges of the 1840s, and many subsequent classification movements, those who have imagined themselves to be *real* Americans, normal Americans, have declared that various groups of abnormal or hyphenated Americans threaten the integrity of the nation.[32]

To be sure, the idea of the culture wars oversimplifies, but it points to the reasons that the entertainment media have become so controversial as vehicles of public discourse.

Thomas Frank notes that the orthodox side of the culture war is energized by what he calls "backlash culture." One looks around and finds alien atti-

Table 7.2. Representative Milestones in America's Ongoing Culture Wars

1963	Supreme Court bans prayer in public schools.
1973	Court's *Roe v. Wade* affirms legality of abortion.
1980	Supreme Court bans posting of Ten Commandments in schools.
1990	Cincinnati museum director is prosecuted for "pandering obscenity" in Mapplethorpe exhibit.
1993	Conservative members of Congress attempt to end funding for the National Endowment for the Arts and the Corporation for Public Broadcasting.
1995	Under criticism, the Smithsonian Institution withdraws plan to show effects of the A bomb on Hiroshima in a fiftieth anniversary exhibit.
1997	Southern Baptists boycott Disney for the company's gay-friendly policies.
1999	Senate begins trial of Bill Clinton for high crimes and misdemeanors.
	Kansas School Board "balances" the teaching of evolution in the state's science classes with "intelligent design" theories.
2000	Boy Scouts ban gays from organization.
2002	Oscar-winning film *Bowling for Columbine* focuses attention on the National Rifle Association and America's gun obsession.
2003	Supreme Court overturns all state sodomy laws, and it bans "moral disapproval" as reason to regulate intimate behavior.
	Massachusetts Supreme Court rules favorably on gay marriage rights.
2005	Responding to White House and congressional pressure, PBS curtails "left-leaning" show and gives news program to conservative analysts.

tudes as reasons to define a different self. In a perversion of the simplest form of identification, we find meaning in *what we are not*. "People in suburban Kansas City vituperate against the sinful cosmopolitan elite of New York and Washington, D.C.; people in rural Kansas vituperate against the sinful cosmopolitan elite of Topeka and suburban Kansas City."[33] The point of this backlash, he argues, is not necessarily to impose a single vision on the rest of the culture "but to take offense."

> Indignation is the great aesthetic principle of backlash culture; voicing the fury of the imposed-upon is to the backlash what the guitar solo is to heavy metal. Indignation is the privileged emotion, the magic moment that brings a consciousness of rightness and determination to persist. Conservatives often speak of their first bout of indignation as a sort of conversion experience, a quasi-religious revelation.[34]

It remains for us to look at a number of issues that flow from this cultural fault line. The sections that follow offer glimpses of several areas of controversy relevant to the focus of this chapter, including fear of internal subversion of entertainment from the political left; resistance to the idea of government support for arts organizations; concern about "antisocial" content in film, television, and music; and suspicions that media decision makers on the nation's coasts have too much power.

Hollywood and the Idea of Hidden Subversion

The oft-quoted maxim of Samuel Goldwyn that "messages are for Western Union" has been repeated by many producers who want to emphasize entertainment as their solitary goal. But even a fast take on key moments in the history of the film industry raises doubts that Goldwyn was expressing anything more than a wish. Among other things, as a Jew and as one of the pivotal figures of early Hollywood, he had reasons to be concerned about public suspicions that popular film entertainment was the perfect environment for planting the seeds of alien belief. The creative entrepreneurs who developed many of the early studios were Jews of recent European ancestry. Louis B. Mayer (MGM), William Fox (20th Century Fox), Carl Laemmle (Universal), and Adolph Zukor (Paramount) were only the most visible early pioneers. As Neil Gabler has pointed out, they shared backgrounds that excluded them and their families from the best WASP American country clubs, the most prestigious city leagues, and the most sought-out private schools and universities.[35] They were victims of not only a quiet anti-Semitism but also nativist suspicions about their European roots. Combine widespread prejudices against Jews and foreigners with the pervasive sense that entertainment could be a vehicle for indoctrination, and the mixture could be volatile. Worriers in Congress, churches, and the press agitated for the protection of American values against the ideas of outsiders.

A related fear was that hidden messages could be smuggled into films consumed by impressionable younger viewers. Immediately after World War II, when the nation's attention shifted to "leftist" writers and directors, some could manage to find even Russian Communists as the agents for all kinds of liberal activism.[36]

One of the interesting things about fantasies of thought control is that they are paradoxically fed by the absence of hard evidence. Add in the reality that many in Hollywood happily joined many left-wing groups, and somehow it made sense that foreigners could be intent on turning Los Angeles into Moscow on the Pacific. Former Screen Actor's Guild president Ronald Reagan was certain of a Soviet plot to dominate labor unions in the film industry. Relying in part on the dubious work of the California Senate's Committee on Un-American Activities, he noted in 1965 that "the Communists . . . used minor jurisdictional disputes as excuses for their scheme. Their aim was to gain economic control of the motion picture industry in order to finance their activities and subvert the screen for their propaganda."[37]

At least on the surface, there is something to be said for the possibility that propaganda perhaps never works more effectively than when it appears in the benign costume of "entertainment." When we think that we are "just" being entertained, our defenses and critical judgments are probably less alert. But as a nation, we tend to overstate the effects of persuasive messages and the arsenals of those who seek our agreement. The concepts of "brainwashing" and "subliminal" (subconscious) persuasion, for example, appeal to us as the plausible outcomes of extensive market research. We tend to assume incorrectly that the accumulated wisdom of the psychology and the social sciences has provided ways to short-circuit what are in reality the surprisingly resilient defenses that exist within us. The idea of easy manipulation of the masses is also aided by self-help industries and advertising agencies, which have a professional interest in presenting themselves as efficient persuaders worthy of their high fees.

The reality, of course, is far more complex. In very simple terms, attitude change is difficult to achieve, even in very well-crafted messages and regardless of whether the appeals are rational or effectively needs based.[38] There can be no doubt that any message or medium that is a constant part of someone's life can produce new or altered attitudes. But anyone who has tried to talk a friend out of smoking or some other self-evidently harmful behavior knows how easily even the best appeals can be ignored.

The point here is not to dismiss the idea that "political" content can be communicated or advocated in the media. But it is worthwhile to remember that the fear of conversion to radical causes probably owes more to the imagination than to hard facts.

Federal Funding for the Arts and Television

The year 1989 turned out to be a pivotal one in the simmering public debate about the role of government in the funding of art and popular entertainment. More than anything else, one work triggered a public brawl about the increasing use of tax dollars to support artists, galleries, orchestras, single performers, and public television programming. However atypical it was, the focus was on a single photograph by Andres Serrano called "Piss Christ," featuring the image of a dime-store plastic crucifix in a container of the artist's urine. Serrano had received a $15,000 grant from a regional group, the Southwestern Center for Contemporary Art, which had itself acquired partial funding from the National Endowment for the Arts (NEA).

Robert Hughes notes that Serrano's work represented a long-established tradition in modern art of using blasphemy to comment on the cheapening of sacred icons.[39] But when the photo traveled to Richmond, Virginia, along with other winners selected by the regional association, it attracted the attention of a self-styled lobbyist for more wholesome media, the Reverend Donald Wildmon. The result was a firestorm. Wildmon's American Family Association had already appointed itself as one of the keepers of the nation's moral values. The organization had received notoriety for its attempts to boycott the sponsors of television programs thought to contain more sex or violence than was good for the American public. It took little time to establish a letter-writing campaign to the media, other conservative religious organizations, and Congress.

In the Senate, the venerable Jesse Helms took up the issue. With a recent history of controversy against funding exhibits that included "degenerate works"—including Robert Mapplethorpe's photographs—Helms nearly succeeded in winning support for a congressional mandate against federal funding of "obscene" material that "denigrates, debases, or reviles a person."[40]

The presence of Serrano's and Mapplethorpe's photos served as a flashpoint in the culture war. However isolated they were from the hundreds of community organizations quietly receiving support for children's television programs, dance, classical and jazz performances, and more traditional art, the NEA came to represent for many conservatives the corruption of culture by a federally supported elite. "Is this how you want your tax dollars spent?" asked the American Family Association in full-page newspaper ads.

Public financing for diverse forms of culture came slowly to the United States, years after it had been a common feature in most European nations.

The NEA was brought into existence in 1965 with a modest $8 million allocation. By 1991, that sum had swelled to $175 million, dispersed throughout the United States to support national and regional efforts in music, dance, art, and drama. Although attacks by Helms and Wildmon made it seem otherwise, the NEA followed a generally safe pattern similar to what had been done at the Corporation for Public Broadcasting (CPB), focusing its support on enterprises that rarely challenged conventional sensibilities.

The CPB was established by the Johnson administration in 1967 to foster arts and public affairs programming that the commercial networks did not want to produce. Today, along with corporate and foundation contributions, the CPB uses a crazy quilt of funding to support program production carried by PBS. The network receives approximately $300 million a year in federal funds.[41]

PBS faces increasing pressure from Congress to support programs from what Bill Moyers has called the "ideological warriors" of the right.[42] For years, Moyers himself incurred the ire of congressional conservatives as the host of PBS's provocative newsmagazine, *Now*. The hour-long look at public affairs from the progressive journalist was a good example of the original idea behind PBS as an alternative network. But after Moyers's retirement in 2004, *Now* was reduced to a half hour, and it became surrounded by programs given to conservative pundits who already had shows on the commercial news channels.[43] All the while, the network once known for taking risks turned to corporate underwriters to support programs that—with a few exceptions, such as *Frontline*, *Independent Lens*, and *P.O.V.*—rarely went beyond "zero sum," "he said/they said" journalism.[44]

The NEA and the CPB continue to exist on an unstable bed of financial quicksand. Americans have a tradition of thinking of art as a distinct arena that should be separate from politics. For those on the orthodox side of the cultural divide, less government and lower taxation are always preferable to the reverse. They have an ingrained suspicion of government and agencies as tools of "progressive" social engineering. Moreover, there is no established tradition of public patronage for the arts in the United States, as there has been in many countries in Europe. French and Italian opera audiences expect state and regional support for major companies; leaders can get themselves into serious trouble over the *neglect* of appointments and funds to performing groups. By contrast, cuts to their American counterparts are hardly noticed.

Life for those who must search for funding is made even tougher when federal money functions to "seed" but not fully support exhibits and programs. Public money frequently pays for part of the costs of mounting performances, exhibits, and broadcasts. But the private sector remains an important—if generally a conservative—influence on much content. As Hughes notes:

> Corporate underwriting has produced some magnificent results for American libraries, museums, ballets, theaters and orchestras. . . . But . . . [the] corporations' underwriting money comes out of their promotion budgets and—not unreasonably, since their goal is to make money—they want to be associated with popular, prestigious events. It's no trick to get Universal Widget to underwrite a Renoir show, or one of the PBS nature series (six hours of granola TV, with bugs copulating to Mozart). But try them with newer, more controversial, or demanding work and watch the faces in the boardroom drop.[45]

The Imposition of a Bicoastal Liberal Bias

The editors of a book described as "a reference guide to media bias" write that "almost all of the Hollywood elite come from cosmopolitan areas, especially California and the Boston-Washington corridor. Very few . . . have roots in middle America."[46] This reflects an old but common complaint that decision makers in the influential entertainment and news media exist in locations that represent limited geographic regions and "liberal" states of mind. Hollywood and New York, the argument runs, are perhaps least likely to reflect the true American zeitgeist, yet they serve as the creative centers for most of our popular media.[47] The programming decisions of the television networks, for example, are made by entertainment and news division chiefs whose offices look out on what is for many Americans the foreign territory of midtown

"Viewers should be advised: the following debate on public funding for the arts contains violence and adult language."

Manhattan. In perfect symmetry, those decisions are often executed on the other coast with its own collection of Malibu exotics.

Without a doubt, actors and others in the entertainment industry sometimes seem to be occupying a very different planet. Not only do the supermarket tabloids remind us of their abnormal appetites and habits, but there is an imprecise but palpable sense that their backgrounds and their chosen line of work have put them *out* of touch with America's geographic and ideological heartland.[48] To many, the polychromatic milieu of Southern California is less centered on the older virtues that are still thought to dominate the vast "fly-over" states between the two great coasts: that hard work is its own reward, that God still matters, and that the family ought to remain at the center of American life. Conservative critic Michael Medved has captured many of the familiar strands of this cultural split:

- Our fellow citizens cherish the institution of marriage and consider religion an important priority in life; but the entertainment industry promotes every form of sexual adventurism and regularly ridicules religious believers as crooks or crazies.
- In our private lives, most of us deplore violence and feel little sympathy for the criminals who perpetuate it; but movies, TV, and popular music all revel in graphic brutality, glorifying vicious and sadistic characters who treat killing as a joke.
- Americans are passionately patriotic, and consider themselves enormously lucky to live here; but Hollywood conveys a view of the nation's history, future, and major institutions that is dark, cynical, and often nightmarish.
- Nearly all parents want to convey to their children the importance of self-discipline, hard work, and decent manners; but the entertainment media celebrate vulgar behavior, contempt for all authority, and obscene language—which is inserted even in "family fare" where it is least expected.[49]

It certainly is true that no one will ever lose an argument asserting that the entertainment industries produce tons of cultural trash.[50] But beyond the obvious, some of this kind of criticism is simple-minded. Few would claim that those making management and creative decisions in the film or television business are "just" average Americans, either demographically or in terms of their training or motivations. Yet the leaders in most industries or occupations would fail the same test. Those who rise to the top in most highly competitive areas of American life carry certain advantages and attitudes. In the entertainment and news businesses, as in others, they are whiter, more male, more educated, and more urban than the population as a whole.[51] And in large numbers, they do indeed tend to be concentrated on the nation's east and west coasts.

But it is also easy to overestimate the idea of bicoastalism. That was more true in, say, the 1950s, than in the twenty-first century. For example, Atlanta is home for the largest American television news organization, CNN. Los Angeles must now compete with Florida, South Carolina, and Toronto for many film projects. And somehow those who have allegedly faced down the heathens of journalism in the New York–Washington corridor have still prospered, including those at the *Wall Street Journal*, the *New York Post*, Fox News, MSNBC, the *Washington Times*, the *National Review, Commentary*, and the *Weekly Standard*. Moreover, it takes a special kind of reverse provincialism to claim that residents of Peoria, Illinois—to pick a famous measure of normalcy—still live in a distinctly different kind of cultural environment than the citizens of New York or Philadelphia. Residents in each city may occupy slightly different geographic and ethnic environments. But they are apt to listen to the same music and news, use the same Internet sources, and see the same films, books, and television shows. Moreover, critics like Medved miss the irony of recent data suggesting that millions of Americans from the heartland apparently are among the most ardent consumers of the salacious content that he decries.[52]

The paradox here is that each side flirts with the abandonment of their ideological roots in the ongoing values debate. Conservatives often attack media corporations for output that corrupts—a view that is at odds with what one would expect to be a baseline faith in the marketplace and corporate freedom. For their part, progressives and liberals tend to be critical of the tastes and preferences of the "ordinary" working people they are normally inclined to champion.

In the end, it is difficult to sustain the view that anyone working in the audience-driven mass media can survive if they are isolated culturally and out of touch with the consumers everywhere whom they seek to reach.

Hegemony in Prime Time: The Triumph of the Incrementalists

If the problem of a "bicoastal liberalism" remains as largely the critique of political conservatives, it can in some ways be paired with a different failure of popular narration alleged by those who might classify themselves as more liberal. Advocates of Antonio Gramsci's original ideas about hegemony—Edward Herman and Noam Chomsky,[53] Michael Parenti,[54] Todd Gitlin, and others—argue that it is in the nature of media organizations to protect themselves and to temporize when dealing with unpopular change. As Gitlin notes, "Those who rule the dominant institutions secure their power in large measure directly and indirectly, by impressing their definitions of the situation upon those they rule, and, if not usurping the whole ideological space, still significantly limiting what is thought throughout the society."[55] The organizational impulse for self-preservation is far more potent than the value of exploring rapid change. There are greater risks in thrusting new perspectives or radical proposals on audiences and advertisers, who largely want predictable forms of entertainment and versions of news that will not disturb settled ways of thinking.[56]

It is useful to think of hegemony as occurring at three levels. *Linguistic* hegemony is a preference for labels and descriptors that sanction the interests of the powerful. *News* hegemony offers interpretations of events in terms of causes and effects that are already sanctioned by mainstream use. And *narrative* hegemony prefers plot devices that define problems as "personal" rather than rooted in deeper social causes.

Regarding linguistic hegemony, Rod Hart makes the point that language sometimes "uses us." "Some of our greatest battles," he states, "are now fought on the field of language, where 'essentially contested concepts' divide people from one another."[57] Should we have a "war on terrorism" or a concerted police action to control it? Was the 2004 presidential election—decided with a close Bush victory in Ohio—a "mandate" for the victor, George W. Bush, or a signal of deep American divisions? Are certain Iraqis or Palestinians "terrorists" and "insurgents" or soldiers in a civil war? (And should the Arab news channel Al Jazeera call them "martyrs"?) Was the war in Iraq an act of "liberation" or "occupation"? What was represented as a "coalition" of various national forces was—from a numbers point of view—at best a generous name for an essentially American operation. And must the United States purge from other nations their own "weapons of mass destruction," overlooking the fact that it owns and sells them itself?

In each case, the words in quotation marks carry a hegemonic presumption. Their use in the heavy traffic of news and political rhetoric makes deep tracks from which it can be difficult to free oneself.

Hegemonic responses within the second form of news focus on ideas sanctioned by regional preferences or familiar ways of thinking.[58] In Robert Entman's words, "The most inherently powerful frames are those fully congruent with schemas *habitually* used by most members of society."[59] We do not welcome changes to the old and familiar topography of our ideas and ideologies. The 1988 shooting down of an Iranian passenger airliner by the U.S. military, for example, was framed largely as an unfortunate *accident*, never drifting into the language of murder or moral culpability.[60] The Bush administration's frame of reference for invading Iraq in 2003—the existence of weapons of mass destruction—was largely accepted at face value by the American press, in sharp departure to the broader reporting and skepticism in much of the rest of the world. At the time, the question of whether the United

States *should* invade Iraq drifted to the margins of most news accounts, largely replaced with various forms of the query "How long will it take to win?" Similarly, attempts by some reporters to draw attention to the role of Saudi Arabia after 9/11 went largely unnoticed, in part because American strategic interests in the kingdom discouraged official recognition of important Saudi connections.[61]

The subject of hegemonic journalism always raises the question "Did we miss the real issue or story?" A nation's news culture must have a broad enough frame to accept views that challenge conventional thinking. For example, why did it take so long for journalists to find the abuses of Abu Ghraib prison in Iraq, with a trail of evidence available for months? Or, more broadly, why was the United States taken by surprise by the collapse of the Soviet Union in 1988 or the lethal attacks in New York and Washington on 9/11? And where was the systematic television coverage of the rise of the European Union as a political powerhouse, with an economy that is now larger than the United States'?

A hegemonic response to events can sometimes be *no* response. Consider the subject of national child poverty rates, a topic that many consider to be a reasonable measure of a society's success in serving its own citizens. A search of LexisNexis academic or newspaper articles touching on "child poverty, the United States," yielded twelve for a one-year period ending on July 1, 2005. On the United Nations' scale of child poverty rates in the world's twenty-six richest nations, the United States was only one step from the bottom—next to Mexico—with a rate of over one in five.[62] Denmark was at the top, with a little more than two in one hundred. That is interesting news, even if it went mostly unnoticed in the nation that incorrectly boasts the world's highest standard of living. In fact, only *one* of the articles dealing with child poverty as a significant problem was from an American source. All of the rest were from Canada, New Zealand, and the United Kingdom, in spite of the LexisNexis database being skewed in favor of American newspapers.[63]

Hegemony of television and film entertainment—our third form—can occur in a variety of ways. We will focus briefly just on the common tendency in popular media to highlight dramatic rather than systemic solutions to conflict.

Prime-time and studio-produced films are usually populated by apolitical figures with little tolerance for negotiated solutions to problems—a significant dismissal of the way the world actually works. In Hollywood versions of life, conflict is usually resolved through coercion, force, or the convenient death of a villain.[64] The stuff of genuine conflict resolution—legislating, mediating, negotiating, or persuading—is underrepresented.[65] If not through force, characters typically deal with problems with spouses or families by summoning various forms of internal courage, rather than by requesting help from service agencies or government programs. With some exceptions, prime-time drama prefers the police to social workers, venal businessmen to effective political leaders, peers to teachers, and lawyers to therapists. One could spend a lifetime consuming prime-time television and never know that battered women sometimes escape to shelters or that 90 percent of crimes against people or property are plea-bargained and never go to trial.

When civic life is addressed at all in the melodramas of our times, it is likely to be more cartoonish than transformational. In films, local elections are more likely to resemble a parade of harmless eccentrics than a group of dedicated volunteers (*Welcome to Mooseport*, 2004). Social activism is similarly neutered by caricature: with flaky but harmless antiwar activists (*Forrest Gump*, 1994), one-issue zealots (*Citizen Ruth*, 1996), or unhinged feminists and environmentalists (*The First Wives Club*, 1996; *I Heart Huckabees*, 2004).

Todd Gitlin has documented this temporizing in a study of the decision-making processes involved in formulating a network prime-time program. He received permission to follow the decisions of the producers of a family situation comedy under development for ABC. The pilot episode of *American Dream* that Barney Rosenzweig and others were creating was intended to be a generally frank but funny look at a family that moved back to Chicago from the suburbs. Their goal was to develop episodes in which the chemistry of the city interacts with the fears and prejudices of the Novak family, an idea that came to Rosenzweig during a football season in which he went from the safety of his home to the tougher Los Angeles neighborhood where USC played its home games. Among other plots, one of the first involved the resentments of Hispanic and African American neighbors, who feared the gentrification of their working-class neighborhood.

But the producer soon ran into trouble with the network. ABC wanted a host of changes to soften the few hard edges that existed in early scripts. The network sought to make the characters of the Novak children more likeable and Donna Novak a less outspoken and self-assured woman. References to birth control pills would also have to go, as would exterior shots of the graffiti-filled Chicago neighborhood. And the original idea of doing a show about middle-class Americans dealing with the issues of the inner city was largely abandoned. As one network executive argued, "at least for the first six episodes," the show would have to play it safer.[66]

That was a number of years ago. One could argue that entertainment in the postmillennium age of three-hundred-channel television comes a bit closer to reflecting the diversity of "real" life. After all, the iconic HBO series *The Sopranos* has both violence *and* therapists, melding traditional Hollywood crime noir with authentic scenes of family dysfunctionality. The uniformity of narrow choices implied in classic hegemony theory would seem to be undermined by more outlets doing more specialized and less formulaic content.

Even so, anyone who surveys the mainstream "products" of the film and television industries will strain to find screenplays that effectively treat the social and economic realities that exist in contemporary America. As such, they will miss the opportunity to fully discover what they need to know about their own society.

CONCLUSION

We have touched on a number of themes tied to the general proposition that there is no distinct threshold that separates the political from the merely "artistic." Our starting points entailed a number of key assumptions, including the basic observation that much of what gives us pleasure in our lives involves portraiture and storytelling. Stories inherently assert values and pass judgments. They give us efficient ways to view ourselves and our choices.

Part of this chapter's argument is that narrative can be political in at least three senses. Artists may take it upon themselves to participate in the civil affairs of the nation by using their work to participate in public debate on an issue. In art as in life, struggles against oppression and injustice are enduring themes. In a second sense, art is political when it re-creates or offers new interpretations of historical events. As the controlling ideas of a culture shift, new narratives replace the old, sometimes converting heroes to villains and fools to victims. Finally, the creators of the representational arts probably cannot avoid at least indirect political commentary in the ways they represent power relationships. Narrative is always its own form of social critique. The expressive arts frequently convert individuals into types: representations of villainy or victimhood, symbols to be admired or maligned.

We also noted that public organizations in these fields are sometimes at the center of debates about how they should be financed and how they and their commercial counterparts should be judged. The culture war that has raged in the United States over the last several decades has increasingly pitted various segments of society against each other over increasingly different conceptions of what American society represents. Sometimes simplified as a debate between "traditionalists" and "progressives," the struggle hinges on a number of differences that yield better questions than answers. Should the arts protect traditional "mainstream" values or challenge them? Should federal tax money be used for arts activities and, in the process, lend legitimacy to groups such as homosexuals who may use their art to critique the prejudices and values of the larger culture? And what is the responsibility of the Hollywood dream machine to the rest of society?

These questions are easier to ask than answer. But it is appropriate that we end a study of political media with questions. Lofty declarations have a way of making certain attributes seem more predictive than they sometimes are. However our queries eventually get answered, it is obvious that future definitions of political discourse will have to include a place for the diverse products of the arts.

NOTES

1. George Gerbner quoted in S. Robert Lichter, Linda Lichter, and Stanley Rothman, *Watching America* (New York: Prentice Hall, 1991), 1.

2. Liesbet van Zoonen, *Entertaining the Citizen* (Lanham, Md.: Rowman & Littlefield, 2005), 15.

3. H. C. Robbins Landon, *Beethoven: A Documentary Study* (New York: Macmillan, 1974), 93–94.

4. David E. Pitt, "Retracing Diego Rivera's American Odyssey," *New York Times*, August 28, 1988, 29–30.

5. Frank Rich, "The Year of Living Indecently," *New York Times*, January 7, 2005, sec 2, 1, 7.

6. I am indebted to the Internet Movie Database (http://us.imdb.com/) for the basic film data cited in this chapter.

7. Hugh Dalziel Duncan, *Communication and Social Order* (New York: Oxford University Press, 1962), 80.

8. Richard Campbell, "Securing the Middle Ground: Reporter Formulas in *60 Minutes*," *Critical Studies in Mass Communication*, December 1987, 325–50.

9. Beth Austin, "Pretty Worthless," *Washington Monthly*, May 1991, 33.

10. Benjamin DeMott, "In Hollywood, Class Doesn't Put Up Much of a Struggle," *New York Times*, January 20, 1991, sec. 2, 1, 22.

11. Jeff Silverman, "TV's Creators Face a New Caution," *New York Times*, December 8, 1991, sec. 2, 1, 31.

12. A contrasting view is offered by the conservative thinker Irving Kristol, who argues that part of what is wrong with America is that it has produced postmodern art that is "politically charged" and "utterly contemptuous of the notion of educating the tastes and refining the aesthetic sensibilities of the citizenry. Its goal, instead, is deliberately to outrage those tastes and to trash the very idea of an 'aesthetic sensibility.'" Quoted in Michael Medved, *Hollywood vs. America: Popular Culture and the War on Traditional Values* (New York: HarperCollins, 1992), 26.

13. See Robert Hughes, *Culture of Complaint: The Fraying of America* (New York: Oxford University Press, 1993), 174–82.

14. For a comprehensive survey of many perspectives within this debate, see Richard Bolton, ed., *Culture Wars: Documents from Recent Controversies in the Arts* (New York: New Press, 1992).

15. Hughes, *Culture of Complaint*, 176–77.

16. See Jessica Werner, "Tim Robbins Pours His Anger into an Anti-war Play—Just Don't Call It Political Theater," *San Francisco Chronicle*, December 6, 2003, http://www.sfgate.com/cgi-bin/article.cgi?f=/c/a/2003/12/06/DDGVG3GCCU1.DTL (accessed May 25, 2006).

17. Interestingly, the political humor from these shows and others is often quoted in the Week in Review section of the Sunday *New York Times*.

18. Kenneth Baker, "A Nightmare of an Exhibition That Really Happened," *Smithsonian Magazine*, July 1991, 86–95.

19. The story of Hearst's attempts to suppress the film is interestingly retold in the PBS documentary "The Battle over Citizen Kane," *The American Experience*, 2000.

20. Randy Shilts, *Conduct Unbecoming: Lesbians and Gays in the U.S. Military* (New York: St. Martin's, 1993). See also Kevin Buckley, "There Was Not Much Worse You Could Call a Man," *New York Times Book Review*, May 30, 1993, 2.

21. See what is usually accepted as Shostokovich's own account in Solomon Volkov, *Testimony: The Memoirs of Dmitri Shostokovich*, trans. Antonina W. Bouis (New York: Harper & Row, 1979), 183.

22. See Francis V. O'Connor, "Symbolism in the Rotunda," http://www.access.gpo.gov/congress/senate/brumidi/Brumidi_10.pdf#search='john20trumbull%20capitol%20 (accessed May 25, 2006).

23. We are more apt to get a sideways view of the American political order from television's penchant for reenacting courtroom dramas rather than its civic affairs. In the early 1990s, there were no fewer than two television versions of the Amy Fisher story, for example, which recounted the story of a Long Island girl who tried to murder the wife of her lover. Add in television films such as *Martha Inc.: The Story of Martha Stewart* (2003), *The O. J. Simpson Story* (1995), or *The Man in the Mirror: The Michael Jackson Story* (2004), and one has a sense of the grip of celebrity culture on the public imagination.

24. Gary Levin, "CBS Drops 'Reagans' amid Furor over Bias," *USA Today*, November 4, 2003, http://usatoday.printthis.clickability.com/pt/cpt?action (March 1, 2005).

25. Alessandra Stanley, "What Hatchet Job? Reagan Movie Is Run of the Mill," *New York Times*, November 30, 2003.

26. Robert N. Bellah, Richard Madsen, William M. Sullivan, Ann Swidler, and Steven M. Tipton, *The Good Society* (New York: Knopf, 1991), 138–44.

27. These applications of Marx are well developed by Duncan, *Communication and Social Order*, 181–88.

28. These categories are suggested by Roger Ebert in *Roger Ebert's Movie Home Companion, 1992 Edition* (Kansas City: Andrews McMeel, 1991), 470.

29. "Memorable Quotes," entry for *Bridget Jones's Diary*, Internet Movie Database, http://www.imdb.com/title/tt0243155/quotes, March 3, 2005.

30. James Davison Hunter, *Culture Wars: The Struggle to Define America* (New York: Basic Books, 1991).

31. Hunter, *Culture Wars*, 126.

32. Todd Gitlin, *The Twilight of Common Dreams: Why America Is Wracked by Culture Wars* (New York: Metropolitan Books, 1995), 2.

33. Thomas Frank, *What's the Matter with Kansas?* (New York: Metropolitan Books, 2004), 35.

34. Frank, *What's the Matter with Kansas?* 121–22.

35. The studio owner's stories are brilliantly told by Neal Gabler in *An Empire of Their Own* (New York: Crown, 1988).

36. For an overview of this period, see Robert Sklar, *Movie Made America* (New York: Vintage Books, 1975), 249–68.

37. Ronald Reagan, *Where's the Rest of Me?* (New York: Karz, 1981), 159.

38. For studies on the forces working against attitude change, see Duane Wegener, Richard Petty, Natalie Smoak, and Leandre Fabrigar, "Multiple Routes to Resisting Attitude Change," in *Resistance to Persuasion*, ed. Eric Knowles and Jay Linn (Mahwah, N.J.: Erlbaum, 2004), 13–38.

39. Hughes, *Culture of Complaint*, 156.

40. Philip Brookman and Debra Singer, "Chronology," in *Culture Wars: Documents from Recent Controversies in the Arts*, ed. Richard Bolton (New York: New Press, 1992), 342–47.

41. Bill McConnell, "A $5 Billion Proposal: PBS Chief Pat Mitchell Posits Plan to Free Public Stations from Federal Funding," *Cable and Broadcasting*, June 14, 2004.

42. See Ken Auletta, "Big Bird Flies Right," *New Yorker*, June 7, 2005, 42–48.

43. The CPB's inspector general later noted that former chairman Kenneth Tomlinson had acted improperly—perhaps with direction from the White House—to recast PBS programming in a more conservative light. Stephen Labaton, "Ex-Chairman of Public Broadcasting Violated Laws, Inquiry Suggests," *New York Times*, November 16, 2005, A17.

44. Auletta, "Big Bird Flies Right," 48. See also John Tierney and Jacques Steinberg, "Conservatives and Rivals Press a Struggling PBS," *New York Times*, February 17, 2005, A1, A24.

45. Robert Hughes, "A Loony Parody of Cultural Democracy," in Bolton, *Culture Wars*, 91.

46. L. Brent Bozell III and Brent H. Baker, *And That's the Way It Isn't* (Alexandra, Va.: Media Research Center, 1990), 271–72.

47. For representative examples explicitly arguing liberal bias in the bicoastal media, see Ann Coulter and Bernard Goldberg, *Arrogance: Rescuing America from the Media Elite* (New York: Warner, 2003), and Ann Coulter, *Slander: Liberal Lies about the American Right* (New York: Three Rivers Press, 2003).

48. See, for example, Ben Stein, *The View from Sunset Boulevard* (New York: Basic Books, 1979), and Michael J. Robinson, "Prime Time Chic: Between Newsbreaks and Commercials, the Values Are L.A. Liberal," in *American Mass Media: Industries and Issues*, 3rd ed., ed. Robert Atwan, Barry Orton, and William Vesterman (New York: Random House, 1986), 360–68.

49. Michael Medved, *Hollywood vs. America: Popular Culture and the War on Traditional Values* (New York: HarperCollins, 1992), 10.

50. For a useful primer that now seems to be an understatement of the problem, see James Twitchell, *Carnival Culture: The Trashing of America* (New York: Columbia University Press, 1992).

51. American Society of Newspaper Editors, "News Staffs Shrinking While Minority Presence Grows," April 12, 2005, http://www.asne.org/index.cfm?id=5648 (accessed May 25, 2006).

52. Cynthia Tucker, "Red States Tuning in to Trash TV," *Baltimore Sun*, January 4, 2005, A11.

53. Edward S. Herman and Noam Chomsky, *Manufacturing Consent: The Political Economy of the Mass Media* (New York: Pantheon, 1988), 1–35.

54. Michael Parenti, *Make-Believe Media: The Politics of Entertainment* (New York: St. Martin's, 1992), 206–7.

55. Todd Gitlin, *The Whole World Is Watching* (Berkeley: University of California Press, 1980), 10.

56. For additional views on hegemony in news coverage, see Allan Rachlin, *News as Hegemonic Reality* (New York: Praeger, 1988), 5–29, and Eric S. Fredin, "Frame Breaking and Creativity: A Frame Database for Hypermedia News," in *Framing and Public Life: Perspectives on Media and Our Understanding of the Social World*, ed. Stephen Reese, Oscar Gandy, and August Grant (Mahwah, N.J.: Erlbaum, 2001), 269–93.

57. Roderick P. Hart, Sharon E. Jarvis, William P. Jennings, and Deborah Smith-Howell, *Political Keywords: Using Language That Uses Us* (New York: Oxford University Press, 2005), 3.

58. For an analysis of news coverage as a function of the broad tendencies of various regions, see John Pollock, *Tilted Mirrors: Media Alignment with Political Change* (Cresskill, N.J.: Hampton, in press).

59. Robert Entman, "Cascading Activation: Contesting the White House's Frame after 9/11," *Political Communication*, October 2003, 422.

60. Entman, "Cascading Activation," 423.

61. Entman, "Cascading Activation," 424–25.

62. Karen Mcveigh, "British Child Poverty Rate Doubles," *The Scotsman* (U.K.), March 2, 2005.

63. The sample period of July 1, 2004, to July 1, 2005, was drawn from LexisNexis Academic, with a base of fifty newspapers, twenty-eight of which were American.

64. For example, the badly abused wife in the film *The Rainmaker* (1997) might have sought help from support services. Instead, the film takes the more conventional, if implausible, route of having the abuser murdered and the abused wife rescued by an idealistic attorney.

65. See James Chesbro, "Communication, Values, and Popular Television Series—A Twenty-Five Year Assessment and Final Conclusions," *Communication Quarterly*, Fall, 2003, 367–418.

66. Todd Gitlin, *Inside Prime Time* (New York: Pantheon, 1983), 86–122.

Selected Bibliography

Auletta, Ken. *Backstory: Inside the Business of News*. New York: Penguin, 2003.

———. "Fortress Bush." *New Yorker*, January 19, 2004, 53–65.

———. *Three Blind Mice: How the TV Networks Lost Their Way*. New York: Random House, 1991.

Bagdikian, Ben. *The New Media Monopoly*. Boston: Beacon, 2004.

Bai, Matt. "Going Deep: With Iowa's Meta-Voters." *New York Times Magazine*, January 18, 2004, 34–39.

Baker, Kenneth. "A Nightmare of an Exhibition That Really Happened." *Smithsonian Magazine*, July 1991, 86–95.

Bellah, Robert, Richard Madsen, William M. Sullivan, Ann Swidler, and Steven M. Tipton. *The Good Society*. New York: Knopf, 1991.

Bennett, W. Lance, and Robert Entman, eds. *Mediated Politics: Communication in the Future of Democracy*. New York: Cambridge University Press, 2001.

Bettig, Ronald, and Jeanne Hall. *Big Media, Big Money*. Lanham, Md.: Rowman & Littlefield, 2003.

Bolton, Richard, ed. *Culture Wars: Documents from Recent Controversies in the Arts*. New York: New Press, 1992.

Bormann, Ernest. *The Force of Fantasy: Restoring the American Dream*. Carbondale: Southern Illinois University Press, 2001.

Boyer, Peter. *Who Killed CBS?* New York: Random House, 1988.

Braestrup, Peter. *Battle Lines: Report of the Twentieth Century Fund Task Force on the Military and the Media*. New York: Priority, 1985.

Burke, Kenneth. *Dramatism and Development*. Barre, Mass.: Clark University Press, 1972.

———. *A Rhetoric of Motives*. New York: Prentice Hall, 1953.

Burston, Jonathan. "War and the Entertainment Industries: New Research Priorities in an Era of Cyber-Patriotism." In *War and the Media: Reporting Conflict 24/7*, ed. Daya Thussu and Des Freedman. London: Sage, 2003.

"Cable and Internet Loom Large in Fragmented Political News Universe." Pew Research Center for the People and the Press, January 11, 2004. http://people-press.org/reports/print.php3?PageID=774.

"Cable TV News Investment." In *The State of the News Media 2004*, Project for Excellence in Journalism, n.d. www.stateofthemedia.org.

Campbell, Richard. "Securing the Middle Ground: Reporter Formulas in *60 Minutes*." *Critical Studies in Mass Communication* (December 1987): 325–50.

Cappella, Joseph, and Kathleen Jamieson. *Spiral of Cynicism: The Press and the Public Good*. New York: Oxford University Press, 1997.

Center for Media and Public Affairs. "Global News: TV News Coverage of Global Issues." *Media Monitor*, November–December 2002, 1–6.

"Changing Definitions of News." Project for Excellence in Journalism, March 6, 1998, http://www.journalism.org/resources/research/reports/definitions/default.asp.

Chesbro, James. "Communication, Values, and Popular Television Series—A Twenty-Five Year Assessment and Final Conclusions." *Communication Quarterly*, Fall 2003, 367–418.

Chiasson, Lloyd, Jr., ed. *The Press on Trial*. Westport Conn.: Greenwood, 1997.

Cohn, Margorie, and David Dow. *Cameras in the Courtroom: Television and the Pursuit of Justice*. Lanham, Md.: Roman & Littlefield, 2002.

Dahlberg, Lincoln. "The Internet and Democratic Discourse." *Information, Communication and Society*, December 2001, 615–33.

Danner, Mark. *Torture and Truth: America, Abu Ghraib and the War on Terror*. New York: New York Review Books, 2004.

Darr, Carol, and Julie Barko. "Under the Radar and over the Top: Online Political Videos in the 2004 Election." Institute for Politics and Democracy & the Internet, October 20, 2004. http://www.ipdi.org/UploadedFiles/web_videos.pdf.

Davidson, Roger, and Walter Oleszek. *Congress and its Members.* 7th ed. Washington, D. C.: Congressional Quarterly Press, 2000.

Dawley, Alan. *Changing the World: American Progressives in War and Revolution.* Princeton, N.J.: Princeton University Press, 2003.

Dedrowski, Karen. *Media Entrepreneurs and the Media Enterprise in the U.S. Congress.* Cresskill, N.J.: Hampton, 1996.

Denton, Robert E., Jr. *The 2004 Presidential Campaign: A Communication Perspective*. Lanham, Md.: Rowman & Littlefield, 2005.

Diamond, Edwin. *Behind the Times: Inside the* New York Times. Chicago: University of Chicago Press, 1995.

Dionne, E. J., Jr., Jean Bethke Elshtain, and Kayla M. Drogosz, eds. *One Electorate under God? A Dialogue on Religion and American Politics*. Washington, D.C.: Brookings Institution, 2004.

Donovan, Robert, and Ray Scherer. *Unsilent Revolution: Television News and American Life*. New York: Cambridge University Press, 1992.

Duncan, Hugh. *Communication and Social Order*. New York: Oxford University Press, 1962.

Edelman, Murray. *Constructing the Political Spectacle*. Chicago: University of Chicago Press, 1988.

Entman, Robert. "Cascading Activation: Contesting the White House's Frame after 9/11." *Political Communication*, October 2003, 415–32.

———. *Democracy without Citizens: The Media and the Decay of American Politics*. New York: Oxford University Press, 1989.

Epstein, Edward. *News from Nowhere*. New York: Vintage Books, 1978.

Fellows, James. *Breaking the News*. New York: Pantheon, 1996.

Fisher, Walter. *Human Communication as Narration*. Columbia: University of South Carolina Press, 1987.

Fleeson, Lucinda. "Bureau of Missing Bureaus." *American Journalism Review*, October–November 2003. http://www.ajr.org/Article.asp?id=3409.

Frank, Thomas. *What's the Matter with Kansas?* New York: Metropolitan Books, 2004.

Frankel, Max. *The Times of My Life*. New York: Random House, 1999.

Frantzich, Stephen, and John Sullivan. *The C-SPAN Revolution*. Norman: University of Oklahoma Press, 1996.

Fredin, Eric. "Frame Breaking and Creativity: A Frame Database for Hypermedia News." Pp. 263–69 in *Framing and Public Life: Perspectives on Media and Our Understanding of the Social World*, ed. Stephen Reese, Oscar Gandy. and August Grant. Mahwah, N.J.: Erlbaum, 2001.

Friedman, Thomas. *The World Is Flat.* New York: Farrar, Straus & Giroux, 2005.

Friendly, Fred. *Due to Circumstances Beyond Our Control*. New York: Vintage, 1968.

Gabler, Neil. *An Empire of Their Own*. New York: Crown, 1988.

Garment, Leonard. *Crazy Rhythm: Richard Nixon and All That Jazz.* New York: Times Books, 1997.

Gitlin, Todd. "Showtime Iraq." *The American Prospect*. November 4, 2002, 34–35.

———. *Inside Prime Time*. New York: Pantheon, 1983.

———. *The Twilight of Common Dreams: Why America Is Wracked by Culture Wars*. New York: Metropolitan Books, 1995.

———. *The Whole World Is Watching*. Berkeley: University of California Press, 1980.

Goffman, Erving. *The Presentation of Self in Everyday Life*. New York: Anchor, 1959.

Gorham, Eric. *The Theater of Politics*. Lanham, Md.: Lexington Books, 2000.

Gowing, Nik. "Journalists and War: The Troubling New Tensions Post 9/11." Pp. 231–40 in *War and the Media*, ed. Daya Thussu and Des Freedman. Thousand Oaks, Calif.: Sage, 2003.

Gray, Chris. *Cyborg Citizen*. New York: Routledge, 2001.

Gronbeck, Bruce. "Citizen Voices in Cyberpolitical Culture." address to the Rhetoric Society of America, May 2002.

Gunn, Joshua. "Refiguring Fantasy: Imagination and Its Decline in U.S. Rhetorical Studies." *Quarterly Journal of Speech*, February 2003, 41–59.

Hariman, Robert, ed. *Popular Trials*. Tuscaloosa: University of Alabama Press, 1990.

Harper, Robert. *Lincoln and the Press*. New York: McGraw-Hill, 1951.

Hart, Roderick, Sharon Jarvis, William Jennings, and Deborah Smith-Howell *Political Keywords: Using Language That Uses Us*. New York: Oxford University Press, 2005.

———. *Seducing America: How Television Charms the Modern Voter*. New York: Oxford, 1994.

———. *The Sound of Leadership: Presidential Communication in the Modern Age*. Chicago: University of Chicago Press, 1987.

Hedges, Chris. *War Is a Force That Gives Us Meaning*. New York: Public Affairs Press, 2002.

———. "The Unilaterals." *Columbia Journalism Review*, May–June 1991, 27–29.

Herman, Edward, and Noam Chomsky. *Manufacturing Consent: The Political Economy of the Mass Media*. New York: Pantheon, 1988.

Hertsgaard, Mark. *On Bended Knee: The Press and the Reagan Presidency*. New York: Schocken Books, 1989.

Hickey, Neil. "Access Denied: The Pentagon's Reporting Rules Are the Toughest Ever." *Columbia Journalism Review*, May–June 2003. http://archives.cjr.org/year/02/1hickey.asp.

Hoge, James, Jr. "Foreign News: Who Gives a Damn?" *Columbia Journalism Review*, November–December 1997, 48–52.

Hughes, Robert. *Culture of Complaint: The Fraying of America*. New York: Oxford University Press, 1993.

Hui, Janice, and Craig LaMay. "Broadcasting and the Public Interest." Pp. 29–57 in *The Business of News: A Challenge for Journalism's Next Generation*, ed. Cynthia Gorney. New York: Carnegie Corporation of New York, 2002.

Hume, Ellen. "Why the Press Blew the S&L Scandal," *New York Times*, May 24, 1990, A25.

Hunter, James Davison. *Culture Wars: The Struggle to Define America*. New York: Basic Books, 1991.

Huntington, Samuel P. "The Lonely Superpower." *Foreign Affairs*, March–April 1999.

Iyengar, Shanto. *Is Anyone Responsible?* Chicago: University of Chicago Press, 1991.

Iyengar, Shanto, and Donald R. Kinder. *News That Matters: Television and American Opinion*. Chicago: University of Chicago Press, 1987.

Jamieson, Kathleen Hall, and Joseph N. Cappella. "The Role of the Press in the Health Care Reform Debate of 1993–1994." Pp. 110–31 in *The Politics of News, the News of Politics*, ed. Doris Graber, Denis McQuail, and Pippa Norris. Washington, D.C.: CQ Press, 1998.

Jamieson, Kathleen Hall, and Paul Waldman. *The Press Effect.* New York: Oxford University Press, 2003.

Judt, Tony. "Its Own Worst Enemy." *New York Review of Books*, August 15, 2002.

———. "The New World Order." *New York Review of Books*, July 14, 2005.

Kalb, Marvin. *One Scandalous Story: Clinton, Lewinsky, and 13 Days That Tarnished American Journalism.* New York: Free Press, 2001.

Kanihan, Stacey, and Kendra Gale. "Within 3 Hours, 97 Percent Learn about 9/11 Attacks." *Newspaper Research Journal*, Winter 2003, 78–83.

Kimball, Penn. *Downsizing the News*. Washington, D.C.: Woodrow Wilson Center Press, 1994.

Klotz, Robert. *The Politics of Internet Communication*. Lanham, Md.: Rowman & Littlefield, 2004.

Knightly, Phillip. *The First Casualty*. New York: Harcourt, Brace Jovanovich, 1975.

Kumar, Martha Joynt. "The Office of Press Secretary." Pp. 224–51 in *The White House World: Transitions, Organization and Office Operations*, ed. Martha Joynt Kumar and Terry Sullivan. College Station: Texas A&M University Press, 2003.

Levin, Gary. "CBS Drops 'Reagans' amid Furor over Bias." *USA Today*, November 4, 2003. http://usatoday.printthis.clickability.com/pt/cpt?action.

Lieberman, Jethro. *The Litigious Society*. New York: Basic Books, 1981.

Lindquist, Julie. *A Place to Stand*. New York: Oxford University Press, 2002.

Lippmann, Walter. *The Public Philosophy*. Boston: Little, Brown, 1955.

Lipset, Seymour Martin. *American Exceptionalism.* New York: Norton, 1996.

Madden, Mary. "America's Online Pursuits, Summary of Findings." Pew Internet and American Life Project, December 22, 2003. http://www.pewinternet.org/reports/.asp.

Massing, Michael. *Now They Tell Us: The American Press in Iraq*. New York: New York Review of Books, 2004.

McCann, Michael, and William Haltom. "Framing the Food Fights: How Mass Media Construct and Constrict Public Interest Litigation." Unpublished paper. http://www.law.berkeley.edu/institutes/csls/McCann%20paper.pdf#search='public%20interest%20litigation.

McChesney, Robert. *The Problem of the Media: U.S. Communication Politics in the 21st Century*. New York: Monthly Review Press, 2004.

———. *Rich Media, Poor Democracy.* New York: New Press, 1999.

McCombs, Maxwell. "The Agenda Setting Approach." Pp. 121–40 in the *Handbook of Political Communication*, ed. Dan Nimmo and Keith Sanders. Beverly Hills: Sage, 1981.

Medved, Michael. *Hollywood vs. America: Popular Culture and the War on Traditional Values*. New York: HarperCollins, 1992.

Meyrowitz, Joshua. *No Sense of Place*. New York: Oxford University Press, 1985.

Mickelson, Sig. *From Whistle Stop to Sound Bite*. New York: Praeger, 1989.

Neuman, W. Russell. "The Impact of the New Media." Pp. 299–320 in *Mediated Politics: Communication the Future of Democracy*, ed. W. Lance Bennett and Robert Entman. New York: Cambridge University Press, 2001.

Nimmo, Dan, and James Combs. *Nightly Horrors: Crisis Coverage in Television Network News*. Knoxville: University of Tennessee Press, 1985.

Nussbaum, Martha, and Joshua Cohen, ed. *For Love of Country: Debating the Limits of Patriotism*. Boston: Beacon, 1996.

"Overview: The State of the News Media 2005." Project for Excellence in Journalism, Journalism.org, n.d. http://www.stateofthemedia.org/2005/narrative_overview_publicattitudes.asp?cat=7&media=1.

Pape, Robert. *Dying to Win: The Strategic Logic of Suicide Terrorism*. New York: Random House, 2005.

Parks, Michael. "The Future of Foreign Coverage." World Press Institute, n.d. http://www.worldpessinstitute.org/parks.htm.

Patterson, Thomas. *Out of Order*. New York: Knopf, 1993.

Petty, Richard, and John Cacioppo. *Communication and Persuasion: Central and Peripheral Routes to Attitude Change*. New York: Springer, 1986.

Pew Research Center. "Americans and Europeans Differ Widely on Foreign Policy Issues." Pew Research Center, April 17, 2002, http://people-press.org/reports/display.php3?ReportID=153.

Pfau, Michael, Michel Haigh, Mitchell Gettle, Michael Donnelly, Gregory Scott, Dana Warr, and Elaine Wittenberg. "Embedding Journalists in Military Combat Units: Impact on Newspaper Story Frames and Tone." *Journalism and Mass Communication Quarterly*, Spring 2004, 74–88.

Phillips, Kevin. *Wealth and Democracy*. New York: Broadway Books, 2002.

Postman, Neil. *Amusing Ourselves to Death*. New York: Penguin, 1985.

Powell, Jody. *The Other Side of the Story*. New York: Morrow, 1984.

Price, David. *The Congressional Experience: A View from the Hill*. Boulder, Colo.: Westview, 1992.

"Public's News Habits Little Changed by September 11." Pew Research Center for the People and the Press, June 9, 2002. http://people-press.org/reports/print.php3?PageID=612.

Putnam, Robert. *Bowling Alone: The Collapse and Revival of American Community*. New York: Simon & Schuster, 2000.

Rachlin, Allan. *News as Hegemonic Reality*. New York: Praeger, 1988.

Reedy, George. *Twilight of the Presidency*. New York: Signet, 1971.

Reid, T. R. *The United States of Europe: The New Superpower and the End of American Supremacy*. New York: Penguin, 2004.

Remnick, David. "Political Porn." *New Yorker*, July 4, 2005, 29.

Rich, Frank. "Iraq around the Clock." *New York Times*, March 30, 2003, sec. 2, 1.

Rogers, Everett, and James Dearing. "Agenda Setting Research: Where Has It Been and Where Is It Going?" Pp. 555–94 in *Communication Yearbook*, vol. 11. Beverly Hills, Calif.: Sage: 1988.

Rosenman, Samuel, and Dorothy Rosenman. *Presidential Style*. New York: Harper & Row, 1976.

Rosenstiel, Tom. *Strange Bedfellows*. New York: Hyperion, 1993.

Sabato, Larry. *Feeding Frenzy: How Attack Journalism Has Transformed American Politics*. New York: Free Press, 1991.

Sabato, Larry, Mark Stencel, and Robert Lichter. *Peepshow: Media and Politics in an Age of Scandal*. Lanham, Md.: Rowman & Littlefield, 2000.

Sanit, Tal. "The New Unreality: When TV Reporters Don't Report." *Columbia Journalism Review*, May–June 1992, 17–18.

Scheuer, Jeffrey. *The Sound Bite Society*. New York: Four Walls, 1999.

Schram, Martin. *The Great American Video Game*. New York: Morrow, 1987.

Schudson, Michael. *The Good Citizen*. Cambridge, Mass.: Harvard University Press, 1998.

Schuetz, Janice. "Introduction: Telelitigation and Its Challenges to Trial Discourse." Pp. 1–18 in *The O. J. Simpson Trials: Rhetoric, Media and the Law*, ed. Janice Schuetz and Lin Lilley. Carbondale: Southern Illinois University Press, 1999.

Schuetz, Janice, and Kathryn Snedaker, eds. *Communication and Litigation: Case Studies of Famous Trials*. Carbondale: University of Illinois Press, 1988.

Serfaty, Simon, ed. *The Media and Foreign Policy*. New York: Macmillan, 1990.

Shanor, Donald. *News from Abroad*. New York: Columbia University Press, 2003.

Simon, Roger. *Road Show*. New York: Simon & Schuster, 1974.

Slater, Don. "Political Discourse and the Politics of Need." Pp. 117–40 in *Mediated Politics: Communication in the Future of Democracy*, ed. W. Lance Bennett and Robert Entman. New York: Cambridge University Press, 2003.

Smith, Hedrick. *The Power Game: How Washington Works*. New York: Random House, 1988.

Sperber, A. M. *Murrow: His Life and Times*. New York: Freundlich, 1986.

Spiro, Peter. "American Exceptionalism and Its False Prophets." *Foreign Affairs*, November 2000.

Steele, Richard. "News of the 'Good War': World War II News Management." *Journalism Quarterly*, Winter 1985, 707–83.

Stuckey, Mary. *The President as Interpreter in Chief*. Chatham, N.J.: Chatham House, 1991.

Thussu, Daya, and Des Freedman, eds. *War and the Media.* Thousand Oaks, Calif.: Sage, 2003.

Trippi, Joe. *The Revolution Will Not Be Televised*. New York: Regan Books, 2004.

Turkle, Sherry. "Constructions and Reconstructions of Self in Virtual Reality: Playing in the Mud." Pp. 143–55 in *Culture of the Internet*, ed. Sara Kiesler. Mahwah, N.J.: Erlbaum, 1997.

Turner, Kathleen. *Lyndon Johnson's Dual War*. Chicago: University of Chicago Press, 1986.

Twitchell, James. *Carnival Culture: The Trashing of America*. New York: Columbia University Press, 1992.

Tyndall Weekly. New York: ADT Research, 2003–2005.

Van Zoonen, Liesbet. *Entertaining the Citizen*. Lanham, Md.: Rowman & Littlefield, 2005.

Vrooman, Steven. "The Art of Invective: Performing Identity in Cyberspace." *New Media and Society*, March 2003, 51–55.

Wallis, Roger, and Stanley Baran. *The Known World of Broadcast News*. New York: Routledge, 1990.

Watts, Duncan. *Six Degrees: The Science of a Connected Age*. New York: Norton, 2003.

Webster, James, and Shu-Fang Lin. "The Internet Audience: Web Use as Mass Behavior." *Journal of Broadcasting and Electronic Media*, March 2002, 6–10.

Welch, Matt. "Blogworld: The New Amateur Journalists Weigh In." *Columbia Journalism Review* (September–October 2003). http://www.cjr.org/issues/2003/5/blog-welch.asp.

White, Curtis. *The Middle Mind: Why Americans Don't Think for Themselves.* San Francisco: HarperSanFrancisco, 2003.

"Who Owns What?" *Columbia Journalism Review*, January 27, 2004. http://www.cjr.org/tools/owners/.

Wiese, Daniell, and Bruce Gronbeck. ""'Campaign 2004 Developments in Cyberpolitics." Pp. 217–40 in *The 2004 Presidential Campaign: A Communication Perspective*, ed. Robert E. Denton Jr. Lanham, Md.: Rowman & Littlefield, 2005.

Williston, Scotti. "Global News and the Vanishing American Foreign Correspondent." *Transnational Broadcasting Studies*, Spring–Summer 2001. http://www.tbsjournal.com/Archives/Spring01/Williston.html.

Wood, Andrew, and Matthew Smith. *Online Communication*. 2nd ed. Mahwah, N.J.: Erlbaum, 2005.

Woodward, Bob. *The Agenda: Inside the Clinton White House*. New York: Simon & Schuster, 1994.

Woodward, Gary. *The Idea of Identification.* Albany: State University of New York Press, 2003.

Zaller, John. "Monica Lewinsky and the Mainsprings of American Politics." Pp. 252–78 in *Mediated Politics: Communication in the Future of Democracy*, ed. W. Lance Bennett and Robert M. Entman. New York: Cambridge University Press, 2001.

Index

About the Author

Gary C. Woodward is professor of communication studies at The College of New Jersey. He has taught and conducted research in Great Britain as well as the United States and has authored numerous books and articles on political media, persuasion, and rhetorical theory. His most recent book is *The Idea of Identification* (SUNY Press, 2003).